The
Ultimate
Border Collie

Edited by Alison Hornsby

HOWELL
BOOK
HOUSE

Copyright © 1998 by Ringpress Books, PO Box 8, Lydney, Gloucestershire, United Kingdom.

Howell Book House
A Simon & Schuster Macmillan Company
1633 Broadway
New York, NY 10019

Library of Congress Cataloging-in-Publication Data

The ultimate border collie / edited by Alison Hornsby WITHDRAWN
        p.   cm.
    ISBN 0–87605–589–7
    1. Border collie I. Hornsby, Alison.
    SF429.B64U58   1998
    636.737'4—dc21   97–38165
                                                                         CIP

Printed in Hong Kong

10 9 8 7 6 5 4 3 2 1

CONTENTS

CONTRIBUTORS

THE EDITOR: Alison Hornsby's interest in the Border Collie began in 1973 when she was working as a trainer for the Guide Dogs for the Blind Association. This involvement deepened when she became puppywalking and broodstock supervisor at the Association's breeding centre, specialising in the training of puppies and the supervision of the GDBA breeding scheme. Ten years ago she founded the Bekkis kennel, in partnership with Jenny Jefferson, and their Border Collies have achieved considerable success in the show ring and as working dogs. To date, they have bred two Border Collie Show Champions, and have made up a third. They have also bred ten working guide dogs, and three dogs for the disabled. *See Chapter 2: The Border Collie Puppy and Chapter 9: The Versatile Border Collie.*

MAX CALDWELL is a lifelong farmer and cattleman. For over 40 years he used horses and dogs of mixed herding breeds to handle livestock. Since 1987 he has been raising and training pure-bred Border Collies, as well as conducting all-breed herding clinics. He uses his dogs daily on 250 beef cows and 300 feedlot cattle. He also trials his dogs and is a trial judge. *See Chapter 8: The Working Border Collie.*

IRIS COMBE: Having been involved with working Collies at grass roots level since childhood, Iris Combe has spent a lifetime researching into the history and development of British herding dogs. She has bred five Rough Collie Champions, two Smooth Collie Champions and three Border Collie Champions, one an International Champion. She has been a Championship show judge of Collies since 1958, including judging both Rough and Smooths at Crufts. When the Border Collie gained KC recognition in 1976 she was a member of the panel that helped to draw up the first UK Breed Standard. She has written seven books on the Collie breeds. *See Chapter 1: Origins and History.*

KAREN DALGLISH has owned Border Collies for some thirty years, and, since Kennel Club recognition, she has made up six Show Champions under her Corinlea prefix. For many years her dog, Sh. Ch. Viber Travelling Matt from Corinlea, was the breed recordholder with thirty CCs. Karen has also bred many Best Puppy winners, Junior Warrant winners, Reserve CC and CC winners, and many of her dogs feature in the pedigrees of today's top winners. Her proudest moment was judging Crufts in 1997, drawing the third biggest entry in the Working Group. *See Chapter 13: Breeding Border Collies.*

ELAINE HILL trains Border Collies and as a hobby enjoys competing with them at sheep dog trials. She also gives sheep dog demonstrations at all types of outdoor events and so has little time to compete in the open trials since they are also held in the summer months. She does try to bring on one or two young dogs and compete with them in the nursery trials which are held throughout the winter. She also does corporate work, where business executives have the opportunity of working a dog. She keeps her own small flock of Swaledale and Hebridean sheep and does shepherding work for local farmers at busy times of the year. Her father, John Chapman, trained, worked and trialled sheep dogs for fifty years, so she has been involved in training and in sheep dogs trials since she was a child. *See Chapter 8: The Working Border Collie.*

JOHN HOLMES, a professional dog trainer specialising in film and television work, is now equally well-known as a distinguished writer on canine matters. He contributes to numerous newspapers and magazines, and has written books on training the family dog and the working dog as well as the award-winning *Pet Owner's Guide to Puppy Care and Training* (published by Ringpress Books in the UK and Howell Book House in the USA). In partnership with his wife, Mary, he breeds dogs under the Formakin prefix, and was responsible for importing the Australian Cattle Dog to Britain. *See Chapter Four: Understanding the Border Collie.*

ALISON JONES BVetMed MRCVS: Alison, an expert in canine nutrition, qualified from the Royal Veterinary College, London, in 1987. After a short period in research, she entered a mixed practice in Gloucestershire where she worked for seven years. She then joined

Hill's Pet Nutrition as a veterinary advisor. *See Chapter Three: Diet and Nutrition.*

BRUCE KILSBY started in Border Collies with his wife Sheena in 1976. Their prefix is Whenway, and they have owned and bred several Champions. Both Sheena and Bruce have awarded CCs in the breed for many years. Although they still show occasionally, and have recently made up another Show Champion in Whenway Royal Highlander, and also own the famous import New Zealand and UK Show Champion Clan-Abby Blue Aberdoone, Bruce's main interest now is in sheepdog trialling. His best achievement in this area to date is in winning an Open Trial with his bitch Polly (Ma Biche of Whenway), enabling her to become the first and only show-bred bitch to date to be registered on merit at the International Sheep Dog Society. *See Chapter 10: The Breed Standards* and *Chapter 11: The Judge's View.*

DICK LANE BSC FRAGS FRCVS: Dick has worked as a veterinary surgeon in practice for the last thirty-five years, and is a consultant to the Guide Dogs for the Blind Association. He was awarded the Fellowship of the Royal College of Veterinary Surgeons in 1968, and the Fellowship of the Royal Agricultural Societies in 1993. Other successes include the BSAVA's Dunkin Award in 1977 and the BSAVA's Melton Award in 1987. Dick's literary work includes joint authorship of the *A-Z of Dog Diseases and Health Problems* (published by Ringpress Books in the UK and Howell Book House in the USA), editing *Animal Nursing*, now in its fifth edition, and joint editor of *Veterinary Nursing*. He is an occasional contributor to the *New Scientist, Veterinary Times* and *Veterinary Practice. See Chapter 17: Health Care* and *Chapter 18: Breed Associated Diseases.*

Griselle Kachina UDX OA, also works as a therapy dog.

BRIAN MCGOVERN has been involved with Competitive Obedience for some twenty-five years as a highly successful handler, as an instructor, and as a qualified Obedience judge. His training seminars have a large and enthusiastic following on both sides of the Atlantic. Brian has his own training school in Holland, and members have achieved remarkable success, winning over 400 first prizes in Obedience competitions. Brian himself has won the Dutch National Obedience Championship on two occasions. *See Chapter 5: The Obedience Competitior.*

ROBYN POWLEY, now in her third term as President of the American Border Collie Club, has been active in Border Collies for well over a decade. She is the former Secretary of the Border Collie Society of America, (the Parent Club for the American Kennel Club), and a current member of the Border Collie Club of Great Britain, the Southern Border Collie Club (UK), the Border Collie Club of Victoria (Australia) and other breed clubs around the world. Her crowning achievement was writing the official AKC Breed Standard. Now the proud owner of twelve Border Collies, Robyn is active in many different pursuits, including conformation, agility and herding. She is also an aspiring judge. Her kennel name of Darkwind is now becoming well known in America. *See Chapter 11: The Judge's View* and *Chapter 15: Border Collies in North America.*

MARY RAY is one of the best-known and most talented dog trainers in the UK. She has won or qualified for every major British Agility final, and she has won both the dog and bitch Obedience Championships at Crufts. Her best-known dogs include Mister Chips, whose name can be found in the pedigrees of many of today's successful dogs. His most famous son was Obedience Champion Red Hot Toddy who won a grand total of 21 Obedience CCs and 15 Reserves. He also won the Crufts Dog Obedience Championship. Another Mister Chips' son, Pepperland Hot Chocolate, competed at the Pedigree Chum Agility Stakes Finals at Olympia on eight occasions, was a winner once and was also a member of the winning team at the Pedigree Chum Team Finals and the Crufts Team Finals. *See Chapter 6: The Agility Competitor.*

JOHN RITCHIE has been breeding Border Collies since 1981, and his small but select Dykebar kennel is well-known and highly respected. His most influential dogs include Sh. Ch. Melodor Flint at Dykebar, the one-time breed recordholder and top stud dog, producing seven

Champion offspring, and Sh. Ch. Dykebar Future Glory, Best in Show at Darlington 1993, and Reserve Best in Show Crufts 1993.

JUDY VOS has been breeding Border Collies for over twenty years, and her Clan-Abby kennel, based in New Zealand, has a worldwide reputation for its outstanding show dogs. Judy has been Border Collie Breeder of the Year in New Zealand since 1980, and dogs bred by her have won CCs at Crufts (UK), awards at Westminster (USA), and Best in Show at the Adelaide Royal Show (Australia). She has also bred the only two Grand Champions in the breed. Judy is a highly respected judge, and has judged Border Collies throughout New Zealand and Australia, as well as in the UK and the USA. *See Chapter 11: The Judge's View* and *Chapter 16: Border Collies in Australasia.*

PATRICIA WILKINSON has been married for nearly 42 years, has four children and seven grandchildren. Her dogs have taken up most of her time, along with her husband's poultry and a small herd of pedigree Ryland sheep. Her other hobby is visiting Antique fairs and collecting dog memorabilia. She has quite a large collection of dog books on every breed and antique paintings and prints of Collies, but her pride and joy is the life-size bronze she has of a Collie. *See Chapter 14: Best of British.*

Other contributions have come from Meike Bockermann (vom Weideland Border Collies) and Angela Seidel in Germany, Michael Darwin (KUSA), and Lesley Scott Ordish.

1 *ORIGINS AND HISTORY*

We accept that man selected and trained dogs to help him in his struggle for survival and, in the process, learned much from them; later they contributed to the economy of the ancient tribes, but very little was written about the ancient herdsmen's dogs after they arrived in the British Isles. They belonged to the poor and lowly and were of little interest to the few academics who could read and write; therefore much of what has been written since is pure speculation.

ORIGINAL HERDING DOGS

It is only from observations of the pastoral scene and from an in-depth connection with rural life and the changing methods of livestock management since the 17th century, that we learn anything about the work and behaviour of the various types of herding dogs. The type that concerns us here is the sheepdog, or Shepherd's dog, one of the earliest canines to build up a mutual trust between dog and master and to cease behaving as a pack animal. Again, we can only speculate on its origin, but ancient history tells of the arrival of one type to the British Isles. It seems that, of the many Celtic tribes wandering across Europe between the 5th and 1st centuries BC, three finally settled in Ireland, bringing with them some livestock and the dogs to manage them, as well as their

hunting dogs. These tribes spoke a common dialect known as Q Gaelic in which the word collie meant useful, thus their generally useful stock/herding dogs became known as 'collies'; the spelling has, of course, changed over the years as the English language altered.

The only description I can find of these dogs is one by an Irish zoologist called W.L.C. Martin who described them as follows:– "Nose, pointed; hair, long and often woolly; form, robust and muscular; aspect, more or less wolfish". It is believed they may have originated with the Basque Celts. After a period of time one of those tribes moved from Ireland to the Western Isles of Scotland. They were followed later by the Christian monks and each brought with them their livestock and the collies to manage them.

EARLY COLLIES

Long ago ships, shipping, livestock farming and all their by-products were the main sources of revenue and employment in Britain and, in the case of farming, dogs were the tools of the trade. For centuries hunting dogs helped to fill larders but were the prerogative of the members of the Royal households and the aristocracy. However, the shepherd and his dogs have always been held in high regard and, before the invention of the sporting gun, in certain environments their instincts and

The collie breeds were selectively bred for the different kinds of herding work that were required.

trainability were invaluable when working in partnership with the hunting dogs. Further down the social ladder came the drovers, graziers and livestock market porters; these men and their dogs were responsible for moving stock along the old droving routes, or sheepwalks, which could take weeks or months, and among these types were dogs trained to hunt to provide meals en route for the men and rations for the dogs, as well as protecting the men while they rested.

As farming methods, laws and modes of transport changed over the centuries, the role of the dogs in these categories became obsolete, but the shepherds' dogs became more and more versatile and, through very selective breeding, they became not only the sheep-herdsman's dogs but also the generally useful farm dog known originally as the Collie.

HIGHLAND COLLIES
There is no doubt that, although the Collie in the British Isles was first recorded in Ireland, it was developed in Scotland as a sheepdog, first as the original rough-coated farm type and then as the special 'eye' dog. From a brief glimpse into its early Scottish history the reason for this will be obvious. The lush pastures of Ireland were suited to the breeding and rearing of horses and cattle, but sheep are domestic animals that can exist, and even show a profit, from the sparsest of grazing on the most inaccessible places and inhospitable weather conditions. The oldest breeds of sheep in Scotland are found on the Scottish islands and the dogs that manage them are descended from those brought there by the monks from Ireland, long before the Viking invasions.

The Scots did not develop their natural resources until the fighting and the feuding among the clans in the glens ceased. The environment, particularly in the Highlands, did not lend itself to agriculture, but sheep farming seemed an ideal occupation. However, in such conditions, this could not have been undertaken without the help of dogs to gather, drive and guard the flocks. We do not know the origin of the true Highland Collies or, indeed, of the Lowland Collies, but we do know that the modern sheepdog, which works with the power of its 'eye of control', was developed by the shepherds of the Border country between Scotland and England. Later this type became known as the Border Collie.

ROMAN SKILLS

The Romans brought numerous types of herding dogs to Britain, mostly from North Africa or countries bordering on the North Eastern Mediterranean shores, but very few survived the climatic conditions; one exception was a short-haired or bare-skinned type of droving dog which is found, even today, in all the collie breeds. To the Romans goes the credit for selecting, breeding and training dogs for specific purposes on the pastoral scene, sheepdogs in particular, sheep and wool being essential to the economy of these invaders.

We know that training a dog to hunt or guard property is encouraging his natural instincts, but training a dog to herd or care for sheep, or other livestock, requires a reversal of these instincts, and it was a skill in which the Romans excelled. Over a period of time they selected and trained dogs to guard, gather and drive livestock to such a high degree of trust that it has remained one of man's greatest achievements.

The method of working used by the modern Border Collie through its 'eye of control' plays a significant part in modern sheep farming. Here man has taken full advantage of the natural instinct of the dog to stalk and wear down its prey by its hypnotic stare, while retaining the ability to guard, gather and drive livestock which were bred into the sheepdogs by the Roman masters.

SELECTION BY COLOUR

Dogs designated for specific purposes by the ancient herdsman were selected by colour. Those kept for guarding the flocks from wild animals or human predators were usually white, or mainly white, and, being brought up from puppyhood with the flock, sheep had no fear of them but they proved efficient guards when the occasion arose. It is interesting that modern shepherds do not like white or mainly white sheepdogs – they say sheep do not respect them – but, as the saying goes, no good dog was ever the wrong colour! The droving or general stock dogs were usually black, black and tan, or brindle, while the blue merles or parti-coloured were selected to blend in with the environment on crags, mountainsides and cliff tops where this natural camouflage assisted when a cautious approach in dangerous conditions was required.

BREED RECOGNITION

For centuries herdsmen's dogs, or collies, had served their British masters with very little recognition, but there is no doubt that it was the introduction of Sheep Dog Trials in 1873 that first brought the working sheepdog or collie to public attention. The first Collie Club was founded in 1881, and it drew up a brief description of the anatomy of a collie, together with a points system for awards of merit in the show ring. It was at this stage that, from the farm collies or working sheepdogs, a show type emerged, selected for its appearance and not its performance, which became known as the pedigree Rough and Smooth.

The formation of the International Sheep Dog Society (ISDS) in 1906 was the biggest step forward and the first real recognition of the Working Sheepdog. It aimed to stimulate interest in the shepherd and his calling, to secure better management of stock by improving the shepherd's dog and to give financial assistance to members (and their wives) in cases of need. In 1915 James Reid took over as secretary and, with the assistance of T. Halsall, he instigated the first Stud

The blue merle colour acted as natural camouflage, and these dogs were used when a cautious approach was required. Photo: M. Bockermann.

ABOVE: Traditionally, white dogs were used for guarding the flock.
Photo: Amanda Bulbeck.

LEFT: The darker black, black-and-tans, and brindles were general stock dogs.
Photo: Keith Allison.

Book. Now the farm dog or working sheepdog could boast a pedigree and, to distinguish what were then known as the 'eye' dog from the other collie types which were being registered simply as Working Sheepdog, Rough, Smooth or Bearded, he gave the name Border Collie to particular entries of working sheepdogs from the Border Counties who were winning at the local trials.

The next step in the development of these Working Collie/Border Collies was in June 1976 when the General Committee of the Kennel Club, after lengthy discussions

with the International Sheep Dog Society and a newly-formed Border Collie Club, decided that the Border Collie "shall be recognised as a breed for show purposes in accordance with KC conditions". Previous to that move, these dogs were registered with the ISDS only as Working Sheepdogs (Border Collies).

I have only touched upon a few stages which transformed the ancient herdsman's dog into an officially recognised breed, but it is sufficient, for the Border Collie is still regarded as the world's finest sheepdog as well as being capable of competing in all

Recognition of the working sheepdog came with the formation of the International Sheepdog Society.
Photo: Keith Allison.

the tests or competitions run by either of the governing canine bodies, and in many roles outside the pastoral scene.

REGISTRATIONS

The names Border Collie and Working Sheepdog refer to one and the same dog which, at times, can be confusing, but the difference is in the registration systems. Since 1976, dogs registered with the Kennel Club (KC) can only be registered as Border Collies if they are already registered with the ISDS, or if both parents are already KC registered. This is the only British breed eligible to be registered with both canine bodies and it can, therefore, have the privilege of competing in the various disciplines or activities of each of these bodies.

A pedigree Border Collie unregistered with the ISDS can only be accepted on the KC Obedience register as a Working Collie or Working Sheepdog. To register a pedigree collie with the ISDS, the breeder or owner must be a member of the Society, but this is not necessary when applying for registration with the KC.

INTERNATIONAL DEVELOPMENTS

As the British Empire faded, confidence overseas in the superiority of the British Sheepdogs strengthened, particularly of the 'eye' dog or Border Collie. In New Zealand, where sheep outnumber people, the shepherd and his dog are essential to the economy, and the country was one of the earliest importers of Border Collies, now usually referred to as 'Heading' dogs. The sheer adaptability of these dogs make them invaluable in the tremendous variation of climatic conditions and environment of both North and South Islands.

Guidelines for testing these dogs at Trials had been in existence for some time, but in 1926 the New Zealand Sheepdog Trial Association, together with the North Island Sheepdog Association, drew up a list of guidelines for the acceptable conformation, or physical appearance, of a Border Collie. This was submitted to the New Zealand Kennel Club and appeared as the Official Working Collie/Border Collie Breed Standard in 1927, this being the Border Collie's first official recognition as a separate breed and not just a sheepdog.

To Australia must go the credit for developing a show type of Border Collie. In fact, in their 1963 list of breeds, the Australian Kennel Control Council claimed it as an Australian breed! The Border Collie, in the field or on the show bench, is big business in Australia and their historical records of those imported from Britain are second to none. Australia issued its first Breed Standard in 1963 and from that time a uniform show type of Border Collie has developed in that country.

Canada and South Africa import a great many Border Collies, mainly for use as stock dogs or to take part in trials. In recent years some excellent local strains have been established from early imports. In European countries the Border Collie is now becoming very popular both as a farm dog and for competing in local sheepdog trials, and many clubs are also scheduling Border Collie classes at their major Championship dog shows.

THE BORDER COLLIE IN THE US

In the United States of America, sheepdog trials, which started about 1920, are now becoming big business and the ISDS-registered Border Collies from trial-winning parents are fetching very high prices. There are four stock-dog registries in the USA and imported ISDS registered collies are accepted by these registries and are, therefore, eligible to compete in Sheepdog Trials. There are also Herding Trials run by the American Kennel Club but, until recently, a Border Collie was not eligible to take part in some of these Tests as the breed was not listed in the AKC Herding Group; that situation changed in 1996.

The majority of American Border Collie

The Border Collie received Kennel Club recognition in 1976.

Ch. Kiwi-Envoy From Clan-Abby; Bred by Judy and Joanna Vos in New Zealand, now a successful show dog in the USA.

owners are strongly opposed to the breed being shown in what they refer to as conformation classes – that is, as show dogs; they want them to remain a working breed. However, after long and heated discussions, some members of the Border Collie Society of America put forward a very lengthy Breed Standard with considerable references to the dog's working ability. It was a brave attempt to combine form and function, but unsatisfactory when a dog is judged on conformation only in competitions run under the rules of different governing bodies. The American Kennel Club agreed to appoint the Border Collie Society of America as the breed's parent Club, but

required them to write a Breed Standard that conforms to the AKC's own approved formula. This AKC Standard differs in many aspects from the British Standard and one wonders if it would have been more acceptable to all parties had the AKC agreed to abide by the ruling on Breed Standards passed by the World Congress of Kennel Clubs in 1981, when all the countries represented, including the USA, agreed that "all canine Breed Standards should be that of the Country of Origin of the breed...."

This is just a thought, but it is interesting that, in the Miscellaneous section of the 1977 AKC Illustrated Breed Standards, there is a brief Border Collie

16

Breed Standard accompanied by a pleasing picture of a Border Collie working sheep. Be it form or function, a Border Collie is capable of making the top grade in any role in which he is required to perform and, as the saying goes, "Handsome is as Handsome does."

Before importing a Border Collie into the USA it is imperative to have all the Registration Certificates and, in the case of a KC-registered Collie, it must also have an Export Certificate – in fact this is necessary for a Collie exported to any country.

AKC IMPORT RULES
Now that the Border Collie has been accepted by the American Kennel Club I give here the requirements for the registration of an imported dog or bitch. A dog whelped outside the USA may be eligible for registration in the AKC Stud Book when imported, provided:-
(A) The imported dog is of a breed eligible for individual registration in the AKC Stud Book.
(B) The imported dog was registered in its country of birth with the registry organization designated on the Primary List of Foreign Dog Registry Organisations before it was exported from its country of birth.
(C) The pedigree for the dog issued by the foreign registry organization contains at least three generations of ancestry, establishing that each dog in the three generations was of the same breed and registered in its country of birth with one of the registry organizations on the Primary List. Each dog named in the three generations must be identified by the registered name and registration number. The pedigree, or any other official documentation issued by the foreign registry organization, must also include the official Transfer of Ownership and date of transfer to the US importer, verifying that the transfer was recorded with the foreign registry organization.
(D) The owner who applies to register the imported dog is a resident of the USA.

An application to register an imported dog with the AKC when completed and submitted, must be accompanied by the original official (export) foreign Pedigree and Certification from the Foreign Registry Organization. The "Certification", which may appear on the Registry's stationery or directly on the pedigree issued by the organization, must reflect the fact that transfer of ownership to the USA importer, including the date of transfer and the importer's USA address, has been recorded with the foreign registry organization. In 1997 the fee to register an imported dog was $25.

2 THE BORDER COLLIE PUPPY

Owning any dog, whatever its breed, is a major responsibility. Before acquiring a Border Collie it is essential to learn as much as possible about the breed's traits and characteristics. Too many people purchase a Border Collie having admired a well-behaved dog performing a specific task – shepherding, Obedience or Agility – little realising how much effort has gone into achieving the end result.

Border Collies require a greater level of commitment from their owners than a lot of other breeds. Their level of intelligence and their herding skills are renowned. If this instinctive behaviour and willingness to learn is left unchannelled, frustration and bad habits can develop. The most valuable commodity you can offer a dog is your time and attention; this, coupled with training and direction, is essential to develop the desirable aspects of the breed's temperament.

The Border Collie is an active, working dog, with the ability to excel in many varied disciplines. As an adult, he requires plenty of physical exercise, mental stimulation and human company. Before acquiring such a dog, be honest and ask yourself whether you are prepared to exercise and train your dog on cold wet days, as well as warm sunny ones? You should also consider the cost of keeping a dog. There is more than just the initial purchase price. There will be food to buy, vaccination and veterinary costs, and boarding fees during holiday times, to name just a few of the expenses.

You may consider the option of choosing an adult dog. Not all Border Collies that require re-homing have problems. However, you should bear in mind that the dog will have established routines and behaviour patterns. In time, and with patience, he should become a well-behaved pet. Only rescue a dog with problems if you are prepared to take on a long-term project; do check his temperament carefully, especially if he is going to live with children. With an understanding attitude, the outcome can be extremely rewarding.

If you are prepared to dedicate the effort, and your lifestyle suits this breed, with the correct approach and handling you can become the proud owner of a uniquely devoted companion.

MALE OR FEMALE?
Having decided that the Border Collie is the right breed for you, further decisions have to be made. What type of dog are you looking for – a dog to work, to show, or to be a companion? Do you have a preference for a particular colour, and would a male or female suit your circumstances? The choice of which sex will need careful consideration, and any

existing male to female ratio in your household must be assessed. As a guide rather than a rule, a female tends to be more tolerant of a male puppy and vice-versa. With the correct approach and handling most adults, males or females, if previously well-socialised with other dogs, will readily accept a new puppy into the household or pack.

If you are purchasing a male for the first time, consider these aspects: males are usually bigger and heavier than bitches, they can be more dominant and display certain male tendencies if not checked at an early age – mounting and wandering. Early castration, around the age of ten to twelve months, can reduce the likelihood of these tendencies developing. If you are considering owning a female, bear in mind the difficulties of the female coming into season every six months. Do not consider keeping unneutered males and females together unless you have suitable facilities for keeping them apart when the female is in season. The neutering of any male or female that is not going to be bred from is thoroughly recommended.

Indianheart vom Weideland: The Border Collie requires a greater level of commitment than other breeds.

COLOUR AND COAT

The choice of colour is personal preference. A variety of colours is available. White should never predominate and mis-marked dogs should not be purchased as potential show stock, although it is an agreed belief, in any breed, that no good dog is a bad colour. Black and white and tricolour are the most popular varieties. Other colours include blue and white, red and white, merles and sables. The availability of certain colours can be limited. The type of coat available varies, from a smooth close-fitting type to a much heavier, rough-coated style. All should have a dense undercoat for warmth and protection.

FINDING A BREEDER

If you are looking for a puppy to work, select a kennel that is known for producing stock with aptitude, willingness and enthusiasm. If you are looking for a puppy with show potential, then you will be looking for good conformation, character, style and markings. If you are looking for a companion dog you are looking for a steadier, quieter type of puppy. It is impossible to foresee with certainty how a puppy is going to develop; all the breeder can do is identify the different personalities and potentials within a litter. Information on breeders that produce working, trials, show or Obedience stock, is available from Breed club secretaries, the ISDS or your national Kennel Club.

Armed with a list of recommended Border Collie breeders, the search for your puppy begins. Arrange to visit as many

Border Collies come in a wide range of colours.   *Photo: Amanda Bulbeck.*

breeders as possible; all good breeders will welcome you. Any opportunity to show off their stock and enthusiastically talk Border Collies is enjoyed. This is the time to ask all those questions you have – and be prepared to answer a few as well. This assessment period is a two-way issue: the breeder should be checking your suitability and circumstances before considering selling you a puppy.

You should ask to meet the dogs. Look at hip-score and eye-test certificates. Ask also about any records of the successes achieved by dogs bred by the breeder. Also, ask about previous litters and their progress to date. This type of information will help you to decide whether the breeder is producing the type and quality of dog you are looking for.

All good breeders with a reputation to maintain will highlight the responsibilities of owning a Border Collie. Expect to be asked certain questions. The breeder will enquire why you want a Border Collie and whether you have owned one before. With this knowledge they can judge if they have a puppy suitable for your requirements and how much information on the pros and cons of owning the breed they need to impart.

The breeder will want to know if you work, as a dog left on its own for longer than about three hours a day will become bored, frustrated, noisy and inevitably destructive. They will ask if you have a garden and whether it is securely fenced. A dog that can escape from the garden is a danger to itself and others. If you have

For show purposes, white colouring should not predominate, but white dogs make very attractive pets or workers.

Photo: Amanda Bulbeck.

ABOVE: Look at the adult dogs before making a choice.

TOP LEFT: Temperament is the most important factor to assess.

LEFT: If you want a family dog, the breeder will direct you to a steadier type.

children and they are present on the visit, the breeder will be observing their behaviour. If the children are well-behaved, the puppy probably will be too. They should also highlight the areas of conflict than can arise when a puppy and child are not taught to respect one another.

CHOOSING A PUPPY

If you are visiting a breeder with a litter, be firm with yourself, especially if you are looking at a litter for the first time. Look at the adults first; if they are unsuitable do not look any further. Avoid, if possible,

buying from the first litter you see, without at least seeing others to compare. Do not let your heart rule your head; have some set objectives before you go and only book a puppy if it meets with your criteria.

Observe the behaviour of the litter. The dam should be relaxed and friendly; any suspicious behaviour is likely to be passed on to the puppies. The litter should appear confident when meeting visitors. They should be friendly, fit and healthy, bright-eyed and well-grown and, like all puppies, full of fun. The environment should be clean and the puppies should have access to

a concrete run or grass, weather permitting.

Do not purchase a puppy from a litter if the dam is unfriendly or aggressive or the puppies appear frightened or excessively shy. They will have learnt this unfriendly behaviour from their mother and will probably grow up to be just like her. It is difficult to walk away from this sort of situation but there are plenty of other puppies around, of a more suitable type and temperament. The size of the puppies within the litter can vary, the males are usually slightly larger than the females. Small puppies in a litter are nothing to worry about, as long as they are healthy, lively and well-covered; the smallest one often ends up the largest. The risk of infection to young puppies is high, so do tell the breeder if you have been to see other litters. The breeder may wisely ask you to look, but please do not touch. The puppies' natural immunity against diseases, acquired from the dam's colostrum (first milk) will be decreasing by the age of six weeks. Any underlying infections in one kennel can be transferred to another, putting the puppies at risk.

If you are a first-time buyer, the breeder will probably advise you about which puppy is the most suitable for you and your particular requirements. Within any litter, for whatever purpose it has been bred, there are variable characters and

If you are looking for a puppy with show potential, the breeder will guide your choice. This is Mobella Team Spirit at Tonkory as a puppy (BELOW LEFT), and (BELOW RIGHT) fulfilling all her early promise, Sh. Ch. Mobella Team Spirit at Tonkory as an adult.

temperaments. Allow the experience of the breeder to steer you in the right direction. Once you have decided to purchase a puppy it is normal to pay a deposit and set a date and time for collection. The breeder should advise you on the pre-puppy preparations.

PREPARING FOR THE PUPPY

Once the puppy arrives you will have little time to yourself, so get organised beforehand. Make all the necessary purchases; track down a supplier of the puppy food recommended by the breeder. Choose a light-weight lead and collar to start with, made of leather or nylon. The range of grooming equipment available is enormous. A metal comb with short teeth set close together is a good one for coping with the fine puppy fluff, and a soft brush to remove mud and dirt is ideal. You will require a comb with longer teeth set wider apart and a brush for an adult coat. Large stainless steel bowls will seem like an expensive purchase, but in the long run they will outlive any plastic or earthenware bowl. When buying toys the cheapest are usually the best. An old stuffed football sock, empty plastic bottles (with tops removed) and empty cardboard boxes are great favourites and are easily replaced if destroyed or if they look unsafe. Kongs and Nylabones are some of the best types of toy to purchase. The safest guide to follow when buying toys or chews is to avoid anything small that can be swallowed

Provide safe toys for your puppy to play with.

or choked on. Decide where the puppy is going to sleep, prepare the bed, buy or borrow a playpen or indoor kennel or crate and, finally, check the garden fence and gate for security purposes. As it is important to provide a safe and secure environment for your puppy to sleep in, the kitchen is usually the best place. The bed should be placed out of draughts and raised off chilly floors. If you have a large kitchen, or an open plan house, it is advisable to restrict the area you allow the puppy to occupy when you are leaving him alone. This encourages settled behaviour, aids successful house-training and provides a safe haven for the puppy during busy times of the day. An old playpen or an indoor kennel or crate are invaluable training aids, used for this purpose. Baby-gates are also useful to restrict access to certain rooms in the house and for blocking access to the stairs. This method confines the puppy to a safe area but he

At last the big day comes when it is time to collect your puppy.

ABOVE: *Supervise introductions with other members of the family – human and canine!*

LEFT: *The new pup will feel bewildered when it first arrives home.*

can still see you and everything that is going on around. This approach can help teach your puppy to feel relaxed when alone, preventing separation anxiety developing.

Most puppies (and Border Collies are no exception) will usually chew their bed. They are very like human babies at this stage, everything goes into the mouth for tasting and chewing. A sturdy cardboard box, with warm bedding, is perfectly suitable until your puppy is more reliable. If it is chewed the box is easily replaced. Moulded plastic beds are an excellent alternative, being reasonably priced, tough and easily cleaned.

It is a good idea to have two boxes for the puppy in the house. One in the normal bed area and one for the sitting room. This provides the comfort and security of a bed in a different place, which should encourage the puppy to settle when you and the family want to relax and watch the television. If you are a first-time dog owner, do not forget to register your pet with a local veterinary surgeon. If you choose a vet that specialises in small animals, he or she is more likely to have broader experience in specific dog-related health problems. If you are in any doubt, ask other dog owners whom they would recommend.

COLLECTING YOUR PUPPY

Moving to a new home is a stressful experience for a puppy. Be prepared to spend a lot of time with him when you first get home – it will be time well spent. When you collect your puppy the breeder should provide you with a diet sheet and general information on worming, inoculations, puppy care and handling techniques. Your puppy pack should also include: a copy of your dog's pedigree; a Kennel Club registration certificate (if applicable); an ISDS registration certificate (if applicable); a copy of any litter eye screening and hearing tests that have been carried out and, finally, a receipt and agreement of sale.

Generally Border Collies are good travellers. As a precaution, most breeders will ensure that your puppy has not been fed before undertaking a journey of any distance; this precaution nearly always reduces the risk of car-sickness. Take someone with you to assist you on this first journey. They can ensure that the puppy is comfortable and secure. Take an old blanket, or a large towel, for the puppy to sleep on. Have the puppy at your feet, in the front passenger footwell. Do discourage the puppy from getting on your lap or looking out of the window. This will help to prevent car-sickness and stop the puppy thinking that it can always travel on your lap.

As soon as you arrive home, take your puppy into the garden for an opportunity to relieve itself. Allow the puppy to explore its new environment and its bed area. Encourage it to walk the route from the house to its designated relief area. If you are using a playpen or crate or indoor kennel, it is a good idea to feed the puppy in it, as part of the introduction period. When and wherever the puppy settles, pick it up and place it in its bed to sleep; this will quickly encourage it to use its bed.

HOUSE TRAINING

It is important to establish a relief routine as quickly as possible. It is also useful to teach your puppy to relieve on command. Choose the word you intend to use – "hurry up" and "be quick" are used a lot. The large quantity of food and liquid required by a growing puppy, in relation to its size, dictates an obvious need to relieve itself frequently. Care and vigilance on your part will achieve quicker results. The essential times for relief are first thing in the morning and last thing at night, immediately after being fed, after waking from sleep and after an active play session.

The key points to remember are that a puppy cannot wait; it takes time for a puppy to learn control. Quicker results will be achieved if your puppy is only allowed into the garden for relief purposes during the first few weeks. Too much access to the garden is inclined to result in play, distracting the puppy from its original task. Correct use of voice and timing of praise, is an essential part of house-training.

Allocate an area of the garden to the puppy for relief purposes. It could be a fenced-off area, a concrete area or a grass area of your choice. The benefits of this are useful to you and the puppy. The puppy learns quickly that this is an approved spot. For reasons of hygiene, children can be

told to avoid this area and, if you are a keen gardener, it will save your lawn from looking pock-marked with burnt brown patches. Always encourage your puppy to walk the route to the allocated area. Stand quietly and, as it begins to relieve itself, with a calm voice, use your chosen command. It will soon learn to associate the command with the act. Praise your puppy, vocally and physically, immediately it has finished.

In the house try to anticipate when the puppy wants to relieve itself. Look for the signs of wandering around sniffing the floor and going round in circles. This will help to avoid accidents. It is inevitable that you are going to react if your puppy has an accident in the house. Avoid telling it off, this will only confuse it. Never discipline your puppy if you discover an accident some time later; it will not remember what it has done wrong. If you catch your puppy in the act, calmly encourage it outside; avoid responding harshly.

Confining your puppy in a playpen or crate will help to achieve quicker results, especially overnight. Most puppies will not foul near their bed area. Place a cardboard box in the playpen or crate, for the puppy to sleep in, and put one thick sheet of newspaper down opposite the bed. Your puppy may use the paper once overnight and then hold on until you appear in the morning. After three to four weeks, if your puppy is still using the paper, remove it. The puppy could perceive the paper as an approved area. By removing it, permission is denied; your puppy should then wait to be let out.

THE FIRST NIGHT

If you have time on the day the puppy arrives, practise leaving it alone for a while, so that being left at night is not such a shock. Having provided a comfortable bed, a soft toy to cuddle, and a stone hot-water bottle (if the weather is cold), when the puppy has relieved itself put it to bed, making as little fuss about this as possible.

It is not unusual for a puppy to cry for the first few nights and this can be very very difficult to ignore. But do try to resist the temptation to go and comfort it. If you can ignore the noise, family and neighbours permitting, it will usually stop after five to ten minutes. If you cannot harden your heart at this point, put a pillow over your head, do anything, but do not go to the puppy. Firmness will pay off in the long run.

The key points to remember are that if you do go to comfort a noisy puppy, it will have won its first battle. It will continue to wake you regularly, for a very long time to come. Do not let your puppy sleep all evening and then expect it to sleep all night. If your puppy sleeps in the evening, wake it up for at least one hour's activity or play, before allowing it to wind down and then settle for the night. Avoid feeding your puppy later than 8pm; they usually need to urinate and defecate again two hours after being fed. Do not leave water available after 8 to 9pm. Too much fluid intake late in the evening will make it difficult for the puppy to stay clean all night.

FEEDING

Opinions and ideas about what to feed vary enormously. Border Collies can be reared successfully on raw meat, cooked meat or a complete diet. Follow the advice given on the diet sheet provided by the breeder. It should give you information on the quantities and on the timing of the feeding regime that the breeder used.

Leaving the dam and litter-mates is a stressful time for any puppy. A new environment, exciting new experiences, a

lot of handling by strangers, even a change of water supply can affect digestion. Feeding little and often for the first few days should prevent aggravating any digestive problems. Resist making any changes to your puppy's diet straightaway. If the need arises it should be done slowly, over a period of five to seven days. Gradually increase the amount of new food and decrease the quantity of the old diet.

When you bring your puppy home, it will normally be on four feeds a day. The breeder should provide you with a small quantity of the diet your puppy has been reared on. Keep to regular feeding times and choose a quiet environment. Border Collie puppies are easily distracted from the task of eating. In their mind, there's far too much to do and see, and they haven't time to stand still and eat.

Avoid hand-feeding at this stage, adding tasty morsels or leaving food down to tempt a picky eater. This approach tends to encourage slow or fussy eating habits. The new environment, and lack of competition from its litter-mates, will often affect a puppy's appetite. A calm, quiet approach from you during these first few days

Resist the temptation of changing your puppy's diet for the first week or so.

should get you both through any feeding difficulties.

FEEDING DO'S AND DON'TS
Store food correctly,
Weigh food accurately.
Ensure all fresh meat products are defrosted thoroughly.
Fresh food should be fed at room temperature.
Do not add supplements to a complete diet, unless advised to by a vet.
Avoid re-offering food or leaving the food down to tempt your puppy to eat more.
Do not feed poultry or fish bones, roast leftovers or chop bones.
Avoid feeding your dog one hour before or after exercise as this could cause bloat.
Fresh water should be available at all times.

It is impossible to give advice on the exact amount of food which should be given; individual growth rate and energy levels have to be taken into consideration. The puppy's stomach should appear mildly rounded without being distended, it should not be fat. Looking down on your puppy, you should see a slight waistline. By twelve weeks most Border Collies will be ready to reduce to three feeds a day. Do not worry if this happens earlier than that; Border Collies seem to put their food to good use.

By eight months most puppies are ready to reduce to two feeds a day. They will have completed their biggest growing curve. Any increase in food now tends to relate to the level of physical exercise and mental activity the individual enjoys. It is a good idea to keep your dog on two feeds a day for the rest of its life. This approach reduces the risk of overloading at one feed and I feel most dogs are happier with a little something in their stomachs at all times. If you have a persistently fussy eater I find that a small amount of a liver-based gravy, made with garlic for added interest,

mixed together with the daily diet, usually does the trick.

GENERAL CARE
The coat of an adult Border Collie is relatively easy to maintain in good condition. Even the heavier-coated dogs, with a little care and attention in the right places, seem to look good. Groooming twice a week with a long-tooth metal comb and a stiff brush should suffice. If your dog is shedding hair, daily grooming will remove the loose hair and get the shedding over with quickly. Extra attention is required on the areas where the coat is at its longest. The back legs (trousers) and tail tend to collect debris such as twigs and brambles, and the softer coat behind the ears is inclined to knot easily.

Your Border Collie puppy will benefit from an early introduction to regular grooming. Choose a time of day when your puppy is quiet and relaxed, and therefore more receptive to being handled. The grooming session should be a pleasurable experience, not a battle. Regular handling in this way will help to build a closer relationship between you and your dog and it will prove very useful on future trips to the vet.

During the grooming session you should take the time physically to examine your puppy. Checking your puppy regularly could prevent a minor problem becoming a major veterinary bill. This should include checking the eyes for any infection or discharge and checking the ears for any waxy discharge. Scratching, or head-shaking, usually indicates an ear infection or a foreign body. Look in the mouth regularly (especially when the puppy is teething) for inflamed gums, rotten or retained baby teeth or adult teeth that may need cleaning. During teething it is not unusual for Border Collies to have a double row of teeth, with new ones erupting before the old ones have fallen

Your puppy should get used to being groomed from an early age.

A puppy that is used to regular handling will learn to relax.

out. Gentle massage of the gums, or an application of baby gum gel, can help to soothe inflamed gums during this difficult period. Check that your puppy has a normal bite; this is known as a scissor bite. Abnormalities include conditions known as an undershot, an overshot or a crooked jaw. These three conditions are unsuitable in any prospective show or breeding animal.

Check the coat for coarseness, dandruff and external parasites; also check the skin for rashes, sore patches or lumps. Puppies and adults usually have dandruff when they are shedding; under normal conditions this is nothing to worry about.

Check the pads for cuts or cracks, and the nails should be kept short. Until your Border Collie is receiving regular exercise on a hard surface, it may be necessary to clip the nails. Just remove the tips, taking care not to cut the quick. If you are in any doubt, seek professional help. Any dog receiving plenty of hard exercise may suffer from soft or cracked pads at some point. Vaseline will soften any hard, cracked pads, and surgical spirit, applied daily, will harden soft pads.

If you own a male puppy, check that he has two descended testicles in the scrotum. When checking be gentle; rough handling or continual checking can cause the testes (in a puppy they are the size of two small peas) to move in and out of the scrotum. Check your bitch's vulva for any abnormal discharge or signs of season. The first season can occur at any time from six months of age onwards. Regular checking will ensure you notice the first day of season.

WORMING
Your puppy should have been treated for roundworm several times by the breeder before leaving the litter. Information on how many times, and which products were used, should be included in your puppy information pack. Your vet will advise you on a suitable worming programme and will provide the medication required. Signs of roundworms (*Toxocara canis*) include poor health, slow growth, a distended stomach and a characteristic sweet smell on the puppy's breath. Diarrhoea and vomiting may occur in cases of heavy infestation. Roundworms are easily identified, should your puppy expel one either by vomiting or within the faeces. They look like thin pieces of white or pinkish string, anything from one to eight inches in length.

It is important to realise that humans can also become infected if they ingest roundworm eggs. A medical condition affecting the eye can result. You should be aware of the risks to your health and your puppy's health if an effective worming programme is not carried out. Effective hygiene will help to prevent re-infestation. Keep areas where the puppy eliminates clean, regularly remove faeces, keep grass short and wash down and disinfect concrete areas daily. Children and adults should be encouraged to wash their hands after handling the puppy and everyone, for hygiene purposes, should discourage the puppy from licking, especially people's faces.

If you think your puppy has tapeworm, ask your vet for advice on effective control. It is important when treating tapeworm that you also begin a flea control programme. Do not forget to spray the puppy's sleeping area with a suitable product, also its bedding, around the house and your car. Remember, all other household pets must be included in this regime. This will break the flea/tapeworm lifecycle. The flea is an intermediate host to the tapeworm. This means that the tapeworm larvae develop inside the flea. The puppy, while grooming itself, can swallow an infected flea, the larvae then develop into tapeworms. Evidence of a tapeworm infection is easily identified. Tapeworms shed segments continuously. These may be seen in the faeces: they look like large, flat, grains of rice. Routine spraying and regular tapeworming of your dog should control this recurring problem.

INOCULATIONS
Your vet will advise you about the age at which your puppy can be inoculated. Certain vaccines can be given earlier than others. You will have to follow the policy guide-lines issued by the vaccine manufacturer your vet uses. Your puppy will be inoculated against distemper, hepatitis, leptospirosis, parvovirus and kennel-cough. Additional inoculation is required against coronavirus and rabies in the countries where this is applicable.

Early socialisation of your puppy is an important part of its development. The earlier you start the inoculation programme the sooner you can take your puppy out and about. Some vets will inoculate a puppy as early as six weeks of age and this will enable you to carry your puppy into public places to gain early experience. Until your puppy has had the complete course of inoculations, avoid going to areas where there is a stray dog population. Do not allow your puppy to run in parks, or other grass areas, or mix with any dogs which might not have been inoculated.

THE LEAD AND COLLAR
The best way to introduce your Border Collie to wearing a collar is to put it on for short periods during play-time or while the puppy is eating. Gradually extend the length of time you leave the collar on, over a period of two to three days. Most puppies, after five to ten minutes scratching and performing, give in and forget it is there.

Once your puppy has accepted wearing the collar, condition it to accept the lead by clipping this on for five to ten minutes and allowing the puppy to trail it around. Only

Introduce your puppy to the collar for short periods until he gets used to wearing it.

do this during a supervised play session, to ensure the lead does not get caught on anything. Occasionally pick up the lead and encourage the puppy towards you, using plenty of verbal encouragement and praise. Repeat the exercise two or three times each session. This will encourage the puppy to follow you, as well as getting it used to the weight and restriction of the lead. Practise this procedure in the garden, as well as around the house, before venturing out on to the streets. Choose a light-weight collar and lead for this purpose.

WALKS AND EXERCISE

Most Border Collie puppies usually accept wearing the lead and collar quite quickly. They will often carry the lead in their mouth for the first few walks and frequent stops are normal. A positive approach from the handler is required. Use plenty of voice and encouragement when the puppy is actually moving. Do not praise your puppy when it stops in an attempt to start it moving again – a sympathetic approach often encourages further reluctance. Avoid getting too far ahead of the puppy and never be tempted to drag or pull it. Use a toy, a tidbit, or have an older dog in front,

to encourage forward movement. Most puppies are reluctant to walk away from the security of the home environment. This is easily overcome. Carry your puppy for the first hundred yards or to the end of the road. As you turn to retrace your steps, put the puppy down and encourage it to walk in the direction of home. Most puppies are like homing pigeons and will walk enthusiastically homeward.

Every puppy is an individual. Age, size and rate of growth will influence the amount of exercise to be given. It is important not to over-exercise your puppy for the first six to eight months. Little and often is the best approach during the early growing period. Remember to monitor all aspects of exercise – walking, free-running and playing with other dogs. Puppies, when enjoying themselves, do not know when to stop. Mental fatigue is far more likely to achieve settled behaviour; excessive physical exercise tends to over-stimulate puppies, especially Border Collies, encouraging hyperactivity. Like children, puppies can become difficult when over-tired; if you see this behaviour pattern occurring, stop it by putting the puppy to bed.

LITTER SOCIALISATION

The importance of early socialisation is now widely recognised. The breeder, or an individual rearing a litter, has a responsibility to ensure that the puppies they have chosen to breed have the best possible start in life. Early influences can affect the development of the pup's senses and learning process. Gentle handling from day one will help to develop the pup's touch and smell senses. During the transitional period from two to four weeks of age, the ears and eyes will have opened.

Do not over-exercise your puppy in the first six to eight months.

A puppy will learn by meeting other dogs.

Though the sight and hearing are not fully developed, the puppy's dam, its litter-mates, and human and external influences, start to have a dramatic effect on the developing senses of sight, smell, touch, taste, hearing and pain.

The weaning period increases the amount of handling the puppies receive. It is noticeable how the puppies' initial response to the human voice develops through food association. It is a very rewarding experience when they start to respond to you calling them, prior to feeding.

During this period interaction with the dam and litter-mates influences skills of communication and play, both pleasurable and dominant. Already the hierarchy within the litter is evident. The larger, more dominant, puppy will display superiority over the more productive teats, denying access to its litter-mates. Maternal punishment will control dominant behaviour within the litter, by growling or holding the puppy down. In addition, the dam's response to external influences can affect the pups' development and character. One common occurrence is when a ringing doorbell triggers the dam to bark at the arrival of visitors. If this occurs in or near the nest area, it is interpreted by the puppies as a warning; they will scatter and hide. This creates a negative, fear-based suspicion in the minds of the puppies about people arriving. This may subsequently develop into a general apprehension of people.

As the puppies grow, their improved mobility and co-ordination enables further exploration beyond the immediate nest area. This provides varied experiences for the developing mind. These may include different floor surfaces, household noises, toys, children, other pets, vehicles coming and going and visitors. The puppy-human relationship really starts to develop now. Through touch and play the puppies will learn to interact confidently with humans, both those already known and visitors. Encourage the puppies to play and explore new opportunities with you, both as individuals and in a group. These are all external influences that need to be experienced by the litter, to help develop characteristics desirable in any adult dog.

From six weeks onwards, the pups are becoming more independent and the relationship with the dam is changing. By now they should be very human oriented, confident and sociable. They are now at their most malleable stage. This important socialisation period lasts until round about 14 weeks of age. New owners should be advised on how to achieve the best results during this steepest learning curve. Socialising your puppy involves you taking it out and about to experience the sights and sounds of everyday life. It needs to meet new people, adults and children, to attend puppy training classes, to meet different types of animals, as well as other dogs, and learn to execute training commands and display acceptable behaviour in different environments and situations. As experienced Border Collie owners know, a puppy learns bad habits as quickly as good ones, so it is important to get it right first time.

HOUSE RULES
It is important to be consistent with your puppy. All members of the household should be encouraged to adopt the same attitude and approach. Decide beforehand on the standard of behaviour you wish to achieve from your puppy, and what you will and will not allow. Unacceptable habits may include jumping up, mouthing or biting, excessive barking, stealing, begging from the table and letting your puppy get on the furniture. Unfortunately, as I have said, bad habits can easily become established and can form part of your puppy's everyday behaviour all too quickly.

Your puppy is a pack animal. It is important to your puppy that you adopt the role of pack leader and make the rules as clear as possible. A puppy that is allowed to assume the role of pack leader will behave like a spoilt child, demanding to be the centre of attention at all times, and soon becoming a nuisance to you and others.

Obedience is the basis of all dog training. Border Collies are usually quick to learn their name and the command 'no'. Keep your training sessions short – five to ten minutes at a time for the essential commands of close or heel, sit, down and come, and these should be worked at regularly. Teach one command at a time; this will avoid any confusion in your dog's mind. Effective use of your voice, and

good timing of commands and praise, will assist your puppy to learn quickly. Error-free learning is the key to success. Reward good behaviour and it is likely to be repeated. Listen to your voice, does it sound cheerful and genuine? Remember, training should be fun for both of you. Practise getting the tone right; women, particularly, find the deeper, stern voice of disapproval difficult to achieve. Men, on the other hand, find the lighter, more encouraging, tone needed for praise equally difficult. Good behaviour can be rewarded with a tidbit, a game with a favourite toy or the giving of physical and vocal praise.

Discourage your puppy if it mouths your hands or clothes. Border Collie pups tend to do perfect heel work attached to your ankle. The natural herding instinct demonstrated by this working breed can develop into habits of chasing traffic or nipping your bottom or heel. This may be interpreted as amusing puppy behaviour at eight weeks of age, but may develop into dangerous behaviour in an adult.

It should not be necessary to shout at your Border Collie; they are usually very responsive and willing to please, with a high level of hearing. It is important to understand that puppies do not grow out of bad behaviour, which is a mistake often made by first-time dog owners. Your puppy must be taught right from wrong, from the start, in exactly the same way that you would teach a child. Discipline should be in the form of a firm disapproving voice, or distraction, or by applying control by attaching the collar and lead, or by ignoring your puppy.

The leash is an important training aid in all situations. It can be used around the home and garden as well for walking out. Put your puppy on the lead for all early learning sessions – this will ensure a more successful lesson your close proximity will give your puppy confidence, you will be in

Children and puppies must learn mutual respect.

control of the situation and your puppy will not be able to evade training interaction.

TOYS AND GAMES

Teach your puppy to chew the toys you have provided. Rotating the choice of toys available will help in keeping your puppy interested and will avoid the search for new items to chew or play with. Your puppy should learn to release the toy on command and should never snatch a toy from the handler. Playtime and games are an important and enjoyable part of your puppy's development. It is important that you initiate the games and, at the end of the play session, the toy is put away until next time. The puppy should not be allowed to run off with the toy. Border Collies, by their very nature, can be obsessive. Control problems can develop if chase-related or wrestling games are taught. These types of game can over-develop the natural herding instincts. This could encourage bullying and play biting, so remember to have fun, but stay in control.

CHILDREN AND PUPPIES

Children and puppies can develop wonderful relationships but it is essential that both puppy and child grow up respecting one another. Children should avoid playing games of strength such as tug-of-war and wrestling unless they are able to control the situation. Your puppy should not be allowed to play to the point of exhaustion. Excitable, enthusiastic children can easily over-excite a puppy, resulting in rough play. The puppy will play with your child in exactly the same way that it would play with another dog. These games are usually rough; sharp claws and needle-sharp teeth can hurt. It will encourage your puppy to be boisterous and excitable. No puppy benefits from this type of encouragement. Children should be taught the following rules when dealing with the puppy.

• Children should be encouraged to leave the puppy alone when it is in its bed. It is important for the puppy to have plenty of opportunity to rest and sleep without being disturbed. Its bed should be a place of sanctuary. If the puppy is constantly disturbed it may become anxious and could show signs of irritability.

• Children should not touch the puppy, or interfere with its bowl, while it is eating. The puppy could perceive any erratic behaviour on the part of a child as a threat. This could lead to the puppy becoming

over-protective of its food or bowl.
• Children should not be allowed to pick up the puppy or to carry it. However, cuddles and affection are enjoyable, as well as being an important part of the puppy's development. Children and adults should sit on the floor before allowing the puppy on to their lap for a cuddle. This will help prevent the puppy thinking that it can jump up and demand your attention ad-lib and it will also avoid the puppy being dropped by mistake.

EARLY SOCIALISATION

Once your puppy has settled into its new home and has accepted the sights and sounds of everyday living, such as the vacuum cleaner, the washing-machine, your children and other pets – to name but a few – it is time to broaden horizons. Make regular short journeys in the car to visit friends and relatives. Carry your puppy around the block or to the local shop. This will give it the opportunity to see and hear traffic and meet larger groups of adults and children.

Once your puppy has been fully inoculated, gradually introduce it to busier conditions. Most puppies take everything in their stride, enjoying their outings, meeting people and, inevitably, receiving lots of attention. If your Border Collie puppy is more cautious, then take your time; introduce it to new conditions gradually; don't let it be overwhelmed by crowds of people or children. Keep to quieter areas for a longer period before slowly introducing the puppy to the busier areas. Puppies can easily be frightened by experiencing too much hustle, bustle and noise too soon. As your puppy gains experience, introduce it to other varied conditions such as steps, shops – banks, building societies and newsagents will usually let dogs in – lifts, slippery floors and swing doors. Vary the areas in which you walk your puppy, go to different parks and different shopping precincts; all these activities will help with the temperamental development of your puppy. The benefits of early socialisation with other dogs are well recognised. Attending a local puppy class will provide the opportunity for teaching your puppy to behave in the company of other dogs.

If you have an older dog do not allow the puppy to pester it continually. A puppy can make an older dog's life a misery, constantly biting and chewing. It is important that your puppy learns during playtime with other dogs that when you say 'enough' you mean it.

Tracking down a good dog training club is not always easy. Contact as many different sources of information as possible. Try your vet, your pet shop, other dog owners or the local library. Before deciding on a suitable club, visit several, without taking your puppy, and observe the methods used. If you do not like them, go to another club. Avoid clubs, or individuals, that advocate the use of punishment or excessive force.

Most clubs will take puppies as soon as they have completed their full course of inoculations. Attending such classes should enable you to improve on your puppy's responses and general behaviour. The instructor should teach you how to implement the basic commands and show you relevant handling techniques. If you wish to work your dog on sheep, or to be more competitive, they will help you to find an individual or a training club that specialises in the field you wish to pursue.

CAR TRAVEL

Most dogs will have to travel in a car at some point. Start training your puppy as soon as possible. Make short, frequent journeys to begin with and, as your puppy's confidence grows, increase the length of each trip. A journey with a fun experience at the destination will soon build up a pleasant association in the dog's mind. The front passenger footwell is usually a good place to start. If you are travelling alone, to prevent your puppy wandering around and getting under your feet, tie it on a short lead, to the seat floor-fixing. Once the puppy is settled and travelling well in the front, you can transfer it to a more convenient place, such as the back seat or the load area of an estate car.

This is a good time to start using a car cage or an indoor kennel or crate if you have one. Feed your puppy in the cage a few times before taking it on a journey. You can also place a sheet over the cage to prevent the puppy looking out of the side windows of the car. This could help to prevent motion sickness, if that tends to be a problem. Leave the front and back of the cage uncovered for ventilation and visual contact with you.

The key points to remember are:
• You must never leave your puppy in the car without ventilation.
• You must never leave your puppy in the car on a hot day. Even parked in the shade, the inside temperature of a car can soar in a matter of minutes.
• Do not feed your puppy before going on a long journey. Travelling on a full stomach is uncomfortable and could increase the possibility of car sickness.
• Do not allow your puppy to put its head out of the window while travelling. Allowing a dog to do this will encourage barking at other dogs, and the chasing instinct, and it also puts your dog at great risk – apart from getting its head knocked off, it may get grit or flies in its eye.
• Do try to keep a bowl and a bottle of water in the car. You never know when you might get delayed on your journey.

Border Collies have a high level of anticipation, so for safety reasons it is a good idea to teach car entry and exit obedience. Some Border Collies are prone to car sickness, but careful introduction to car travel can reduce the likelihood of this happening. As already mentioned, a pleasant experience at the end of a very short, straight journey is the most successful method, building gradually on success. Not allowing your puppy to look out of the windows will also help. Travelling your puppy with another dog, experienced at travelling, can give confidence. Travel-easy tablets, or skullcap and valerian tablets, given before the journey can help. Only use travel tablets if your dog has time to sleep off the effects at the end of the journey.

The aim is to train your dog to be a well-behaved, integral member of the family.

3 DIET AND NUTRITION

Nutrition has never been the sole domain of the medical practitioner or of the veterinary surgeon. It is relatively recently that the medical profession has developed clinical nutrition to the point where there are professors in the subject, and that veterinary surgeons in companion animal practice have realised that they have an expertise to offer in this area of pet health care. This is curious, because even the earliest medical and veterinary texts refer to the importance of correct diet, and for many years veterinary surgeons working with production animals such as cattle, pigs and sheep have been deluged with information about the most appropriate nutrition for those species.

Traditionally, of course, the breeder, neighbours, friends, relatives, the pet shop owner and even the local supermarket have been a main source of advice on feeding for many pet owners. Over the past fifteen years there has been a great increase in public awareness about the relationships between diet and disease, thanks mainly to media interest in the subject (which has, at times, bordered on hysteria), but also to marketing tactics by major manufacturing companies. Few people will not have heard about the alleged health benefits of 'high fibre', 'low fat', 'low cholesterol', 'high polyunsaturates', 'low saturates' and 'oat bran' diets. While there are usually some data to support the use of these types of diets in certain situations, frequently the benefits are overstated, if they exist at all.

Breeders have always actively debated the 'best way' to feed dogs. Most Border Collie owners are aware of the importance of good bone development and of the role of

The pet dog is entirely dependent upon its owner to provide for its nutrition needs.

Photo: Carol Ann Johnson.

When choosing a diet, it is important to assess the amount of energy in the food that is available to the dog.

Photo: Keith Allison.

nutrition in achieving optimal skeletal characteristics. However, as a veterinary surgeon in practice, I was constantly amazed and bewildered at the menus given to new puppy owners by breeders. These all too frequently consisted of complex home-made recipes, usually based on large amounts of fresh meat, goat's milk, and a vast array of mineral supplements. These diets were often very imbalanced and could easily result in skeletal and other growth abnormalities.

Domesticated dogs usually have little opportunity to select their own diet, so it is important to realise that they are solely dependent upon their owners to provide all the nourishment that they need. In this chapter, I aim to explain what those needs are, and in the process to dispel a few myths, and hopefully give some guidance as to how to select the most appropriate diet for your dog.

ESSENTIAL NUTRITION
Dogs have a common ancestry with, and are still often classified as, carnivores, although from a nutritional point of view they are actually omnivores. This means that dogs can obtain all the essential nutrients that they need from dietary sources consisting of either animal or plant material. As far as we know, dogs can survive on food derived solely from plants – that is, they can be fed a 'vegetarian diet'. The same is not true for domesticated cats, which are still obligate carnivores, and

whose nutritional needs cannot be met by an exclusively vegetarian diet.

ENERGY-GIVING FOOD
All living cells require energy, and the more active they are the more energy they burn up. Individual dogs have their own energy needs, which can vary, even between dogs of the same breed, age, sex and activity level. Breeders will recognise the scenario in which some litter-mates develop differently, one tending towards obesity, another on the lean side, even when they are fed exactly the same amount of food. For adult maintenance a Border Collie will need an energy intake of approximately 30 kcal/lb body weight (or 65 kcal/kg body weight). If you know the energy density of the food that you are giving, you can work out how much your dog needs; but you must remember that this is only an approximation, and you will need to adjust the amount you feed to suit each individual dog. This is best achieved by regular weighing of your dog and then maintaining an 'optimum' body weight.

If you are feeding a commercially prepared food, you should be aware that the feeding guide recommended by the manufacturer is also based on average energy needs, and therefore you may need to increase or decrease the amount you give to meet your own individual dog's requirements. In some countries (such as those within the European Community) legislation may not allow the energy content to appear on the label of a prepared pet food; however, reputable manufacturing companies can and will provide this information upon request.

When considering different foods it is important to compare the "metabolisable energy", which is the amount of energy in the food that is available to a dog. Some companies will provide you with figures for the "gross energy", which is not as useful because some of that energy (sometimes a substantial amount) will not be digested, absorbed and utilised.

There are many circumstances in which your dog's energy requirement may change from its basic adult maintenance energy requirement (MER):

Work

Light	1.1 – 1.5 x MER
Heavy	2 – 4 x MER
Inactivity	0.8 x MER

Pregnancy

First 6 weeks	1 x MER
Last 3 weeks	1.1 – 1.3 x MER
Peak lactation	2 – 4 x MER
Growth	1.2 – 2 x MER

Environment

Cold	1.25 – 1.75 x MER
Heat	Up to 2.5 x MER

Note that there is no increased energy requirement during pregnancy, except in the last three weeks, and the main need for high energy intake is during the lactation period. If a bitch is getting sufficient energy, she should not lose weight or condition during pregnancy and lactation. Because the energy requirement is so great during lactation (up to 4 x MER), it can sometimes be impossible to meet this need

by feeding conventional adult maintenance diets, because the bitch cannot physically eat enough food. As a result she will lose weight and condition. Switching to a high-energy diet is usually necessary to avoid this.

As dogs get older their energy needs usually decrease. This is due in large part to being less active caused by getting less exercise, e.g. if their owner is elderly, or there are locomotor problems such as arthritis, but there are also changes in the metabolism of older animals that reduce the amount of energy that they need. The aim should be to maintain body weight throughout old age, and regular exercise can play an important part in this. If there is any tendency to decrease or increase weight this should be countered by increasing or decreasing energy intake accordingly. If the body weight changes by more than ten per cent from usual, veterinary attention should be sought, in case there is a medical problem causing the weight change.

Changes in environmental conditions and all forms of stress (including showing, which particularly affects dogs with a nervous temperament) can increase energy needs. Some dogs, when kennelled for long periods, lose weight due to a stress-related increase in energy requirements which cannot easily be met by a maintenance diet. A high-energy food containing at least 1900 kcal of metabolisable energy/lb dry matter (4.2 kcal/gram) may be needed in order to maintain body weight under these circumstances. Excessive energy intake, on the other hand, results in obesity, which can have very serious effects on health.

Orthopaedic problems, such as rupture of the cruciate ligaments, are more likely to occur in overweight dogs. This condition, which often requires surgical intervention, is not very common in the Border Collie but it may occur in older dogs that have been allowed to get overweight, or following repeated trauma to the stifle joint due to jumping and twisting on exercise. It presents as a sudden-onset complete lameness or a gradually worsening hind-leg lameness. Dogs frequently develop heart disease in old age, and obesity puts significant extra demands on the cardiovascular system, with potentially serious consequences. Obesity is also a predisposing cause of non-insulin dependent diabetes mellitus, and has many other detrimental effects on health, including reducing resistance to infection and increasing anaesthetic and surgical risks. Once a dog becomes obese, activity tends to decrease and it becomes even more necessary to decrease energy intake; otherwise more body weight is gained and the situation is made worse.

Energy is only available from the fat, carbohydrate and protein in a dog's diet. A gram of fat provides two-and-a-half times as much energy as a gram of carbohydrate or protein and so high energy requirements are best met by feeding a relatively high-fat diet. Dogs rarely develop the cardiovascular conditions, such as atherosclerosis and coronary artery disease, that have been associated with high fat intake in humans.

Owners may think that protein is the source of energy needed for exercise and performance, but this is not true. Protein is a relatively poor source of energy because a large amount of the energy theoretically available from it is lost in 'meal-induced heat'. Meal-induced heat is the metabolic heat 'wasted' in the digestion, absorption and utilisation of the protein. Fat and carbohydrates are better sources of energy for performance.

For obese or obese-prone dogs, a low energy intake is indicated, and there are now specially prepared diets that have a very low energy density; those which are most effective have a high fibre content.

Your veterinary surgeon will advise you about the most appropriate type of diet if you have such a problem dog. Incidentally, if you do have an overweight dog it is important to seek veterinary advice in case it is associated with some other medical condition.

CHOOSING A DIET
The first important consideration to make when selecting a maintenance diet is that it should meet the energy requirements of your dog. In some situations, specially formulated high-energy or low-energy diets will be needed to achieve this. Other nutrients that must be provided in the diet include essential amino acids (from dietary protein), essential fatty acids (from dietary fat), minerals and vitamins. Carbohydrates are not an essential dietary component for dogs, because they can synthesise sufficient glucose from other sources.

Do not fall into the trap of thinking that if a diet is good for a human it must be good for a dog. We only have to look at a dog raiding the dustbin or eating faeces to see that what tastes good to a dog would not be so appealing for the owner. There are many differences between a human's nutritional needs and those of the dog. For example, humans need a supply of vitamin C in the diet, but under normal circumstances a dog can synthesise its own vitamin C, and so a dietary source is not essential. The amount of nutrients that a dog needs will vary according to its stage of life, environment and activity level. For the rest of this section life-cycle feeding will be discussed.

FEEDING FOR GROWTH
Growing animals have tissues that are actively developing and growing in size, and so it is not surprising that they have a relatively higher requirement for energy, protein, vitamins and minerals than their adult counterparts (based on the daily

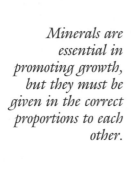

Minerals are essential in promoting growth, but they must be given in the correct proportions to each other.

intake of these nutrients per kg body weight).

Birth weight usually doubles in seven to ten days and puppies should gain 1-2 grams/day/lb (2-4 grams/day/kg) of anticipated adult weight. An important key to the successful rearing of neonates is to reduce the puppies' energy loss by maintaining their environmental temperature, as well as by ensuring sufficient energy intake. Bitch's milk is of particular importance to the puppy during the first few hours of life, as this early milk (called colostrum) provides some passive immunity to the puppy because of the maternal antibodies it contains. These will help to protect the puppy until it can produce its own immune response to challenge from infectious agents.

Survival rate is greatly decreased in puppies that do not get colostrum from their mother. Orphaned puppies are best fed a proprietary milk replacer, according to the manufacturer's recommendations, unless a foster mother can be found. Your

veterinary surgeon will be able to help if you find yourself in such a situation.

Obesity must be avoided during puppyhood, as so-called 'juvenile obesity' will increase the number of fat cells in the body, and so predispose the animal to obesity for the rest of its life. Overeating is most likely to occur when puppies are fed free choice (ad lib) throughout the day, particularly if there is competition between litter-mates. A better method is to feed a puppy a daily ration, based on its body weight, divided into two to four meals per day – the number decreasing as it gets older. Any food remaining after twenty minutes should be removed.

In 1987 growth studies were carried out using two groups of puppies, one group fed free-choice and the other group fed twice daily for 30 minutes. This showed that the time-restricted group consumed less food but still achieved similar adult size to the group fed ad-lib. By consuming less food the puppies were less likely to develop diseases of overnutrition.

Limiting food intake in growing puppies has also been associated with fewer signs of hip dysplasia.

Proper growth and development is dependent upon a sufficient intake of essential nutrients, and, if you consider how rapidly a puppy grows, usually achieving half its adult weight by four months of age, it is not surprising that nutritional deficiencies, excesses or imbalances can have disastrous results, especially in the larger breeds of dog. Deficiency diseases are rarely seen in veterinary practice nowadays, mainly because proprietary pet foods contain more than sufficient amounts of the essential nutrients. When a deficiency disease is diagnosed it is usually associated with an unbalanced home-made diet. A classical example of this is dogs fed on an all-meat diet. Meat is very low in calcium but high in phosphorus, and demineralisation of bones occurs on this type of diet. This leads to very thin bones that fracture easily, frequently resulting in folding fractures caused simply by weight-bearing.

Development of a good skeleton results from an interaction of genetic, environmental, and nutritional influences. The genetic component can be influenced by the breeder in a desire to improve the breed. Environmental influences, including housing and activity level, can be controlled by the new puppy owner with good advice from the breeder. However, nutrition is one of the most important factors influencing correct development of the puppy's bones and muscles.

In growing puppies it is particularly important to provide minerals, but in the correct proportions to each other. The calcium:phosphorus ratio should ideally be 1.2-1.4:1, and certainly within the wider range of 1-2:1. If there is more phosphorus than calcium in the diet (i.e. an inverse calcium:phosphorus ratio), normal bone development may be affected.

Care also has to be taken to avoid feeding too much mineral. A diet for growing puppies should not contain more than two per cent calcium. Excessive calcium intake actually causes stunting of growth, and an intake of 3.3 per cent calcium has been shown to result in serious skeletal deformities, including deformities of the carpus, osteochondritis dissecans (OCD), wobbler syndrome and hip dysplasia. These are common diseases, and while other factors such as genetic inheritance may also be involved, excessive mineral intake should be considered a risk factor in all cases.

If a diet already contains sufficient calcium, it is dangerously easy to increase the calcium content to well over three per cent if you give mineral supplements as well. Some commercially available treats and snacks are very high in salt, protein and calories. They can significantly upset a carefully balanced diet, and it is advisable to ask your veterinary surgeon's opinion of the various treats available and to use them only very occasionally.

A growing puppy is best fed a proprietary pet food that has been specifically formulated to meet its nutritional needs. Those that are available as both tinned and dry are especially suitable to rear even the youngest of puppies. Homemade diets may theoretically be adequate, but it is difficult to ensure that all the nutrients are provided in an available form. The only way to be sure about the adequacy of a diet is to have it analysed for its nutritional content and to put it through controlled feeding trials.

Supplements should only be used with rations that are known to be deficient, in order to provide whatever is missing from the diet. With a complete balanced diet nothing should be missing. If you use supplements with an already balanced diet, you could create an imbalance, and/or provide excessive amounts of nutrients, particularly minerals. Nutritional management alone is not sufficient to prevent developmental bone disease. However, we can prevent some skeletal disease by feeding appropriate amounts of a good-quality balanced diet. Dietary deficiencies are of minimal concern with the ever-increasing range of commercial diets specifically prepared for young growing dogs. The potential for harm is in overnutrition from excess consumption and supplementation.

FEEDING FOR PREGNANCY AND LACTATION

There is no need to increase the amount of food being fed to a bitch during early and mid-pregnancy, but there will be an increased demand for energy (i.e. carbohydrates and fats collectively), protein, minerals and vitamins during the last three weeks. A bitch's nutritional requirements will be greatest during lactation, particularly if she has a large litter to feed. Avoid giving calcium supplementation during pregnancy, as a high intake can frustrate calcium availability during milk production, and can increase the chances of eclampsia (also called milk fever or puerperal tetany) occurring.

During pregnancy a bitch should maintain her body weight and condition. If she loses weight her energy intake needs to be increased. A specifically formulated growth-type diet is recommended to meet her nutritional needs at this time. If a bitch is on a diet formulated for this stage of her life, and she develops eclampsia, or has had previous episodes of the disease, your veterinary surgeon may advise calcium supplementation. If given during pregnancy, this is only advisable during the very last few days of pregnancy when milk let-down is occurring, and preferably is given only during lactation (i.e. after whelping).

FEEDING FOR MAINTENANCE AND OLD AGE

The objective of good nutrition is to provide all the energy and essential nutrients that a dog needs in sufficient amounts to avoid deficiency, and at the same time to limit their supply so as not to cause over-nutrition or toxicity. Some nutrients are known to play a role in disease processes, and it is prudent to avoid unnecessarily high intakes of these whenever possible. The veterinary surgeons at Hill's Science and Technology Centre in Topeka, Kansas, are specialists in canine clinical nutrition and they are particularly concerned about the potential health risks associated with too high an intake of the following nutrients during a dog's adult

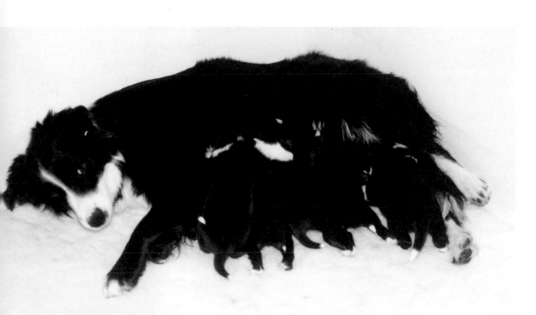

A bitch's nutritional needs will be maximum during lactation.

Photo: Carol Ann Johnson.

As your dog gets older its energy needs will decrease, and diet should be adapted accordingly.

Photo: Keith Allison.

life – protein, sodium (salt) and phosphorus.

These nutrients are thought to have an important and serious impact once disease is present, particularly in heart and kidney diseases. Kidney failure and heart failure are very common in older dogs and it is believed to be important to avoid feeding diets high in these nutrients to such an 'at risk' group of dogs. Furthermore, these nutrients may be detrimental to dogs even before there is any evidence of disease. It is known that salt, for example, can be retained in dogs with subclinical heart disease, before there is any outward evidence of illness. Salt retention is an important contributing factor in the development of fluid retention (congestion), swelling of the limbs (oedema) and dropsy (ascites).

A leading veterinary cardiologist in the USA has claimed that 40 per cent of dogs over five years of age, and 80 per cent of dogs over ten years have some change in the heart – either endocardiosis or myocardial fibrosis (or both). Both of these lesions may reduce heart function. Phosphorus retention is an important consequence of advancing kidney disease which encourages mineral deposition in the soft tissues of the body, including the kidneys themselves, a condition known as nephrocalcinosis. Such deposits damage

the kidneys even more, and hasten the onset of kidney failure.

As a dog ages there are two major factors that determine its nutritional needs:
1. The dog's changing nutritional requirements due to the effects of age on organ function and metabolism
2. The increased likelihood of the presence of subclinical diseases, many of which have a protracted course during which nutrient intake may influence progression of the condition.

Energy requirements usually decrease with increasing age, and food intake should be adjusted accordingly. Also the dietary intake of some nutrients needs to be minimised – in particular, protein, phosphorus, sodium and total energy intake. Dietary intake of other nutrients may need to be increased to meet the needs of some older dogs, notably essential fatty acids, some vitamins, some specific amino acids and zinc. Unlike humans, calcium and phosphorus do not need to be supplemented in ageing dogs – indeed to increase them may prove detrimental.

NUTRITIONAL AIDS FOR BLOAT
Many Border Collie owners are aware of a condition called gastric dilatation and torsion, commonly known as bloat. This potentially life-threatening condition was previously thought to be the result of

eating a high fat or carbohydrate meal. Current thinking is that bloat is due to aerophagia (the intake of large amounts of air with a meal), common in greedy individuals, and the predisposing factors may be: genetic make-up, competitive feeding, strenuous exercise around meal times and excitement at feeding time. The last three factors encourage rapid eating.

Special highly-digestible diets are available from veterinary surgeons to feed to at-risk individuals. It is especially important in the working Border Collie to allow a sufficient period of rest after exercise and before feeding to allow full recovery. Feeding a very tired, out of breath dog can predispose to aerophagia and increase the risk of the dog developing bloat.

FEEDING FOR PERFORMANCE
This is an area of nutrition that is of special importance to the owner of a working Border Collie. Light to moderate activity (work) barely increases energy needs, and it is only when dogs are doing heavy work, such as pulling sleds or working for prolonged periods in the field, that energy requirements are significantly increased. A large amount of research has been carried out to determine the optimum dietary characteristics for dogs subjected to prolonged hard physical work. This is particularly relevant when looking at the demands put on a working Border Collie out in the fields all day on a busy sheep farm.

The working Border Collie should be treated and fed like a human athlete. Energy demands will be high, up to four times that required for maintenance, and these calories should be provided in a readily accessible form. It is also preferable that the weight of food consumed is minimised to reduce the bulk within the intestines. Running puts stresses on the dog's ability to control the level of acid within the blood. A build-up of lactic acid within the muscles will cause reduced performance and should be avoided. Some

The working Border Collie should be fed like the human athlete.

Photo: Keith Allison.

diets have the addition of a buffer to help control exercise-induced acidosis. If the work is being done under conditions of temperature stress (such as in severe cold winter weather) then the calorie needs will be even greater.

The extra calories that are needed to sustain this level of work must be supplied to the Border Collie in a form that delivers them rapidly to the organs that require them. In a dog that is running and herding sheep, this means ensuring that a constant supply of energy reaches the muscle cells. The food must be digested before the calories become available to the muscle cells. So, a highly digestible diet is recommended. This becomes even more important in dogs that work regularly, since frequent exercise causes the intestines to speed up the rate at which they move the food through. The diet must be digestible to maximise the amount of calories the dog is able to extract from a food that is moving more rapidly through the intestinal tract.

It is for these reasons that the fuel of choice for the working dog is fat and not carbohydrate. Not only does fat provide two-and-a-quarter times the number of calories than the same weight of carbohydrate (mainly cereals) but they are more easily and efficiently digested, allowing the diet to be of a much smaller bulk. A dietary level of a least 20 per cent fat (as measured on a dry matter basis) is considered to be the minimum requirement for work.

It has recently been found that psychological stress also plays an important role in the efficiency of food conversion. Many Border Collies show overt excitement at the prospect of doing the work they so enjoy. These stresses also include transportation (say to a trialling event), spectators, noise and atmospheric temperature. Just as energy needs rise with exercise, they also appear to rise with increasing stress. It has been suggested that it is preferable to keep dogs in a quiet place prior to their being needed for work. This is often not done, especially in competition, but it may cause reduced efficiency of energy utilisation.

It must also be remembered that the working Border Collie should only receive a diet balanced for extra work while that work is actually being done. If the dog is allowed to rest for prolonged periods, then the diet should be switched back to an ordinary maintenance diet. A full week should be allowed for the transition from performance type diet to maintenance diet.

INTERPRETING FOOD LABELS
Labelling laws differ from one country to the next. For example, pet foods sold in the USA must carry a Guaranteed Analysis, which states a maximum or a minimum amount for the various nutrients in the food. Pet foods sold in Europe must carry a Typical (as fed) Analysis, which is a declaration of the average amount of nutrients found from analysis of the product.

COMPLETE v. COMPLEMENTARY
In the UK a pet food must declare whether it is Complete or Complementary. A Complete pet food must provide all the nutrients required to satisfy the needs of the group of pet animals for which it is recommended. At the time of writing there is no obligation for a manufacturer to submit such a diet to feeding trials to ensure that it is adequate.

In the USA some manufacturers submit their pet foods to the feeding trials approved by the Association of American Feed Control Officials (AAFCO) to ensure that they meet the nutritional requirements of the National Research Council (e.g. the Hill's Pet Nutrition range of Science Plan products). A Complementary pet food needs to be fed with some other foodstuff in order to meet the needs of the animal. Anyone feeding a complementary food as a substantial part of a dog's ration is obliged to find out what it should be fed with, in order to balance the ration. Failure to do so could result in serious deficiency or imbalance of nutrients.

DRY MATTER

The water content of pet foods varies greatly, particularly in canned products. In the USA there is a legal maximum limit (78 per cent) which cannot be exceeded, but no such limit is in force in Europe and some European canned petfoods contain as much as 86 per cent water. Legislation now makes it compulsory for the water content to be declared on the label and this is important, because to compare one pet food with another, one should consider the percentage of a nutrient in the dry matter of food.

For example, two pet foods may declare the protein content to be 10 per cent in the Typical Analysis printed on the label. If one product contains 75 per cent water it has 25 per cent dry matter, so the protein content is actually $10/25 \times 100 = 40$ per cent. If the other product contains 85 per cent water, the protein content is $10/15 \times 100 = 66.6$ per cent. This type of calculation (called Dry Weight Analysis) becomes even more important when comparing canned with dry products, as the water-content of dry food is usually only 7.5-12 per cent.

You can only effectively compare pet foods if you know:
1. The food's energy density
2. The dry weight analysis of the individual nutrients.

COST

The only valid way to compare the cost of one food against another is to compare the daily feeding costs to meet all the needs of your dog. A high energy, nutritionally concentrated type of diet might cost more to buy per kilogram of food, but it could be cheaper to feed on a cost per day basis. Conversely, a poor quality, poorly digestible diet may be cheaper per kilogram to buy, but actually cost more per day to feed, because you need to feed much more food to meet the dog's requirements. The only valid reason for feeding a food is that it meets the nutritional requirements of your dog. To do that, you need to read between the marketing strategies of the manufacturers and select a diet that you know provides your dog with what it needs.

HOME-MADE DIETS

What about home-made recipes? Well, theoretically it is possible to make a home-made diet that will meet all the nutritional requirements of a dog, and all foodstuffs have some nutritional value, but not all published recipes may actually achieve what they claim. The reason is that there is no strict quality control of ingredients, and the bio-availability of nutrients may vary from one ingredient source to another. If you feed a correctly balanced home-made diet, they are often time-consuming to prepare, usually need the addition of a vitamin/mineral supplement, and if prepared accurately can be expensive. Variations in raw ingredients will cause fluctuations in nutritional value.

4 UNDERSTANDING THE BORDER COLLIE

No breed of dog that I know is subject to so much misunderstanding as the Border Collie. It is this misunderstanding, rather than the dog itself, that gets so many of the breed into trouble. Fans of the breed claim that it is the most intelligent of all breeds and point to its success in Obedience competitions and Sheepdog trials as proof of this claim. But Obedience competitions, or trials as they are known in America, are no test of intelligence. They can be compared to "square bashing" in the Army – essential if men are to react quickly and accurately to a variety of different commands, but never regarded as an IQ test.

THE POWER OF INSTINCT
Success in Sheepdog Trials depends much less on intelligence than on instinct – something which I find the average dog owner has great difficulty understanding. Indeed, many people are convinced that an animal is using its intelligence when, in fact, it is responding to an instinct. The new-born puppy squirms around until it finds the "milk bar" and starts to suck – driven, not by intelligence, but by the instinct to survive. Its dam, who may never have seen a new-born puppy before, will start to clean it up and bite off the

umbilical cord with amazing accuracy. This has nothing to do with intelligence either: stupid bitches do this just as well as clever ones – sometimes better.

The young Sheepdog (the Border Collie is by no means the only Sheepdog) which has never seen a sheep before may, suddenly and unexpectedly, take off, run round a flock of sheep and fetch them to the handler. That is known in sheepdog circles as "starting to run". It has nothing to do with intelligence and everything to do with instinct. Once the dog starts to

The Border Collie – the most misunderstood of all breeds.

Photo: Keith Allison.

At seven months, this Border Collie is driven by the herding instinct.

run it is the trainer's task to teach him what he should and should not do. Until he starts to run – instinctively – there is no point in even trying to train him except to teach him to drop on command and come when called, something which every dog should be taught.

The age at which a young dog starts to run varies enormously between individuals. I have seen six and seven week old puppies creeping about after hens in the farm yard and I have known several well-bred young dogs which showed absolutely no interest in any stock until well over a year old. Four to six months is the age at which the herding instinct usually shows signs of developing.

This book is aimed mainly at the pet dog owner, few of whom are likely to want to work their dogs, but my reason for dealing with the subject is because I hear of so many problems with Border Collies which are due entirely to a complete lack of understanding of what makes the dog 'tick'. Among those I have met who seem to be mesmerised by the Border Collie behaviour have been instructors at training classes and well-known Behaviour Counsellors.

All animals, including humans, have instincts of one sort or another. Instinct cannot be seen and it is impossible to tell what instincts an animal possesses, or how strong they are, simply by looking at it. The Greyhound curled up on the couch shows no signs of any hunting instinct, but

the instinct may be so strong that it makes the dog chase a dummy hare, which it never catches, round a racetrack once or twice every week. Looking at a class of Border Collies in the show ring I would assume that they all had some herding instinct, even those bred from several generations of dogs which had never had the opportunity to work. But I could not be sure, and I would have no idea how strong that instinct was. I defy anyone to tell, simply by looking at a dog in a show ring, whether or not it has any herding instinct and, if so, how strong that instinct is. To the puppy buyer who wants a prospective sheepdog trial winner it cannot be too strong. To the buyer who wants a pet, the stronger the instinct the more necessary it is to train the dog.

Instinct is something which is there or, on rare occasions, is not; e.g. occasionally a puppy will not suck and in the wild it simply dies. If an instinct is there it can be strengthened by use or it can be allowed to lie dormant so that it may appear to be absent altogether. But it can be diverted into other channels and it should never be forgotten that all instincts have been handed down to the domestic dog from the wolf. The sheepdog herding sheep, the gundog flushing or retrieving game, or the police dog tracking and catching a criminal, are all responding to the wolf's instinct to hunt and catch its prey.

Apart from being strengthened with use, instincts can be and have been, strengthened by careful selective breeding. The modern Border Collie is the extreme example of how this can result in a quite abnormal herding instinct. At one time I had a very keen, strong-eyed bitch called Jean. Quite by accident I discovered that, if I rolled a log of wood along the ground, she would cast out round it and take up a position at "12 o'clock" from where I stood and "eye" the log. She would move left or right on command and, if I left her, I could return an hour later to find her still "eyeing" the log and patiently waiting for it to move! I tell that story when I get involved in an argument with someone who claims that the Border Collie is the most intelligent of all breeds, but the moral of the story is much more significant. It shows that what intelligence the dog has may be completely over-ruled by an abnormally strong instinct.

THE VALUE OF INTELLIGENCE

Intelligence is usually over-rated and, to many people, is the be-all and end-all of any dog. Very often it is measured by whether a dog does or does not do what the owner wants. If it does what the owner wants, it is intelligent; if it does what it wants to do, it is stupid! This type of owner is very often too stupid to realise that he has failed to teach the dog what he wants it to do. There is an erroneous belief that the more intelligent a dog is, the easier

it will be to train. That depends on whether it is willing to learn, in which case intelligence will be a great asset. But some dogs just do not want to learn and are very good at using their intelligence to find ways to evade the wishes of their trainer!

To suggest that a dog is not quite as intelligent as it might be is regarded by some owners almost as an insult. Why, I don't know. Some of my best friends are not very clever and some of the nastiest people I know are extremely intelligent. An exceptionally intelligent dog is frequently over sensitive and highly strung and is rarely reliable in a difficult situation. The less intelligent dog with a firm, steady temperament is far more likely to try and try again, even if he does not get it quite right the first time.

THE HERDING INSTINCT

As I have said, the first sign that the herding instinct is developing is when the pup starts to run and the age at which that happens varies greatly between individuals. If encouraged at this stage the instinct will rapidly become stronger. Every time the pup is taken towards sheep he will be keener to run than he was the time before. But if he is not encouraged, or is actually discouraged, this desire to herd is unlikely to develop and may die altogether. An example of this is the well-bred pup allowed the freedom of the farmyard. One

The majority of Border Collies will never be called on to herd, and so it is an instinct that should be actively discouraged.

Photo: Carol Ann Johnson.

day he responds to his herding instinct and singles out a hen from the flock. Eventually the hen makes a desperate effort to escape. In the excitement the pup's hunting instinct takes over and he grabs the hen and kills it. The owner who has allowed the pup to do "what comes naturally" then punishes it far more severely than necessary. A pup with an abnormal herding instinct, as I already mentioned, may get over this but many pups with excellent potential have been put off working for life by tactics of this sort.

Even if a pup is not "cured" by the above tactics, if it is prevented from "running" when the instinct "tells" it to do so, it is quite likely that the instinct will weaken and possibly die out altogether. A pup that is keen to run at six months but prevented from doing so may show no inclination to run by the time he is a year old. It should be noted that I have in mind a pup with a normal herding instinct.

I dislike the term "pet dog" and it hurts me to think of a Border Collie being kept as "just a pet". However I have to accept the fact that many of the breed are kept as pets and many of them provide a great deal of pleasure to their owners. Others certainly do not. Generations of wise men have, by careful selective breeding, produced a dog superior to all others for certain types of work. It is sad that the very qualities they strove to preserve are now the cause, directly or indirectly, of so many problems.

Though many of these problems are difficult to cure, most of them can be avoided. But the first essential to avoiding them is to be aware of them. Sheep are by no means necessary for the herding instinct to make itself apparent. With no legitimate "quarry" to herd the well-bred sheepdog will happily divert to something else. Cars, buses, push-bikes, motor bikes and children rushing about playing are all readily available as substitutes.

OBSESSIVE INSTINCTS

Few people seem to realise that the vast majority of young sheepdogs have to be cured of "gripping". From a practical point of view, a dog which grabs hold of a sheep is much to be preferred to one which lets the sheep escape. Bearing that in mind it should be easy to understand why a dog which is really fond of children and gentle with them when indoors suddenly nips one when games become too rough. Such dogs are often accused of being nasty and vicious and often sentenced to death as "dangerous". The poor dog is merely responding to an instinct, strengthened by man's skill as a breeder, but not kept under control by the owner.

During 40 years training and handling animals for films and television, one of our best dogs was Tuck, a Border Collie who, among other parts, played 'Clive', Leslie Sands' faithful companion in 21 episodes of the BBC series *Cluff*. Tuck was given to us at the age of three-and-a-half because she chased bikes and motor bikes. Because she was intelligent she soon learned that these things could easily be stopped by grabbing the front wheel! Now I am fairly certain that, had Tuck been corrected the very first time she did that, she would not have become so obsessed with such a dangerous occupation. As I have said, instincts tend to weaken if not used, but, when they have developed to the extent that this one had, they will always be there. Tuck lived and worked with us until she was over 12. Right to the end if she heard a motor-bike starting up in the distance she was for off. But she never did go off because I had taught her the two basic exercises – to drop on command and to come when called. But although she remained with me physically, mentally she was after that motor-bike. So long as she could hear it, it was difficult, sometimes impossible, to get her to concentrate on anything else. Fortunately there are seldom any motor-bikes in television studios and it was only on location that this weakness sometimes proved a problem.

PROVIDING ALTERNATIVES

If you don't want to use an instinct then try not to let it develop but, more importantly, try to provide the dog with an alternative – not chasing bikes! That this policy is effective can be seen in many Search and Rescue dogs, which find lost hill walkers and mountaineers. Most of the wild open space where they have to work is sheep country. Quite a high proportion of the dogs used for this work are bred from generations of keen, working sheepdogs. But once trained these dogs will search for a human "body" on ground where sheep are all around.

From an early age they are familiarised with sheep but discouraged from showing the slightest interest in them. Just as important they are given an alternative which makes use of the dog's instinct. Not the herding instinct which the handler is trying to suppress, but the hunting instinct itself, from which the herding instinct is evolved. A wild dog frequently picks up the scent of a prey animal (either on the ground or on the wind) and follows the scent to where the prey is. This is similar to a Search and Rescue dog picking up the scent of a person and following it until he finds the "body". Just as the wild dog is rewarded by finding something to eat, so the domestic dog is rewarded with a tidbit and praise. Once trained, these dogs can be sent out on their own to search a wide area, ignoring any sheep they meet on the way. An excellent example of how an instinct can be diverted.

Potential problems should always be nipped in the bud. Correct your pup the very first time and every other time that he shows the slightest interest in chasing car or bike. If you do have the opportunity, do not be tempted to see if he will work

sheep. If you aspire to qualifying your dog as a full Champion as opposed to a Show Champion, then he will have to qualify as a worker. But, unless you have regular work for him, don't let him start to run and, above all, provide an alternative.

POSITIVE ACTION

There is nothing most dogs hate so much as doing nothing. All the TLC about which we hear so much is no substitute for something positive to do. Unemployment is the direct cause of many good dogs going mad   and I do mean literally mad. I know of no breed to which this applies so much as the Border Collie; but this is compensated for by the breed's quite exceptional versatility.

The aforementioned Tuck was a good example. I knew that she had never seen any sheep but from her pedigree I felt sure she should work. I found I was right. With very little encouragement she quickly became an excellent sheepdog with great eye and style. She also excelled in what is known as "power", so often lacking in today's sheepdogs. Tuck also took to "man work" like a duck to water. Her last film part was in *Casino Royale*, when she was 12 years old.

In a pub brawl a stunt man was thrown on top of the bar. Tuck had to rush through the crowd, jump up on the bar, grab the man by the seat of his pants and hang on while he stood up and spun round several times. She really enjoyed that part! When we first had her she was very noisy, so I taught her to bark on word of command or a hand signal and to stop barking to a verbal command or hand signal. She became so good at this that I could rely on her to bark and cease barking on cue on a live TV programme.

When asked for a dog on a boat on the Thames, barking at passers by on the bank, Tuck was the obvious choice. Mary, my wife, was handling Tuck. She told her to stay on the boat with the picnic party, then stayed beside the camera on the bank and signalled to Tuck to keep barking. Dead easy until the Director said the next shot would be with the tablecloth. What tablecloth? Hadn't they told us? There are always a lot unidentifiable "they" in film and TV offices and they had made no mention of a tablecloth. The director, whom we knew very well, explained that the picnic party were now to have a picnic on the river bank with all the food etc. spread out on the tablecloth on the ground. When they were all enjoying their picnic Tuck was to appear from nowhere, grab the tablecloth and drag it away scattering the picnic in all directions. Did Mary think she would do it? It wasn't the sort of thing dogs are normally taught to do. Had "they" told us about it Mary was sure she could have taught Tuck to do it. But one thing she could say was that, if Tuck wouldn't do it, we didn't have a dog that would and she was quite happy to have a go.

So the tablecloth was laid out and the picnic party sat around it. Mary put Tuck down, just out of camera and walked over to the picnic, picked up the edge of the tablecloth and shook it while Tuck concentrated on her every move. She then walked back to Tuck and, as soon as the camera rolled gave a low hiss – our signal to attack. Like a flash Tuck flew at the tablecloth, grabbed it exactly where Mary had shaken it and dragged it away, scattering everything exactly as required – all in one take!

Before coming to us Tuck had been encouraged to retrieve and would pick up anything a dog of her size could pick up. She wasn't at all keen on giving anything up, but that problem was soon overcome. On a film called *Postman's Knock* she ran along a platform at Paddington station, through a crowd just alighting from a train, and snatched a letter from Spike

Milligan's hand. At the time we had a kennel maid who had a small boy of about four who played ball with Tuck for hours at a time.

With the provision of a variety of outlets for her boundless energy, both mental and physical, Tuck lost much of her obsession about bikes and led a happy and contented life. The same outlets are not available to many Border Collies but the number and variety of activities in which dogs can take part have increased greatly in recent years, especially for owners with competitive minds.

OBEDIENCE TRAINING

Obedience classes immediately come to mind. These were well established before World War II but did not take off until dog shows restarted after the war. I was very much involved and had a good deal of success with my Corgies. In those days, judges adhered to the Kennel Club guidelines which say that a dog and handler must behave in a natural manner. A dog was penalised for "crowding" if it touched the handler's left leg. Strangely enough the same guidelines still apply but, today, unless a dog curls itself round the handler's left leg and gazes up into his or her face, it seems to stand little chance of success. To encourage this a new command – "watch me" has become popular. I like a dog which watches where he is going and I can not stand one that keeps tripping me up as some Border Collies do. This tendency to cling to the handler has, in my opinion, played a big part in the breed's success in Obedience. We already have "Obedience strains" in the breed and my fear is that, just as breeders have produced dogs with abnormal herding instincts, so breeders of the future may produce strains with an abnormal tendency to cling to their owners. Any intelligence or initiative which such dogs might have could be completely overpowered by the "watch me syndrome". I think that breeders, like their dogs, should watch where they are going!

Some people are surprised when I point out that an Obedience-trained dog is not invariably an obedient dog. Of course it should be, but it is no secret that outside the ring the behaviour of some successful Obedience winners leaves much to be desired. It seems to me that this has become worse in recent years due, in part at least, to a changed approach to training. All training must be fun we are now told. It is certainly important that a dog enjoys being trained and even more important that he enjoys doing what he has been trained to do. This fun philosophy has also been applied to school children, one result being that there are now many young people looking for jobs and wishing they had spent a little less time having fun and a little more learning the 3Rs!

The Border Collie, as a breed, has a strong tendency to become excited and quickly become rowdy. Great fun for the dog and for some owners too – some of whom become as excited and rowdy as their dogs! Carried to extremes, as it often is, this fun training can have the opposite to the desired result – an obedient dog. A sensitive dog, and most Border Collies are very sensitive, responds to the touch of the hand and can be rewarded by stroking the head, cheeks and round the ears. This is not so very different from the way wolves show affection towards members of their pack, by licking and caressing each other. By applying the same principle an excitable or tense dog can be calmed down, when he will be much more likely to listen to what the handler has to say. "Hyping up" before going into the Obedience ring may help to gain an extra half-point but will do nothing to produce a more obedient dog.

AGILITY AND FLYBALL
Agility has become very popular in recent years both with the competitors and the

Am Ch/OTCH Heelalong Jalapenna UDX (Pepper), working with Sandra Davis. Heelwork to music is proving an entertaining option.

general public. Here again the Border Collie excels and the sport provides both physical and mental exercise for dog and handler. As an onlooker, I have noticed that the quiet handler with a dog that listens to instructions, is very often more successful than the "screamers and shouters" who comprise the majority of the competitors. Flyball has fairly recently been introduced to this country from America and is proving just as popular as Agility with competitors and spectators and, very obviously, with the dogs.

TRAINING CLASSES
Both of those sports are best suited to clubs where members can meet regularly,

Griselle Kachina UDX, OA notching up points in her Agility Excellent class. Agility provides an ideal outlet for the Border Collie's boundless energy.

Ch. Borderbreeze Lionheart competing in agility in Germany.

Photo: R.C. Franck.

learn from instructors and other members and see how their dogs compare with the others. But remember, a training class is only as good as its instructor(s). Some are very good, some not so good and, unfortunately, some are very bad. So if you are thinking of taking your dog to classes, whether for Obedience, Agility or Flyball, always go along, without your dog (with permission of course) for at least one session before deciding whether it is the right one for you and your dog.

Most clubs have a tendency to cater for the competitive-minded. Those with potential as team members, who can take part in competitions, receive a lot of help and encouragement, while those with no such potential tend to be left out in the cold; which does not mean that these people cannot provide an outlet for their dog's mental and physical energy, at the same time providing pleasure for both dog and owner. Contrary to common belief, training classes are not the best place to

The retrieve can be the basis of a number of tasks which will stimulate the Border Collie's mind.

train a dog. They are good places to learn how to train a dog but it should then be taken home and the advice given put into practice in an area familiar to the dog. Next week it can return to the class, when the Instructor should be able to assess what progress has, or has not, been made and offer advice on how to proceed.

One advantage of classes is that they provide an opportunity for your dog to mix with other dogs. This is something that should really be started when the pup is quite young and puppy socialisation classes have certainly been one of the best ideas of recent years. The age at which puppies are allowed to attend is usually governed by the age at which they were vaccinated. So far as the puppy is concerned the earlier it is socialised, the better. There is no doubt that a six-week old pup will tolerate strange sights and sounds which might terrify an unsocialised puppy of six months old.

Being quite a new idea, it is not surprising that there is considerable variation in the way puppy socialisation classes are run. In some cases a lot of puppies are simply let loose in a confined space and left to get on with it. Fine if all the pups are the same size and age; but if a big, boisterous four-month old Labrador puppy wants to have a game with a rather sensitive eight-week old Border Collie, it can have disastrous results. Common sense is what is needed, but I have heard of instances where it appears to have been in short supply.

ENCOURAGING THE RETRIEVE

While classes of one sort or another can be a great help to some owners, they are not essential in order to have a well-behaved dog. Standard obedience exercise should help to produce an obedient dog, but they do not provide an outlet for the exceptional energy of most Border Collies. The only instinct which is brought into play is the retrieve, when a dumb-bell is thrown by the handler to land a few feet away and in full view of the dog. A sensible dog could be excused for saying to himself "Well, you threw the thing, so you can go and pick it up!"

I have found that a dog which is not too keen on retrieving will, usually, become enthusiastic if he has to hunt for the object instead of simply picking it up off the open ground. This is because he is using his hunting instinct and, as I said, instincts develop with use. A dog which will hunt for an object can be very useful. Once, when I was exercising Flush, a Cocker Spaniel, in a London Park, I returned to my car to find I had dropped my car keys. I called Flush up to me and told her to "seek", pointing back the way we had just come She went off at the gallop and quickly returned with the keys.

Griselle, and her daughters Roostie, Marble and Muskie, based in the US. Border Collies like being involved in all types of activity.

So, if you want a really useful dog, teach him to hunt for various objects in long grass or other cover. Start by throwing them where he can see them fall but, once he is happy with that, start hiding them when he is out of sight. You can also encourage him to seek back for objects that you have surreptitiously dropped as you walked along. As shown with the example of Flush, this has real practical value and the dog will enjoy it too.

Most Border Collies take readily to retrieving, provided they are encouraged to do so at the right time. The retrieving instinct, like the herding instinct, may weaken, and possibly die, if not encouraged when it wants to develop. This is one reason why dogs from rescue kennels are sometimes difficult to encourage to retrieve in play. No one has ever played with them and they may even have been shouted at for picking up objects which their owners did not want them to have. If you throw an object and your dog will not even look at it, don't just say "Oh, he won't retrieve." When someone says to me "He won't do this," or "He won't do that," I invariably reply "What you mean is that you have failed to teach him how to do it." Unfortunately there are many people who have just no idea of what their own dog is capable of doing – if only they would take the time and trouble to teach him.

THE SENSE OF SMELL

When it comes to a sense of smell, the dog has us licked to a standstill – so why not allow him to use it and develop it? Don't start until the dog is retrieving reliably then, when out walking, with the dog running ahead of you, to start with on a track or path, drop something obvious, like a glove. Walk a few metres, stop, call the dog back to you and send him for the object, which he can easily see. When he retrieves it and comes back, make a great fuss of him and continue your walk. Repeat the process but each time walk a little further before sending the dog back. Continue until he will go back 25-35 metres.

Once he is keen on this game, drop the object out of sight, in some heather or tufts of long grass. Call him back to you and give him the same command; he should run back and use his nose to find the object. It does not require a brilliant dog to do this. When a dog cannot see an object it is as natural for him to use his nose as it is for you to put out a hand to find a light switch in the dark. Once the dog finds the object easily, gradually increase the distance until he will go back quite a long way; vary the distance and send him back on crooked tracks as soon as possible. If a keen dog is always sent back on a straight track of 200-300 metres, he is liable to over-run completely an object left just 25m in front of him.

TEACHING AN ADULT DOG

When teaching an adult to retrieve in play

Weidelands Sita, based in Germany. Develop your dog's sense of smell so that you can play search and retrieve games.

Photo courtesy: Meike Bockermann.

there are certain points to consider. First of all you *cannot make* him play. You can only encourage or persuade him to do so, which means that, in the initial stages you must use every ploy possible to encourage him to play. Eventually you should find something on which he is really keen. It doesn't matter what it is so long as he likes it. You should then be able to use that object to start him retrieving properly.

Elton, one of the first dogs to pass as a Dog for the Disabled, was a Labrador/Golden Retriever who would probably have retrieved naturally if encouraged as a puppy, but he had more likely been discouraged and, when he went into training as a DFD, he just did not want to know about retrieving. His trainer kept on trying new objects with no avail, then one day she threw a Kong which bounced in all directions and Elton ran and picked it up. He was immediately praised and rewarded

Arnpriors Trader (Tay) works as an explosives search dog.

Photo courtesy: Maggie Peacock.

and very soon he would pick up the Kong and retrieve it to hand.

Picking up objects for his disabled owner is a very important part of a service dog's duties. Elton will now pick up and carry virtually anything to his owner. This includes bringing in from the doorstep the small milk crate with full bottles of milk – and taking their empties out again. I am not suggesting that a Kong is necessary to teach a dog to retrieve – some dogs may not like them – but what I am saying is that you must find something which the dog really likes and use it. It does not matter what it is so long as he is keen on it.

KEEPING TRAINING FUN

The retrieving instinct is that part of the hunting instinct which makes the dog carry his prey to some safe place before settling down to eat it. But some people, when they are teaching the retrieve, appear to be trying to suppress this instinct. They are far too concerned about how the retrieve is done – pick up cleanly, deliver to hand, finish to heel etc. – instead of concentrating on getting the dog to run out happily, find the object and bring it straight back. Once he is enjoying that and can be relied on to do it every time, then you can add polish if you want to.

"Playing ball" can usually be put to much better use than is normally the case. If a tennis racket and ball are used it is possible to provide much more exercise for the dog – and rather less for yourself – than if you just throw the ball about. It can also be used to instil discipline. Have the dog sitting in front and facing you. Now hit out three balls, left, right and over the dog's head. Keep the dog sitting for a short while and then send him for whichever ball you want, making sure that he does not go for another one. When he has brought the first, he can be sent back for the other two, in whichever order you choose. If you can do this in cover, such as long grass or heather, the dog will have to use his nose as well as learning to mark where each ball has fallen.

Retrieving, in any of its many forms, may not seem much like an alternative to herding, but it does provide a positive outlet for some of the dog's hunting instinct and there are few owners who cannot put it into practice. Remember, there is nothing a Border Collie hates as much as doing nothing.

RETAINING CONTROL

In my opinion the Border Collie is prone to obsessions and one of the most frequent is retrieving. Take a walk on any beach or public space where people walk their dogs and you are almost certain to see at least one dog rushing after a stick, or maybe a stone, and carrying it back to its owner. There, the object is dropped at the owner's feet and the dog proceeds to bark. The

If you provide mental and physical stimulation for your Border Collie, and establish control, you have the key to a great partnership.

Photo: Keith Allison.

owner, being much better trained than the dog, obediently throws the object for the dog to retrieve again and again and again! So it goes on for the whole duration of the walk and every other walk too. These owners believe they are playing with the dog when, in fact, the dog is playing with them, sometimes becoming quite hysterical in its demands. There are other obsessions but that is a good example.

For some reason I cannot understand, there are people who like a dog which is constantly tearing round like a lunatic and disturbing the peace for all concerned. They say that it shows he is enjoying himself. That is quite probably true but it is not natural behaviour. Wild dogs do not behave like that. Of course they play a lot – when the pack leader gives permission. I am not the only person who likes a dog which goes for a walk with me as opposed to me going for a walk with the dog; a dog which listens to what you have to say and tries to understand what you want him to do. If you like that sort of dog by all means play with him but make him understand, right from the start, that he only plays with your permission. When you decide that enough is enough, the game stops right there, until you decide to start another one.

5 THE OBEDIENCE COMPETITOR

The Obedience world generally accepts that the Border Collie, and its non-pedigree counterpart the working sheepdog, is probably the most suitable breed for competitive Obedience. Certainly in the United Kingdom it is the most popular choice and is gaining popularity in almost all countries with a competitive Obedience programme. The Border Collie's inherent willingness to work makes this breed an almost automatic choice for anyone seriously interested in Obedience as a hobby or sport. Sadly, all too often we see many Border Collies competing in Obedience with an expression of abject boredom in their eyes, and I believe that this is because too many competitors change breeds, wrongly believing that a Border Collie is synonymous with success.

Nothing could be further from the truth. As any Collie owner will testify, this breed is an extremely complex animal and a thorough understanding of how this breed thinks is essential both to success in the ring and to the welfare of the dog. Few dogs, and even fewer Border Collies, will naturally take to and enjoy the strict regime of the Competitive Obedience ring. All breeds, but especially the Border Collie, have to be taught to enjoy what is, from the dog's point of view, a series of pointless, abstract exercises. This is why I spend a lot of time in 'preparation training'

before actually teaching the formal exercises. I develop my dog's natural ability to play, until the single most important activity in my dog's life is playing with me. I then use play as motivation and reward during training with, as the end result, a well-trained dog that loves training and working. This preparation training often takes many, many months to develop, but I believe that the dog's attitude and willingness to work are paramount to success in teaching the exercises. As an alternative to play, one can also use food as reward with equal success, and the choice of whether to use play, food, or both during training is a matter of personal preference.

Border Collies can be very single-minded and, when they have formed an attitude towards something, it can be very difficult, if not impossible, to alter their outlook. Bearing this in mind it is easy to understand that once a Border Collie has decided that Obedience training is boring, negative or such like, it will take many months, if ever, to alter his opinion. In short, it can be said that, if trained correctly and with the right attitude, the Border Collie makes an excellent Competitive Obedience dog that will work with style and enthusiasm throughout his working life. However, without the right demeanour combined with a thorough understanding of the Collie mind, and without careful and patient training with motivation as priority, the end result will be a submissive, bored animal.

PREPARATION TRAINING

As stated earlier, I spend a great deal of time 'preparing' my dogs prior to teaching the actual exercises. In this phase of training I want to develop my dog's attitude towards work, and bond him to me. This may take a few weeks or many months, depending on the dog's character. With puppies I always start off using both food and play as motivation and reward. Play periods are just that, play, with almost no actual training of the formal exercises to be taught for competition. Only when the puppy is playing happily with me, and has been taught to share his toys with me, rather than playfully competing against me for possession of the toy, will I attempt to channel the play into formal training. All this means careful observation to see how the puppy is reacting during the play sessions. Unfortunately, this requires a basic understanding of puppy behaviour that only comes with experience. This is why I advise beginner handlers to start off training using food as reward and

motivation. Food training is simpler for the beginner handler and, as progress is made and experience gained, play rewards may replace food if the trainer wishes to do so.

A 'rule of the thumb' that can be employed to see if your play sessions are developing along the right lines is the following: during your play session have a tug of war with your puppy, then throw the toy a few feet away and let the puppy run after it. If the puppy picks up the toy and immediately runs back to you to continue the tug of war, your play is developing nicely. On the other hand, if the puppy picks up the toy and runs off every time, then there is probably something amiss in your play. This, of course, is purely an indication and puppies may react in different ways on different days. However, I would want my puppy to bring the toy back every time to play with me before I attempted to progress. Initial advancement with play training may seem slow but the end result will be worth waiting for.

With young puppies, or when starting initial training with older, untrained dogs that have lost the willingness to play, I use

Play sessions are a time for bonding, and for assessing your puppy's reactions.

food to introduce them to the exercises. Food has, initially, an advantage over play as technique because the preparation stage is far shorter – normally a week or two is long enough – whereas developing the play to use as a training technique can take many months. Furthermore, some breeds of dog are less suited to play training. However, with the Border Collie this is not the case, as this breed seems to live just for play. Therefore the decision to use food or play is normally just personal preference.

GETTING STARTED

The first thing that we must teach a dog to do is to pay attention. To attempt to teach a dog a command or exercise while he is unable or unwilling to give us his complete and undivided attention would be wrong. When communicating with a person we would never dream of asking a question, or starting a conversation, while that person was distracted, or their attention was elsewhere, and the same principle applies to communicating with a dog. The dog

must first be taught to pay attention willingly, then, as training progresses, basic attention must be further developed into concentration, with the dog watching our every move for the slightest command or signal. To obtain this level of co-operation we must teach the dog that paying attention will be rewarded and that giving attention always leads to pleasure, so that, in time, the dog will learn that giving attention is one of life's most pleasurable activities.

This may all sound a little exaggerated; however I firmly believe that the foundation of all training lies in the willingness of the dog to pay attention, and a dog cannot be taught anything if he is not paying attention. Furthermore, I want my dog to pay attention willingly. If a dog is forced to pay attention by correction and punishment, i.e. by correcting him every time that he looks away, he may quickly learn to keep paying attention in order to avoid correction but I doubt that he will ever learn to *enjoy* paying attention. I admit that this method works and some dogs seem to accept correction with little damage; however, I prefer to see a dog that loves to work and shows this by dancing around the competition ring. I see so many Collies that work with their heads hung low, wrapped around the handler's leg, hating every minute of the sport. I want my dogs to enjoy Obedience as much as I do, and therefore I want to introduce the dog to every exercise without the use of correction, thus ensuring that the dog will learn to enjoy being trained.

FOOD, PLAY, OR BOTH

Before actually starting to teach the dog to pay attention we should have decided whether we will use food or play as a

Always start training sessions with a game: Ria McGovern with Stillmoor Dark Shadow known as Stevie.　　　　*Photo: McGovern.*

reward. If we have chosen the play method, the dog should already have been taught the 'rules of play' in the preparation phase of training, i.e. he wants to play with us and share his toy, and he will willingly take and leave the toy on command. As stated, I usually advise beginner handlers to start off training with the use of food, as this allows them to start teaching the actual exercises much earlier than if they have to spend several weeks, or even longer, teaching the dog how to play in a way that can be used as a training technique.

However, as the Border Collie adapts so readily to play training, I always advise my pupils to finish off each training session with play. In time, once the dog understands the rules of play training and has also been taught the exercises with food, the decision can always be made to replace the food with play as motivation and reward at a later date.

WHERE TO TRAIN
We must also decide where we will be doing all initial training. I believe that the worst place to teach a dog a new exercise is at a dog club with all its distractions. A dog club is where the handler gets advice on how to train the dog. However, the dog should be trained in a quiet place that is well-known to him and where there are no distractions whatsoever. Border Collies are, by nature, very strong eye dogs, and are easily distracted by any movement, and often get over-excited while watching other dogs being played and trained. Therefore, it is extremely important that we carefully select a training area that is quiet with no distractions. I use a quiet part of the garden or, if it is available, a garage or spare room to teach my dogs to pay attention.

To simplify matters I will be describing how to teach the dog the exercises using food as reward. This does not imply that I prefer food – in fact I prefer play, as Border Collies adapt so well to play training. To explain both methods simultaneously could be confusing. The basic principles are the same, with only minor differences in the techniques. One of the initial disadvantages of play training is that the dog must be released from the exercise to receive his reward, whereas with food training the reward can be given during the exercise.

TEACHING ATTENTION
To compete in Obedience we will need to teach the dog to pay attention in three situations – while moving, when sitting and in the heel position. Once the dog will pay attention in these three situations we can start to teach the basic exercises. Once again I must emphasise that the dog should not only pay attention but must do so willingly and happily and the success of this will be determined by the trainer's attitude. Always remember that the technique will teach the dog what he must do, but our attitude will decide how willingly he will do it. Border Collies are usually very sensitive dogs and, if the attitude of the handler is negative or boring, the dog will react accordingly, which is why we must at all times avoid correcting the dog.

If there are no distractions the dog will have no reason to look away and, therefore, we can devote our time to praise and reward. If we are willing to spend the time in developing the dog's attitude during initial training until such times as the dog has formed the opinion that training is fun, this positive attitude will be carried forward into further training. Once a Border Collie has made his mind up regarding a particular situation or activity it is very difficult to change his mind. This can be put to good use in initial training, and so we must carefully observe the dog and be convinced that he is enjoying training while at the same time doing what is required of him. It would be wrong to teach the exercise while ignoring the dog's state of mind and then try at a later date to alter his attitude towards the exercise. Our priority must always be attitude rather than technical perfection.

Attention on the move
Put the dog on the lead and take him into the training area. Have about twenty pieces of food with you and attract the dog's attention by offering him the food. Do not demand anything of the dog but just talk to him in a happy, motivational voice while feeding him the food. As you are doing so, keep walking about, a few steps in one direction and then a few steps in another, so that the dog has to follow you in expectation of receiving another piece of food. Do not make him wait too long for the next piece of food; four or five seconds between pieces is more than enough. You will soon find that the dog looks at you in expectation of another reward and you can then introduce the watch command,

Learning to pay attention on the move.

Photo: McGovern.

together with verbal praise, prior to giving him the next piece of food.

Remember to introduce the command and praise only when he is actually watching you. Do not make the mistake of giving the command when the dog is looking away. A dog learns by association and, if he associates the watch command with looking at you, he will soon understand what is required. If he does look away, just tempt him to look up by placing a piece of food under his nose, and then repeat the command, together with verbal praise, once you have regained his attention. Do not try to correct the dog for looking away at this time. In the next stage of training we will teach the dog to keep paying attention, but only after he has been taught what we want in this stage.

Once the dog has been given the twenty or so pieces of food you can end the training session with a game. The whole session should only have lasted for two or three minutes. This initial training should, preferably, be repeated two or three times a day for a week. At the end of the week the dog should be happily and willingly paying attention in expectation of his food reward. After all, from the dog's point of view, he has been taken to the training area and has been spoken to in a happy manner while receiving lots of lovely food. Nothing frightening or negative has happened, so there should be no reason why he would not be completely willing to repeat the experience.

Once you are totally happy with the dog's attitude you must teach the dog a subtle, but very important lesson. He must learn to watch you to receive his reward, rather than watch the food (or toy). This should be very simple to teach if the first week's training has been properly taught. Take the dog into the training area with your twenty pieces of food, just as you did in the first week. This time, keep about five pieces of food in sight in your hand,

As Stevie becomes more experienced he focuses his attention on the toy, without actually playing with it.   *Photo: McGovern.*

reward him with the food that is out of sight in the other hand. If he looks away you should call his name in an exciting tone and, when he looks back, give him the watch command together with praise and food reward. Either reaction from the dog is acceptable. He will soon learn that the reward will come even if he cannot see it. Once the out of sight food has been used up, show the dog that both hands are empty: once again he will either keep watching or will look away. You should react as previously described, this time rewarding the dog with the food in your pocket. The dog will soon learn that if he keeps watching you he will be rewarded, as you are an endless source of pleasure and reward even if he cannot see the reward.

By the end of the second week's training the dog should be capable of happily paying attention for two or three minutes without the visual aid of actually seeing the reward. He will learn that watching you will earn him a reward and he will have realised that the watch command is the command to pay attention.

Obviously, if you are using toys instead of food, the toy should be small enough to be hidden in the hand so that the dog cannot see it. You must also remember to release the dog into play every four or five seconds and not just at the end of the exercise.

The three basic stages of reward – in the hand in sight, in the hand out of sight, and in the pocket – should be used each time we teach a new step of training and should be implemented throughout the dog's working life, to maintain motivation and enthusiasm.

Attention in the sit
Once the dog is happily paying attention on the move, the Sit command can be introduced. Start off as in the previous step and, once the dog is paying attention, introduce the sit command. The dog

another five pieces in your other hand out of sight, and the rest of the food in your pocket. Encourage the dog to watch, as you did in the first week, and begin to feed him the five pieces of food while encouraging him to pay attention. Once the food in your hand has been given, show him your empty hand. The dog will do one of two things; he will keep watching you, hoping for more food even though he cannot see any, or he will look away.

If he keeps looking at you, praise and

Attention in the Sit: The same result can be achieved using a food reward.
Photo: McGovern.

Attention at Heel.
Photo: McGovern.

should already know the command from puppy training and this, combined with his willingness to pay attention, should result in an immediate reaction. If the dog does not sit immediately, place the food above his head, which will encourage him to do so. When he does sit, praise and reward him before releasing him.

Once he is sitting happily each time he is commanded, the command can be given with the food out of sight, and then in the pocket, as previously described. The secret of an instant response is attention and attitude, and this simple sit command should easily be incorporated into the training.

Gradually increase the duration of the sit until the dog will happily sit for four or five seconds while paying attention. Do not attempt to make the dog sit for longer than this because you are teaching attention in the sit, not the sit stay exercise,

and, by keeping the exercise short, motivation will still be the priority.

Attention at heel

Once the sit has been incorporated to the attention training, the sit at heel can be taught. Hold the food in the left hand above the dog's head and command him to sit, then swivel back and position yourself in the heel position next to the dog. As you do this, ensure that the dog does not move, by keeping the left hand above his head. Once you are in the heel position give the dog your chosen command, i.e. Heel or Close, then praise, reward and release him. As you progress, the three phases of food should be used, until the dog will sit happily at heel without the visual aid of food in the hand. Once again, do not let the dog sit at heel for more that a few seconds. Bear in mind that you are teaching attention in the heel position, and to make the dog sit for longer than a few seconds would serve no useful purpose.

By the end of this phase of training the dog should be happily paying attention while on the move, in the sit and in the heel position. He should be able to do so without the visible aid of food or toy, and he should be doing so happily and with lots of confidence. All of his training to date has been carried out in the same place with no distractions whatsoever. This should have resulted in a happy, willing worker that is ready to commence further training. During this whole phase of training the priority at all times should be motivating the dog to want to work. I have found that the Border Collie accepts this method extremely well, as there are no corrections or punishments used.

By now the dog will have understood the basic rules of training, i.e. command, response and reward, and this basic understanding will be invaluable in further training. All training sessions should be kept short, with lots of enthusiasm. Collies are workaholics and, once they have learnt to enjoy doing something, are willing to go on for hours at a time, but to maintain motivation, each session should be broken up in short sections and each session should end while the dog is still having fun.

TEACHING THE EXERCISES
Prior to actually starting to teach the dog the exercises required in Obedience, I always evaluate the progress that has been made. By now we should have built up a good relationship with the dog without actually having taught him any of the formal exercises. The dog should be happily paying attention and should understand the rules of play and work. There should be no fear or hesitancy and the dog should be full of confidence. We can now proceed to teach the dog the exercises required for the particular Obedience programme in which we will be participating. Most countries have their own set of rules and regulations, although some exercises are common to all programmes, i.e. heelwork, recall to handler, retrieve, and stay exercises. Other exercises, such as jumping, scent discrimination, sendaway (go outs) vary in interpretation from country to country.

As trainer and competitor, each individual should be aware of the particular requirements for their national programme and should train the dog to these standards. The attention training described above can be used for any Obedience programme and is not an exercise as such, but is common to all. Other attributes that are not laid down in the rules but which are, in my opinion, prerequisite, are style, happiness and attitude which should be required in whichever programme we are competing in. My chosen Obedience programme is British Obedience in which seven different exercises have to be taught in various forms. The UK heelwork test is far longer and more demanding than the American version. We do not have to jump our dogs and our scent discrimination is on cloths instead of dumbbells. However, as this book is intended for an international market, I will restrict my description of how I teach an exercise to those exercises common to all lands.

HEELWORK
Heelwork is a combination of three components, attention (dog), heel position (dog), and deportment (handler). A dog that pays absolute attention, and has been taught a correct heel position, will be guided around the ring and receive his signals from a handler with good deportment.

Basic Heelwork. Position on the move.
The first stage of teaching heelwork is devoted to teaching the dog his correct

heel position and combining this with attention that has already been taught. I teach this in four exercises:

The left-hand circle. Is used to teach the dog the heelwork position on the move and is taught after the dog has learnt and understands the heelwork position during attention training. In the left hand circle the handler will be working towards the dog, which makes eye contact easier and will help give the dog confidence, as it is easier to communicate with him.

The right-hand circle. Teaches the dog to maintain the heelwork position while the handler has broken eye contact and is moving away from him. Eye contact initially helps but, if carried on too long, is one of the major causes of forward working, as the dog will come forward when working in a straight line in an attempt to regain eye contact. Border Collies, more than any other breed, are strong 'eye contact' dogs and this can cause problems if not kept under control. The right-hand circle is where this potential problem is controlled before it develops.

The figure of eight. Combines both left and right hand circles and helps the dog understand and maintain his heel position while moving in alternating directions with fluctuating body signals and posture from the handler. As the figure of eight is a combination of both the left and right circles, the handler will, in one exercise, make and break eye contact, thereby combining the previous steps.

The weave. Teaches the dog constantly to adapt to alternating left and right curves while maintaining the heelwork position. The weave also prepares the dog prior to teaching the left and right turns. The most important aim of teaching the weave is to get the dog to react to subtle body language as we constantly change direction. Initially the dog receives no lead help or commands, just lots of verbal encouragement so that he has to take his

clues from the body language. Not until the dog is doing this should gentle guidance from the lead be introduced to tighten the dog up and, as this is done, the commands for left and right turn can be introduced as the dog turns to the right and left. This prepares the dog for learning the turns in the next phase of training.

All of the above steps will teach the dog to read body language while maintaining the heel position, and will give him the confidence to do flowing heelwork. Once this point has been reached we can start to teach the next phase of heelwork training.

Novice Heelwork.
Starting from the halt. This step is a combination of two exercises already known to the dog. He has been taught to sit at heel during the attention training, and he has been taught to heel during basic heelwork training, so all we have to do is combine the two. Starting with the dog at heel, give him the command and step off with the left foot and immediately praise him as he moves off, and then release him. He should be praised for moving off from the sit, not for doing heelwork, which he has already been taught. Gradually increase the number of off steps he can do, up to about fifteen to twenty steps.

Incorporating a sit into the halt. To teach the dog to sit correctly at heel as we halt is a matter of correct timing. The command to sit should be given as the left leg closes up to the right. The command is given prior to closing up, which results in the dog doing two things; he obeys the command to sit and he tries to maintain his heel position, which will result in a correct sit at heel. Crooked sits are, as often as not, caused by the handler first stopping and then giving the sit command. If the dog goes into the sit while still moving forward the crooked sit can be avoided.

Figure of eight: Brian McGovern working with Whackie on the inside (ABOVE LEFT) and on the outside (ABOVE RIGHT).
Photos: McGovern.

The weave: Whackie, handled by Lenie Kastelijin, learns to react to body language as she changes direction.
Photo: McGovern.

Now working on the outside, Whackie curves to the right.

Photo: McGovern.

Teaching the turns. Prior to attempting to teach turns the handler should have developed perfect deportment, which will result in each turn being carried out in the same way each time with the same timing. Consistent deportment by the handler, combined with complete attention and correct heel position, are all that is needed to teach correct turns. Turns should be taught one at a time, each one being perfected before going on to the next.

Leaving off the aids. There are two sorts of aids applied during training, which I call the intentional aids (lead technique, verbal praise, commands etc.) and the unintentional aids (body movement, exaggerated signals etc.). The intentional aids do not normally cause problems, as the handler is aware of them, and these aids should be consistently applied until the dog is working well, and then alternately left off and then reapplied, so that the dog can, if required, work without them. It is the unintentional aids that can cause the problems simply because many handlers do not realise that these aids exist. The solution is to ask an experienced trainer to watch you work your dog and observe your deportment, and then to make a list of all body signals that would be unacceptable in the ring. Once you are aware of the unintentional aids, they can be alternately removed and applied, as with the intentional aids. Border Collies are extremely clever in clueing into the most subtle body movements and, therefore, this part of training should not be underestimated.

Advanced Heelwork.
This phase of training will include:
Changes of pace (slow and fast pace).
Changes of pace should not be introduced into training until the dog is confident and happy at the normal pace. I prefer to teach the fast and slow pace using the same basic steps (i.e. left and right circle, figure of eight and the weave) that I have found so successful in teaching normal pace. Extreme care should be taken when teaching a Border Collie, that the handler does not lean forward (in fast pace) or backwards (in slow pace), as our breed tend to react to this more so than other breeds. The secret is to maintain the same upright body posture for all three tempos.
Stand, sit and down positions. Most obedience programmes have the stand, sit, and down positions in heelwork in one form or another. The secret of training these positions correctly is to teach them as a separate exercise until the dog is confident and then continue to do so to maintain perfection. Border Collies are renowned for 'taking over' once they have

learnt an exercise and this is normally caused by the handler either not being aware of the unintentional aids, or by practising the complete exercise. A Collie will soon learn to recognise the circumstances relating to a certain exercise and start anticipating what is going to happen. This anticipation, is of course, unacceptable both in training and in competition.

Bear in mind that heelwork is not one exercise but a series of movements, joined together to make one whole entity. In training, this series of exercises should be broken up into separate, small steps to be taught and trained. Border Collies learn extremely quickly and, while this can be an advantage, it can also cause problems if we fail to understand that the quick-thinking, intelligent Collie can become bored very easily if training becomes too repetitive and uninteresting. The danger of taking a Collie out and doing ten minutes of continuous heelwork is that, through boredom, the dog will lose concentration and motivation. If we then correct the dog for not paying attention, or for not trying hard enough, he will soon decide that training is negative and, once a Collie has made this decision, the damage has been done.

RECALL
This is one of the first exercises that I teach a dog, because it can be so much fun and helps build up a relationship with the dog. When first introducing the dog to the recall exercise the priority must be enthusiasm rather that precision. The method for teaching a puppy or a mature dog is almost identical, with only minor adaptation for the size of the dog. The exercise can be split into four sections: the Sit, the Wait, the Recall and the Present (front).

Upon presenting, the dog must be taught to go to heel, but I do not include this as

Teaching the Present: Ria places her feet slightly apart to guide Stevie into the correct position.
Photos: McGovern.

part of the recall, as it is a separate exercise and should be taught as such. Furthermore, although the four parts that make up the complete exercise are numbered in order of sequence, we do not have to train them in this order and can, in fact, teach the dog the recall long before he is capable of doing the sit and the wait. Being intelligent and sensitive creatures, many Collies would get upset if we were to insist on a correct present after he had happily rushed up to us on the recall command. As always, our priority must be attitude before precision and, therefore, I teach the dog to want to come as quickly as possible and do not insist on a sit in the present until he has been doing so for some time.

The Recall

To teach the recall I make use of a friend to hold the dog while I run off prior to calling the dog with the help of a tidbit or a toy. Depending on the size of the dog, I either sit on the ground with my legs spread open (for small puppies), on my

knees (for larger puppies) or on a chair (for adult dogs). Once I see that the dog fully intends to come when told, and is paying absolute attention, I signal the 'helper' to release the dog and then I excitedly call him as he runs towards me. By placing my hands containing the reward close to the front of my body, I can ensure that the dog runs right up to me. At this time I only want the dog to rush up to me as quickly as possible. If the assistant is well known to the dog, then the dog can be turned around and held, prior to being called back. In this way the dog will soon learn to run to and fro to receive his reward. If we wish, the trainer can introduce the sendaway command as the dog is sent back to the assistant and, in this way, we can very simply introduce the dog to another exercise.

The Present

As preparation for teaching the present, I prefer to sit in a chair while ensuring that my feet are positioned slightly apart with

71

just enough room for the dog to sit between my legs. I then call the dog into the present using my feet as a guide to ensure a straight sit. In this way I can call the dog from any angle and teach him to straighten up before sitting. The dog does not have to be called from the sit, and can just be walking around the room or sitting next to my leg. Once again, bear in mind that we are teaching the present and not the recall. Once the dog will come in and sit between my legs from any angle we can teach the present from the stand.

Place the dog in the sit and position yourself in front of the dog so that he is presenting as you want. Take a step back with one leg while simultaneously calling the dog. Step back with the other leg while giving the sit command. If you take just one step backwards the dog will not have enough room to walk into the present and will 'bunny hop' into the present, thereby learning to tuck his rear end in rather than sitting back. The dog will learn to sit in the present while moving forward, rather than stopping first then sitting. If the dog sits while still moving forward he will be unable to do other than sit straight. Crooked sits are, as often as not, caused by the dog first stopping and then sitting. The 'bunny hop' avoids this habit.

The sit and wait

The sit should already be well estab-lished, as it has been taught in steps one and two of attention training. The wait should not be taught until the dog has been taught the sit-stay to avoid any confusion. Once the dog has been taught the sit-stay we can begin to teach the sit and wait. Place the dog in the heel position and command him to sit, and then step away and turn and face him, walk backwards to the end of the lead and then praise before returning to the present. Continue praising the dog while walking backwards to the end of the lead. Repeat this three or four times, then return to the present, step back into the finish and then release the dog. Initially the dog should not be called until he is capable of sitting and paying full attention while you leave him. Once he capable of doing so, the wait, recall and present can be combined.

Putting it all together

Place the dog in the sit, command him and walk off to the end of the lead, and turn and face him. Call the dog and walk quickly backwards to encourage the dog to come promptly. As the dog approaches the present position, command him to sit before taking the last step back into the

Stevie must be confident in the Sit-Stay before graduating to the Wait.

halt, to ensure that the dog goes into the sit while still moving forwards. Praise the dog for presenting and release.

A common mistake is to call the dog into the present and to keep moving back for a few steps. This only encourages the dog to slow down, as he has to reduce his speed of return to the speed at which you are moving backwards. The secret is to stop just as the dog reaches you, thereby avoiding this bad habit. Do remember to vary the training and to teach each step as a separate exercise, only combining them occasionally. Otherwise, Collies soon realise that the present is coming and will slow up in anticipation.

THE RETRIEVE

Most Border Collies love this exercise and, if not taught carefully, will tend to 'take over' and do it their own way. The recall is an integral part of the retrieve exercise and, therefore, it should be thoroughly taught before the retrieve. The retrieve is, in fact, a combination of five exercises of which only one will be new to the dog. The sit, recall, present and finish should all have already been taught to the dog. The retrieve, placed between the sit and the recall, is the only new step. Once the dog has run out and picked up the article, the exercise reverts back to the recall exercise. I prefer to teach the exercise in six separate steps, with a specific goal in mind in each step. The six steps are: the Hold, the Take, the Reach, Take around the arm, Take around the leg, Retrieve at the end of the lead. Each step is carefully taught and then they are all joined together for the complete exercise.

The Hold

In this step the dog is taught to hold the article firmly but gently, without mouthing. To do this, gently open the dog's mouth and place the article just behind the canine teeth, and, with the index finger of each hand, gently hold the article in the dog's mouth, while praising and giving the hold command. Do not punish or correct the dog if he resists. Just remove the article, calm the dog and start again. This step will lay the foundation for all further steps and the dog will form his opinion of the exercise based upon your attitude. The key words are positive praise. You must gently force your will upon the dog without upsetting him. Do not force the dog to hold the article for more than a few seconds. The moment the dog accepts the article without resistance the article can be removed. Continue with this step until the dog will happily accept the article without resentment.

The Take

In this step the dog will be taught to take the article on command without the article being placed in his mouth. Place the dog in the sit with your left hand in his collar. Place the article in your right hand and keep it out of sight behind your leg. Excite the dog with your voice and bring the article into view. The moment that the dog glances at the article, praise him and quickly hide the article back behind your leg. Keep repeating this game of hide and seek until the dog gets quite excited. Once he is actually looking for the article, bring it into view a few inches from his mouth. As the dog reaches forward towards the article, release the pressure on the collar in your left hand and give him the hold command. Your powers of observation are extremely important here, as the dog should not be given the hold command unless his attention is fixed on the article and he really wants to chase it. If the dog is not interested in the article, you should continue the hide and seek game without actually letting the dog get the article. Once the dog has been given the hold command and takes the article, revert immediately to step one to ensure that the

THE RETRIEVE
Demonstrated by Brian McGovern and Coolabri Tricky Woo, known as Woolie.

*Step One –
The Hold:
This exercise
lays the
foundation
for the
complete
retrieve
exercise.*

*Step Two –
The Take:
Woolie takes
the article on
command.*

*Step Three – The Reach: Woolie takes
the article at arm's length.*

*Step Four – Around the arm: Woolie has to go
around the arm to take the article.*

dog holds the article correctly. It is extremely important that this step is fully developed and that the dog is really keen to take the article before you proceed to the next step. Any reluctance or hesitation on the dog's part must be fully overcome; if not, this attitude will be carried forward to the next steps.

The Reach

This step is an extension of step two, the only difference being that the dog must now actually move forward out of the sit to take the article which is held in the right hand at arm's length in front of the dog. All hesitation or reluctance should have been overcome in the previous step and, therefore, this step, and all further steps, are designed to teach the already willing dog how to retrieve the article in the correct way. The moment the dog moves forward and has taken the article, give him the sit command and revert to step one, applying the hands to ensure that the dog holds the article without mouthing.

Take around the arm

To ensure a correct pick-up of the article in competition I prefer to teach the dog to go around the article and pick it up from the far side. This teaches the dog self-control. I want my dogs to retrieve quickly and correctly. Unfortunately, speed often causes faults such as snatching and running on after the pick-up. All of these habits cost points in competition and therefore, by teaching the dog the far-side pick-up, these faults can be avoided.

Sit the dog at heel and place your left hand in the collar to control the dog. Hold the article in your right hand fairly close to, and in front of, your body. Hold the article between thumb and index finger, with the article sticking out to the right, so that your hand will act as a barrier and the dog will not be able to take it. Give the dog the hold command and guide him out

past the article with your left hand, so that he turns and takes the article from the far side. The secret is how the article is held in the right hand; if held correctly the dog can only take the article from the far side. This step must be repeated many times until the dog has formed the habit of going around the arm and does not attempt to take the article from the near side. A dog that has been taught to enjoy retrieving will try to retrieve as quickly as possible, which means taking the shortest route, straight up to the article. Only by constantly training this step throughout the dog's working life will you be able to suppress this instinct. Border Collies make excellent retrievers, usually completing this exercise at top speed. However, speed without control can be very costly and great care should be taken to teach the dog to retrieve the way you want to and not the way he would prefer.

Take around the foot

Up until now the dog has only retrieved from the right hand and, in this step, the dog is taught to pick up the article from the ground. If the dog has been taught the previous steps correctly, this will only be a matter of showing the dog what is required. If the dog shows any reluctance, then the solution will be found in step two, where the dog is taught to enjoy retrieving, and in step four, where the dog has been taught the far-side pick-up.

Place the article on the ground about twelve inches in front of your feet. Hold the dog on a short lead in your left hand. Give the dog the hold command and, simultaneously, step forward with your left leg past the article and guide the dog around the leg for the far-side pick-up. As the dog picks up the article, give him the sit command and position yourself in front of the dog in the present. Do not insist that the dog presents, as this will distract from the step being taught. This step, once

ABOVE: Introducing the dumb-bell: Repeat the first three steps using a dumb-bell.

RIGHT: Woolie is happy to take the dumb-bell going around the arm.

again, will be repeated throughout the dog's life, in order to suppress his natural instinct to pick up the article via the shortest route, i.e. straight up to the article.

Retrieve at the end of the lead

By now the dog should be taking the article off the ground from the far side and should be happy to do so. We can now throw the article for the first time. Sit the dog at heel and throw the article a few feet away. Command the dog to sit and walk out and position yourself in front of the article, as in the previous step. Look back over the left shoulder and command the dog to retrieve the article. As he runs past the left leg, place the foot to the left and past the article, to ensure a far-side pick-up. Once the dog has taken the article,

finish off the step by placing yourself in the present, as in the previous step.

By carefully adhering to the above steps, and repeating them throughout the dog's working life, I have found that my Collies are fast, correct retrieve dogs. I never practise the finished exercises by throwing an article and sending the dog (off lead) to retrieve. At most I will let the dog do one or two retrieves occasionally, but I always have him on a flexi-lead to maintain control. To ensure accurate recalls and presents during retrieves I repeat all the basic recall steps with the dog holding an article. Border Collies have a highly developed instinct to chase. This can been put to great advantage in teaching a fast retrieve; however, this same instinct can create many problems if not controlled.

ABOVE: Now Woolie must pick up the article from the ground.

RIGHT: Step Five – Take around the foot.

Step Six – Retrieve at the end of the lead.

THE STAY EXERCISES

In general these exercises, the stand, sit and down stay, should not cause any undue problems with a Border Collie. There are several reasons why a dog will break stays and, for the Border Collie in particular, two possible problems can exist.

Collies are often, by nature, extremely active and excitable dogs with excellent eyesight and they see everything that is going on around them. In every other Obedience exercise we want the dogs lively and happy. For the stay exercises we need them calm and quiet. If we have play-trained our dogs they will quickly become excited if they see other dogs running about and playing while they have to stay while this is going on. The solution to this problem is the same as when teaching all other exercises. The exercise should be taught in a quiet area with no distractions whatsoever. The length of the stay exercises should be gradually increased, while the dog is constantly praised for doing right, thereby building confidence. Gradually distractions such as toys, and such like, can be introduced until the dog has learnt to ignore them. Only when he will do this should the dog be introduced to other dogs and the excitement of club and show environment.

Another common stay problem particular to the Collie is nervousness. Collies can be very sensitive and are often upset by sudden noises. Often a Collie will break a stay exercise for no obvious reason. I believe there is always a reason for a dog breaking a stay exercise; unfortunately the reason is, as often as not, obvious only to the dog. Once this problem has developed there is often nothing that can be done about it and, therefore, the solution lies in careful confidence-building and de-sensitising before the problem arises.

In general, Collies are good stay dogs, with the exception of a certain type of Collie with the character that can have the inherent problems described above. It is difficult to estimate how many of the nervous types of Collies with stay problems could have been 'cured' with careful training. However, I firmly believe in the principle that prevention is better than cure, and train all stays with the utmost patience and care.

IN SUMMARY

The Border Collie is an Obedience dog 'par excellence'. His intelligence, agility, build, and natural willingness to work make him an obvious choice for anyone wishing to compete in Competitive Obedience. He matures earlier than most other breeds and can often work until an advanced age. One of my Collies, Woolie, is still competing at almost twelve years of age and loving every minute of it. This means that we can reasonably expect a working career of ten years, far more than most other breeds. It also means that we can take the time to train slowly and with patience. On the down side, Collies can be very complex and it is quite common to see Collies with extremely strange habits and behaviour. Handled carefully, with an understanding of the Collie mind, the breed will enjoy Obedience. Collies are intelligent and sensitive and, wrongly handled, they will be difficult and will develop behaviour problems. Great care should be taken in developing the dog's attitude towards his work; teaching him to enjoy working must be our priority. Being sensitive, they do not adapt well to harsh handling – oh! they will still work, but it will not be a pretty picture.

6 *THE AGILITY COMPETITOR*

A group of enthusiasts from the North of England got together in 1977 to discuss some ideas they had for a new dog sport. They wanted it to be a fast action sport, but also wished it to retain an element of Obedience. They decided to put together a sport called Dog Agility, which would have elements of Obedience, working trials and show jumping. The Obedience part of Agility would mean having the dog under control to the extent that it would negotiate obstacles without the benefit of a lead. A 30-cm-high square table, or a down box, was part of the course and the handler was required to put the dog in the down position for five seconds without actually touching the dog. The disciplines taken from working trials were the ability to redirect the dog from a distance, the long jump, the hurdle and the scale, although this was modified into the "A" frame obstacle. The third element was show jumping. From this came show jumps, numbered courses and the fact that it could be a timed event with faults awarded for obstacles taken incorrectly. Obviously a few new obstacles were thought up, and this new sport had its first public showing at Crufts in 1978. The following year a proper team competition was held at Crufts and, since that time, it has been the fastest growing canine pursuit we have ever known.

In the early days of Agility the main breeds competing were Border Collies, working Sheepdogs and German Shepherds. There were, of course, a lot of other breeds as well, but the working background of Collies and Shepherds meant that they did most of the winning. As the sport has got faster over the last fifteen years it has become dominated by Border Collies and working Sheepdogs. They are fast, agile, intelligent and, most importantly, can "turn on a sixpence".

STARTING AGILITY TRAINING

To teach a dog all the agility obstacles, I believe it is easier to have the handler plus a helper – preferably an experienced instructor.

The dog should be fitted with a flat, leather collar and a lead that is comfortable to hold. As an experienced trainer and instructor, I have always preferred to be the one that holds the dog's lead. There are three reasons for this:

1. As I am used to handling beginner dogs, I can react quickly, anticipating their movements and not allowing the lead to interfere with the dog's balance.
2. If I am holding the lead, the handler's hands are free to encourage the dog with praise, to give food treats, or to use toys at the correct time and with the correct body signals.
3. I am stronger and more comfortable with a dog on my lefthand side, and thus,

Agility is now an international sport – and the Border Collie reigns supreme.
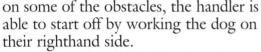
                                    Photo: Keith Allison.

on some of the obstacles, the handler is able to start off by working the dog on their righthand side.

What age should the dog be when you start training? The fact is that you cannot compete until the dog is 18 months old. If you want your dog to last for many years, it is not advisable to start training before 12 months of age. You need a degree of Obedience, so you will have plenty to work on up to the age at which they can start on the equipment. The only items of equipment to practise on before 12 months of age are the tunnels, but beware of making the dog tunnel-crazy; this can be a real problem. You could also get the dog used to passing between jump wings with a pole on the floor, and you may put them on a contact area near to the ground and practise a Wait.

OBEDIENCE TRAINING FOR AGILITY

It is a tremendous advantage for yourself and your instructor if your dog is under basic control before you start your Agility training. This will mean that once your dog has got his balance and has learned to negotiate each item of equipment, you will be able to dispense with the lead quickly; this will enable you to start training sequences without the dog running off or being disobedient.

USEFUL OBEDIENCE TRAINING

Sit Stay Invaluable for training your dog to wait on the start line.

Recall When you start building up from one jump to several, the dog can be left in a Sit Stay and then recalled over several jumps.

Sendaway The dog can be taught to work away from you or ahead of you and, when you build up from one jump to several, a Sendaway will help you send the dog on over several jumps.

The Down For a good, fast Down on the table it will be much easier if you have trained a Down command in Obedience using the floor instead of the table.

Retrieve A toy can be an excellent reward for a dog during its Agility training, but it is important that the dog plays with you with the toy and does not just run off with it. A retrieve game with a toy, where the dog brings the toy back to you, or a game of tugging, will be very beneficial.

Heelwork Basic heelwork is a must. The dog can be trained to come to heel or to your righthand side without having to be pulled about and physically handled. The ultimate aim is to have the dog walking, running or turning and staying quite close

– all of this being done in a smooth manner without getting in your way.

BEHAVIOUR

Bad behaviour should not be allowed to start. One of the worst examples in Agility is a dog who barks while competing on a course of equipment. The excitement of Agility can easily encourage a dog to bark and if this becomes a habit, it is very hard to cure. The best advice about this habit is not to let it start. What may take a simple verbal correction initially will be a major corrective problem if left to become a habit. If a dog barks while competing on a course, he will not be able to hear your commands over the noise he is making himself! If the initial verbal correction does not work, I suggest filling a small washing-up liquid container with water and squirting the dog with it every time he barks. It is not cruel, it just shocks the dog, especially when he believes it will happen every time he barks! One other important point about barking – do not let your dog bark while waiting on the start line or while queuing up to work.

BITING

Some dogs will jump up and nip your arm or bite the back of your legs or feet. This can happen in between obstacles or when you leave the arena. This is normally caused by excitement and should be corrected as soon as it starts and before it becomes a habit.

COMMANDS

When teaching a new dog Agility, it is important to have separate verbal commands for each item of equipment. For the A frame and Dog Walk I use the command Walk On. For the See-Saw I use the same command, Walk On, but add the word See-Saw. An inexperienced dog can sometimes get the Dog Walk and See-Saw mixed up and they can lose confidence if

they run straight up the See-Saw, not expecting the tip when it occurs.

My command for Jumps and Hurdles is Over, but for Spreads, Long Jumps and Wishing Well it will be Right Over. The connotation of a jumping obstacle is still there but the word Right in front of it tells the dog it is something different.

It is quite common for the word Through to be used for the Tyre. However, an inexperienced dog may go under the Tyre with this command, especially if there is a tunnel as the next obstacle. For this reason I use the command Tyre Over.

For both the Rigid Tunnel and Collapsible Tunnel I use the command Through. For the Weaving Poles it is a straightforward Weave and for the Table it is Table Down; thus we are telling the dog which piece of equipment is next and also the position for the dog to assume once he is on the table.

Direction commands are of critical importance. Competitions are rarely won by handlers who run all the way round a course with the dog, especially if your physique is such that you cannot run quite like the wind! There will be certain parts of each course where you can command the dog at a distance and then cut a corner yourself to save precious seconds.

You will have already taught the dog commands for the separate items of equipment. You will now need to teach the dog directional commands. For the Left Turn use the command Back, for the Right Turn use Come; for the dog to be on your Left use Heel, for the dog to be on your right use Side. The Heel and the Side commands are used to keep the dog close when passing between obstacles. To send the dog straight ahead, I use the command Go On; and, at all times, to get the dog's attention, I just call his name.

BODY LANGUAGE

In all canine training body language is very

COMMANDS
Photos: Keith Allison

ABOVE: The Dog Walk – "Walk on."

RIGHT: The Seesaw – "Walk on seesaw."

ABOVE: Hurdles – "Over."

RIGHT: Tyre – "Tyre over."

Rigid tunnel – "Through."

Collapsible tunnel –
"Through."

Weaving poles – "Weave."

Table – "Table down."

important. Our bodies give lots of signals to dogs. One of the commonest faults to be seen is using the wrong hand to signal to the dog. By this I mean that if the dog is working on the left, any signals made should be with the left hand; and the same, obviously, if the dog is working on the right – the signals should be made with the right hand. A lot of handlers do not realise that when a dog is working a course, it will be watching the handler's body language. If the dog is on the left and you signal with your right hand, your right side will come forward and your left shoulder will drop back slightly. The dog will then assume, incorrectly, that you are turning left and he may turn in an unwanted direction and thus waste valuable time or, indeed, on a tight course, the dog could take the wrong obstacle and be eliminated.

Handling should be, at all times, straight and smooth.

THE START
We will now move on to the individual obstacles. We will first talk about the start. Although this is not an obstacle as far as course judging is concerned, you can still be eliminated or waste valuable time. It is of paramount importance that the dog stays behind the start line until you have commanded him to start. This would usually happen after the timer has said that he, and hence the judge, is ready. If your dog starts prematurely and takes the first obstacle, you will be eliminated.

With a slower type of dog it can sometimes make it worse if you try to make him wait on a start line and then walk on to the course and call the dog to

Direction commands are of critical importance.

Despite the speed the dog is going at, he will still have his eyes on you, watching your body language and listening for the next command.

you. With this type of dog it is generally better to start off the line together.

For the faster type of dog a good stay on the start line puts you in control and allows you to position yourself to the best advantage. If you have taught your dog the Sit Stay thoroughly, you will have no problems. However, the dog can get over-excited and try to take over from you on the start line.

I train a dog to Stay with just one command. I then walk confidently away to the position on the course that will give me the best advantage. Anticipation can often be caused by the handler that constantly tells the dog to Stay, almost winding it up in the process. A hand signal held up while walking away can also be a problem as, when the dog is called, the hand will drop and this, along with the verbal command, is the signal for the dog to start. So, if you walk away holding your hand up and your hand drops slightly, the dog will take this as a Start signal.

If you do have a problem with anticipation, have a training session. Set the dog up on a start line, walk away, then

return to the dog and praise it, while keeping it in the Sit position. Then break off and together walk away. You can do this while other dogs are working on a course. Also, to make the training situation more like a show, arrange for someone to act as a timekeeper, even to the point of saying "when you are ready" or "in your own time" as a prompt for you to go. Remember, a good Obedience Sit Stay exercise is invaluable on the start line.

RIGID PIPE TUNNEL
This tunnel should have a minimum diameter of 2ft and should be a minimum 10ft in length. In practise the tunnel is normally a minimum of 12ft in length and is of the concertina type, usually made of heavy-duty vinyl, with metal or plastic ribs. When Agility first started piping was obtained from coal mines, as it is the same as they used for ducting fresh air underground. In some cases, if the clubs did not wash it well after they had obtained it, they ended up with some very black dogs!

When you initially start this training, the

RIGID TUNNEL

Frankie's view of the tunnel.

Barbara kneels at the other end of the tunnel and calls Frankie.

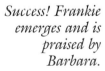

Success! Frankie emerges and is praised by Barbara.

tunnel should be compressed to its smallest length and kept straight. Put the dog in the Down position at one end of the tunnel, facing it and as close as possible to the entrance. The instructor stays with the dog. The handler goes to the other end of the tunnel and calls the dog. It may be necessary for the handler to put his head into the end of the tunnel and he may also need to have the dog's lead passed to him by the instructor. After the dog has gained confidence and is passing through the tunnel without the lead, the tunnel can be gradually lengthened and a slight bend put in it.

COLLAPSIBLE CLOTH TUNNEL
This tunnel should be a minimum of 2ft in diameter and have a maximum span of 2ft 6ins, again with a 10ft minimum length. It has a solid entrance of at least 1ft 6ins in length and 1ft 7ins high, normally constructed with a flat board and a piece of plywood, or a similar material, bent over to make a tunnel entrance fixed to the board. Attached to the rear of this would be a length of canvas tunnelling. The front edge of the tunnel should be suitably padded.

The training principles are the same as for the pipe tunnel. The main training difference is that the cloth can be rolled up to shorten the length of the tunnel, and the tunnel exit should be held open by the handler. Once the dog has gained confidence, the end of the tunnel can be let down and the tunnel unrolled to its full length.

DOG WALK
This can be best described as a bridge. The dog goes up a slope, over the top of the bridge and down a slope on the other side. The height of the middle plank should be approximately 4ft 6ins from the ground, with firmly fixed ramps on either side of it. Each of these three planks should be between 12ft and 14ins long and a minimum of 10ins, maximum 12ins, wide. There are normally two piers, or supports, holding the top plank secure.

The initial training takes place with the lead on the dog (plain leather collar and sturdy leather lead). The handler and instructor approach the dog walk with the dog between them. It is important that the dog approaches in a controlled manner. Dogs that pull and rush up the plank will take over when the lead is removed. Try to keep the dog motivated with commands and keep the lead loose. Walk the dog up the plank and ensure that you and the trainer stay each side of it. You can obviously then catch the dog if he falls off but, more important, you will give him confidence in these early stages. Once the

COLLAPSIBLE CLOTH TUNNEL

The same training methods are used as for the rigid tunnel, but Barbara holds the end of the tunnel open.

DOG WALK

Initial training takes place on the lead.

Mary and Barbara walk on either side of Frankie encouraging him to move in a controlled manner. Barbara is encouraging him with a treat.

As Frankie approaches the contact (marked in red), Barbara encourages him to lower his head by giving him a treat.

Frankie is put in the Down the moment he leaves the contact.

Frankie, on the lead, is encouraged down the A-frame.

On the contact Frankie is given a treat.

Frankie is put in the Down and rewarded.

dog has found his balance, encourage him to trot across while on a loose lead, but always, right from the beginning, ensure that the dog waits on the contact. After this, the speed can be built up while still retaining control on the contacts.

A-FRAME
The A-frame consists of two ramps 9ft long by 3ft wide. These two ramps are hinged at the apex and the apex should stand 6ft 3ins from the ground. Each ramp should have a non-slip surface and anti-slip slates at intervals.

There are various methods of starting the training for this obstacle. As the dog cannot see the other side when he is on the ascent, you may need to go up the A-frame yourself, leaving the dog being held by the instructor, and then call the dog up to you. It may give the dog more confidence if he has a lead on; if it is long enough the instructor could pass it to you.

Another method is to have two leads on the dog. Both handler and instructor hold a lead and walk either side of the A-frame. This keeps the dog central and the even pull stops the dog falling off one of the sides. Another method is the training A-frame. The normal height of the A-frame is over six feet but you can obtain an adjustable one for training. If you do start the initial training on one of these frames, it is important to get the height up to competition size as soon as possible.

Once the dog has confidence about going over the apex, and he knows what is on the other side, then there are usually no further problems. Always ensure that the descent is taken in a controlled manner. Do not let the dog get into the habit of rushing down the slope and jumping off early.

SEE-SAW

This obstacle should consist of a plank firmly mounted on a central bracket. The plank should be a minimum of 12ft and a maximum of 14ft long and the width should be between 10ins and 12ins. The height of

the central bracket should be a maximum of 2ft 3ins from the ground and, as with the A-frame, it should have a non-slip surface and have anti-slip slats at intervals.

Never train for this obstacle until the dog is confident on the dog walk. Initially the instructor should hold the dog on the lead. The handler should give verbal encouragement and, as the dog walks up the plank, the handler should hold the plank to stop it banging down when the dog passes the point of tip. The handler should gradually lower it down. After the dog has had a few tries then the handler can let go of the plank when it is a couple of inches from the floor. The distance from the ground at which the handler lets go of the plank can gradually be increased until it is not necessary for the handler to hold the plank at all. The end result should be that the dog walks up the see-saw, slows for the plank to tip, then walks down to the

SEE-SAW

Do not start see-saw training until your dog is confident on the A-frame.

Frankie is rewarded when he reaches the off contact.

contact. While the dog waits on the off contact this is a good time to give him a treat.

CONTACT POINT TRAINING

This may be a good time, before going on to the training of contact points, to explain fully what they are and what purpose they serve. There are three prime obstacles in Agility, the A-frame, the see-saw and the dog walk. On the on and off sides of all of these there is a contact area, which is normally painted in a different colour to the rest of the obstacle. The reason why it is called a contact area is that the dog's paw must make contact with this area. The reason for the introduction of contact areas, back in the very early days of Agility, was not just to catch the dog out and find fault with it, there was also a safety measure involved. It was thought that, by introducing a contact area, handlers would train their dogs to the ends of the higher pieces of equipment and, I have to say, it has fulfilled its original purpose. Very rarely now do you see a dog leap off one of the prime obstacles from a great height. The dog walk and see-saw would have a contact area covering the last 3' from the end of each on and off plank, and the A-frame would cover an area of 3' 6" from the bottom of each ramp.

The two methods I use for training to achieve good contacts are either to make the dog wait standing on the contact, or for the dog to be in the Down position on the contact. I also put the dog in the Down position on the ground immediately after the contact area. Whichever method I use I expect the dog to have a low head carriage on the contact area; so, if it is just the wait on the contact, I give a treat to the dog on the contact at a low level, encouraging him to lower his head. It is a fact that dogs which keep their heads high at the end of a contact obstacle are more likely to jump off and miss the contact.

Border Collies have a definite advantage in keeping a low head carriage. If you watch them working sheep you will notice that when they are concentrating on their work their necks are lower than their shoulders, and you want the same action on contacts.

If the handler is going to use a treat or toy as a reward on the contact area of the A-frame, dog walk or see-saw, this should be given to the dog by using the hand nearest to the dog while keeping the body straight. The dog will not then have to watch the hand returning to the other side of the handler's body, and this will help to keep the dog's head straight. In the early stages of training, the handler may have the dog on a lead. The lead may be held with the hand nearest the dog and so the bad habit of giving the reward with the wrong hand can develop. Contact training should be done in a controlled manner. Speed will come later.

JUMPS AND HURDLES

The maximum height allowed is 2ft 6ins and the displaceable bar should have a minimum width of 4ft. The top bar or plank must be easily displaced by a dog, and a wall should have displaceable units on the top. Certainly, most hurdles would have a significant 'wing' on each side, very similar to show jumping hurdles.

To start hurdle training, the ideal height at which to set the hurdle bar for a Collie-size dog is 15 inches. The trainer should hold the dog on a lead while the handler stands on the other side of the hurdle and calls the dog over the low jump. It is fairly rare for a dog to try and go under the jump with the bar height set at 15 inches.

For the second stage of training it is preferable to use a wingless hurdle. Once the dog is happily taking the jump from both sides, you can move on to approaching the jump together but still with the dog on a lead. If you have to use a winged hurdle, you should have a longer

JUMPS AND HURDLES

Mary holds
Frankie on
the lead.

Barbara calls
Frankie over
the jump,
giving the
"Over"
command.

LEFT: Mary
demonstrates another
method using a toy to
encourage Kizzy over
the jump.

RIGHT: Teaching
the dog to jump and
turn left or right.

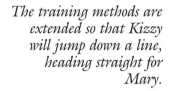

Now Mary can rely on the verbal command and a hand signal.

The training methods are extended so that Kizzy will jump down a line, heading straight for Mary.

than normal lead on the dog. This is to ensure that you do not upset the dog's balance and that you can allow the dog to land comfortably. Once the dog is taking the jump from both sides with the lead on and the handler passing the side of the hurdle without the dog trying to go under the bar or round the side of the hurdle, the handler can remove the lead and try without it. It is important with all obstacle training to use the correct command when you start the initial training. In this case every time the dog approaches the hurdle you say 'over'.

TYRE
In the early days of Agility, the only thing you ever saw suspended in a frame was a real rubber tyre. These are still to be found now, but the modern way of constructing a tyre obstacle means that you replace the tyre with a life-buoy. This is much smoother for the dog, should it brush past it on its way through, and as it is so smooth with no openings, it is much safer. The life-buoy or tyre should have a minimum aperture diameter of 1ft 6ins and, for a standard dog, the centre of the aperture should be 3ft from the ground. When the tyre or life-buoy is mounted

Frankie, on the lead, is encouraged to go through the tyre which is at its lowest height.

Once the dog is confident, try without the lead.

with an A-frame mechanism, then any chains or bars that are used to hold the tyre secure should be covered in suitable padding.

All the same principles apply to this obstacle as apply to hurdle and jump training. Drop the tyre to its lowest height, sit the dog very close to it. Pass the lead through the tyre and call the dog through. Without being harsh, you should be able to ensure that the dog goes through the tyre because you will have the lead on. Once the dog passes through the tyre easily, gradually raise the tyre height. If the dog tries to go underneath the tyre, drop the height again until he regains his confidence. The handler should decide at what point the lead is removed during the training session, but do not be afraid to put the lead back on if the dog loses confidence.

LONG JUMP
Three to five separate units comprise a long jump. The maximum overall length at which these units can be placed is 5ft and the maximum height of any of the units should be 1ft 3ins. Marker poles with a minimum height of 4ft should be placed at all four corners. These should not be attached to any part of the long jump. It is

very difficult to visualise a long jump, but the long jump units are usually made up of a flat plank, around 6ft wide and 4ft long. Supports are put on each end of the plank to make it stand at an angle on the ground. Then another four units would be made the same, but with the supports made slightly longer on each one, so, in essence, what you have are between three and five separate planks, rising up in height, so the dog would jump over the lowest one at the front and clear the highest one at the back. The dog would also be required to jump straight through the obstacle, hence the need for having four corner poles.

When starting training use just three of the elements. It is important that there is a definite gap between these elements, otherwise, when approaching the obstacle, the dog may think it is a solid obstacle and try and walk on it.

The four corner posts should be used to ensure that the dog jumps straight over, but with the dog on a lead the poles may get in the way. For this reason it is best to leave the training for this obstacle until the handler has a wait and recall without a lead over an ordinary hurdle. Sometimes a dog may need more height in the obstacle to stop it stepping on the elements. I sometimes put the small front element on to the back one, thus increasing its height by 25 per cent. Gradually increase the length and add the other elements as the dog becomes more confident.

WISHING WELL

The wishing well is a very pretty obstacle and a little bit similar to the one you may have in your garden, including having a pretty roof over it. The big difference, of course, is that you will get no water out of this one! The bar that the bucket would normally hang off is a displaceable bar, similar to the top bar of an ordinary hurdle, and the dog has, obviously, to clear this bar and jump through the middle of the two uprights which hold the roof up, to successfully complete the obstacle.

Only when the dog can jump two foot six inches and a spread should this obstacle be attempted. The only problem that usually occurs is with the dog stepping on the base (banking) as he goes over. If this should occur, put some short poles on the base that will roll when the dog's paws make contact with them.

TABLE

This should be a solid construction, with a non-slip surface. The table top should be a minimum 3ft square and the height for standard dogs should be 2ft 6ins (for minis it should be 15ins).

The table should be stable, of sound design and must not wobble. To start the training the instructor should hold the dog on a lead, while the handler goes to the other side of the table and calls the dog up. Put the dog in a quick Down once on the table. Never allow the dog to jump on and then straight off the table. When teaching the table I always make sure the dog lies down on the hip and not in the upright Down. I believe this helps to stop the dog skidding off the table. Also, as with a Down Stay, it takes two movements for the dog to get up. You may have already started table training at home without realising it, with the dog jumping on chairs or beds. I must confess to sometimes using my bed as a table for training.

WEAVING POLES

There should be a minimum of five and a maximum of twelve poles in each set. Although poles can be hammered into the ground, it is preferable to fix them into a frame, especially when they are to be used for a show. The poles should be of a rigid construction and, although the Kennel Club rules state that they should be between 1ft 6ins and 2ft apart, it is

TABLE

Mary holds Kizzy steady in the Down Stay.

LEFT: Barbara starts with Frankie on the lead, encouraging him to weave through the poles.

RIGHT: A toy is a useful aid to keep the dog moving.

Kizzy is now weaving at speed, following the toy through the poles.

generally recognised that the ideal width apart is 21ins The poles should be a minimum of 2ft 6ins high and, ideally, 1ft in diameter.

There are several ways of teaching the dog to weave. The quickest method is to teach the weave as it is, without any attachments. To explain: wires can be purchased to aid the training. These guide the dog in and out of the poles in the required direction, and also two sets of weaves can be gradually put together to achieve the same purpose. I have always found that the quickest method is to teach the dog without these attachments. It would normally take longer to teach this obstacle than any other, therefore it is in the handler's best interests to have a set of weaving poles at home. This should be a standard set, of the dimensions given above, and a few minutes can be spent practising daily, always, obviously, being careful not to overdo it. This will quicken the learning process and speed up the dog. If you only practise once a week, achieving show standard will be a slow process.

95

Apart from a couple of hurdles which I use for turn training, weights, recalls, sending over etc., the only piece of major equipment I own and keep at home is a set of weaves.

When teaching the dog the weave for the first time, I show the dog the way through while it has a lead on. I approach the weave initially in a straight direction so that the dog will learn, from the beginning, which side of the weave to enter first. This should be with the first pole next to its left shoulder. I will hold the lead short and control the dog's head by keeping it close to the poles, so that its body will follow without being pushed and pulled through too far. After I have accomplished this, I will get him to follow a tidbit or toy by, again, keeping my hand nearest the dog close to his nose and taking my time, in order to give him the chance to follow. If you initially move your hand too fast, he will start missing out poles and getting in a mess. If he follows easily, the lead can be removed and, if you have your timing right, he should weave correctly.

At the end of each weave, I will play with his toy with him, or maybe throw it, or feed him the tidbit I have in my hand. When training the weave, I would keep my feet away from the dog, as I do not believe in blocking each pole with your foot and leg. I find the dog is then not learning for himself, and will miss out poles if you do not block them. You will also stop his speed through the poles, because your foot cannot keep up with his speed and style and, of course, the dog will need the speed to develop his style. If you watch a dog that weaves slowly, you will notice that his feet cross over each other and look untidy. If a dog is weaving fast, he will either use the two front feet together in a push-jump fashion, or use each leg individually in a swimming motion.

To train for a correct entry, I will try to excite the dog by holding him back, about 12ins away from the first pole, telling him to weave. I then let him go just ahead of me and, if he enters the wrong side, I will call him back to heel. If he got it right, I will follow up and encourage him on through the weave. It is probably best to teach the dog to weave on the left and right-hand sides of the handler from the beginning. However, a dog that has learnt to weave ahead of you by itself should not worry which side you are on.

The dog that has been taught initially to weave on the left will, when the handler swaps to the other side of the weave, weave so far down the poles and then pull out halfway. The interesting thing that has happened to me, and I have seen many times in training, is that when the dog is weaving on the left and misses the last two poles, the handler then stops and gets the dog to come back and do the last two poles, so the handler only corrects what has been missed. However, if a handler is weaving with the dog on the right and the dog misses the last two poles, the handler generally goes back to the beginning and starts the poles all over again. The dog is then, of course, not being taught how to come back to the handler's right side to do the last two poles. When I have asked the handlers just to correct the last two poles when the dog has been on their right, they then cannot get the dog in the correct position to do this.

Teaching the dog to come back to your right side as a separate exercise will help with this problem because, if the dog is continually being taken back to start the poles from the beginning, it is not learning where it went wrong and, of course, dogs have short memories and any correction should be immediate, at the place where the mistake was made.

Then, of course, there is the dog that misses the last two poles because it wants to get on with the other equipment. A tunnel as a next obstacle may be a favourite for this. If the dog does miss the last poles to rush on to the next item of equipment, it is best to turn round and make the dog weave back in the opposite direction.

SEQUENCES

This means putting several obstacles together to run one after another, but it is not a full course. Any number of obstacles, from two upwards, would constitute a sequence. You know the time when your dog has learned to negotiate all the equipment. The dog has also learned to turn left, right, straight on and wait, when commanded, from whichever side you are handling on, and you can also change sides without making the dog pull up. Now is the time to start putting together several pieces of equipment and building up sequences with the dog off lead.

It may be wise to leave the jumps at 15" when beginning sequences. I myself prefer to have a proper course set out and then to pick out parts to use as sequences. There are normally many ways you can think of to use four to six obstacles together. When you have worked your way around the course, completing various obstacles in sequence and it is coming together smoothly, you should put the jumps up to 2ft. I would then start working on half the course and then, ultimately, run the full numbered course. After achieving this, I would then revert back to the sequences but this time with the dog jumping 2ft 6ins.

If this all went smoothly, I would then try running the full course with the jumps at full height. If any problems do occur during this training session, such as the dog going under the jump pole or hesitating in its take-off, or losing confidence on any other piece of equipment, I would revert back to the basic rule of dog training – do not be afraid to go back to basics, it will solve any

problem much more quickly and will give the dog back the confidence he needs. In the case of hurdles, this would mean lowering the height again until the dog has regained confidence.

WALKING THE COURSE

Agility started with a sprinkling of show jumping input, and one of the things both sports still keep in common is walking the course. In the early days of Agility it was a case of rushing round a set of equipment as fast as possible, with the dog on your left hand side. Nowadays, course walking is absolutely critical in order to decide where you are going to save the split seconds required to win a class.

When walking a course, whether it be for training purposes or competitions, it should always be done with care. Probably three times is best: the first to see the numbers and to memorise the position of the obstacles, the second to work out the most economical path for the dog, and the third to work out your own path and where you will need to change sides. Usually there will be a choice of handling changes at least a couple of times on each course. Everyone has to work out which will suit their dog best. Some dogs naturally sweep out wider on corners, giving you time to cut across. Others turn extremely tightly and the handler will not have time to swap correctly. In training, you can try different ways to see which ends up the smoothest. If you stand and watch any open Agility competition, it will very quickly become apparent that the winning dogs do not run round the whole course on their handlers' lefthand sides. You will note the handlers swapping sides, with the dogs responding at a distance to various commands. It must be remembered that there can be hundredths of a second between 1st and 20th place, and any split seconds saved on a course could bring you a red rosette.

7 *THE FLYBALL COMPETITOR*

One of the most popular and fastest growing dog sports is Flyball. This fun competition originated in the United States and is one of the few dog sports that is a wholly team event. The competitions are run on a knock-out system with two teams competing against each other in each round. Each team consists of four dogs, with each dog, in turn, having to run out and jump four low hurdles before pressing a pedal on a special apparatus with his front paws which will then release a tennis ball that the dog must catch and carry back to his handler, again jumping over the same four hurdles on the return. Once that dog has returned, the next dog in the team is released and so on, until all four team members have successfully completed the course. Each round of the competition has three legs and the winning team qualifies through to the next round. The winner of each heat is the team that completes the run correctly in the fastest time. Any dog that fails to return with the ball, or misses a hurdle, or makes any other fault, must run again. All four dogs must complete the course correctly and as quickly as possible.

The Border Collie is an ideal choice for this sport. His athletic build and alert, spirited character are perfect for a competition requiring speed and agility combined with a certain amount of enthusiastic control. However, although the Border Collie is perhaps the most popular breed seen in Flyball competitions, care must be taken during training, because the inherent characteristics which make the Border Collie so suitable can also, if not properly channelled and controlled, lead to over-excitement and even hysteria. Care should also be taken to ensure that the dog is physically fit and healthy, as the amount of physical effort needed to compete in Flyball competitions is, I believe, underestimated. Obviously the dog should have first class eyesight, and have no hip problems or other physical disabilities. Border Collies are often willing to suffer great pain and discomfort in their obsession to 'do the job'. However, just because the dog does not seem to show any signs of discomfort during an activity, this does not mean that we should allow him unrestricted access to activities that can cause problems. Flyball is an excellent hobby for a physically fit dog.

THE TRAINING
To compete in a Flyball competition a dog must be taught to jump over hurdles and operate the Flyball box to release the ball. He must learn to catch the ball in mid-air and run back to the handler while carrying the ball, and he must learn to do all this while suffering the distraction of other dogs doing the same things and in direct competition with him.

Each phase of training should be broken down and taught as a separate exercise until the dog is experienced and proficient in each step. Only then should the separate steps be combined into the finished article. The actual training of the individual steps is quite straightforward and should not cause any undue problems for a Border Collie. However, care should be taken to prepare and teach the dog to complete the exercise while coping with the distraction of other dogs. The rules of competition allow the next dog to be released as the preceding dog crosses the finish line. This means that two dogs are on the racing lane at the same time.

Most dogs get into a high state of excitement during Flyball competitions and must be taught to keep their minds on the job in hand and to ignore all fellow team-members and competitors. The training should, therefore, be split into the following phases:
Teaching the dog to catch a ball in mid-air.
Teaching the dog to operate the Flyball box.
Teaching the dog to retrieve a ball.
Teaching the dog to jump hurdles.
Teaching the dog to run out and return as quickly as possible.
Teaching the dog to do all of the above amid the distraction of many other excited and barking dogs.

CATCHING A BALL IN MID-AIR
I have watched many instructors trying to teach a dog to operate a Flyball box without first having ascertained whether or not the dog enjoys chasing and playing with a ball. Obviously a dog that is completely disinterested in catching a ball will be quite useless in Flyball competitions. Luckily most dogs enjoy, or can be taught to enjoy, chasing a ball. The Border Collie usually does not have to be taught and will willingly play with almost any object. However, not all Collies are natural 'catchers' and some dogs may have to be taught how to catch a ball in mid-air.

Start off by having a game with him and roll the ball along the ground, allowing the dog to run after the ball and collect it. As he does so, run backwards while calling the dog. This will encourage him to turn as he picks up the ball. This will be very important in later training, as the dog can save precious seconds in competition if he has been taught to turn quickly once he has caught the ball. As soon as the dog is happily playing with the ball, he can be put on a flexi-lead and told to fetch the ball. As he picks up the ball he can be called and, simultaneously, be given a tug on the lead to assist with the quick turn-around while, at the same time, by using the flexi lead, the distance from dog to handler can be gradually increased.

Within a few days the dog should be happily chasing a thrown ball and quickly bringing it back to his handler. One should not make the mistake of insisting on obedience-type precision when teaching this 'retrieve'. The priority is keenness and speed, not accuracy. Once this goal has been achieved the dog can be taught to catch the ball in mid-air.

To teach this, place the dog on the flexi-lead and let him walk about on a loose lead; call his name and, as he looks at you, throw the ball to him in an underhand throw so that the dog can easily catch it. As he catches the ball call him, while simultaneously tugging on the lead and running backwards to encourage him to return to you the moment he catches the ball. As in the previous step, gradually increase the distance until the dog can catch the ball at the full eight-metre length of the flexi.

Some dogs are so keen to play this game that they will not go more than a yard or two away. If this happens the dog should be placed in the sit and the handler should gradually back away to the end of the lead to increase the distance. Once the dog is adept at catching the ball, and is extremely enthusiastic to do so, he can be taught to operate the Flyball box.

OPERATING THE FLYBALL BOX
Prior to actually teaching the dog to operate the box, it is worthwhile allowing the dog some time to get used to seeing the machine in operation. Occasionally some dogs are initially frightened of the noise the machine makes and, as Border Collies can be noise-sensitive, it is advisable to play catch with the dog at a few yards distance from the box while an assistant operates the mechanism without actually releasing a ball. The vast majority of dogs will not even react to this noise but it is better to play it safe and allow the dog time to get used to the noise. Once you see that the dog is quite happy in the vicinity of the machine, he can be introduced to the pleasures the machine can give.

Place the dog on a soft leather collar that can be used to restrain him, and give the ball to your assistant, who will be operating the machine, which is a yard or two away. With one hand hold the dog by the collar, and with the other hand hold the lead which is attached to that collar. Do not speak to the dog. The assistant should attract the dog's attention by calling his name and, when the dog is paying attention to him, he can operate the box to release the ball. As the ball flies out encourage the dog to get it and, as he picks it up, run off backwards, while excitedly calling the dog and praising him. It does not matter if the dog fails to catch the ball at first; just allow him to chase and collect it. His ability to catch will improve with experience.

After backing away from the box for a few yards, remove the ball from the dog's mouth and give it back to the assistant. Make sure that the assistant comes to collect the ball, rather than you taking the ball back to the box. The dog should *not* learn to take the ball back to the box. This step should be repeated another two or three times, with the dog being encouraged to catch the ball by the assistant standing at the box, rather than by the handler holding the dog. The dog will learn that it is the assistant and the box that controls his ball and he will soon learn to give them his full attention. The dog will then realise that the ball is in the box and is not thrown by the assistant and, once he understands this, he can be taught how to operate the box and release the ball. In this phase it is extremely important that the dog does not have any opportunity to walk around to the far side of the box in an attempt to get the ball. He should be encouraged to be interested in the box, and should be shown that the box contains the ball, but he should never be allowed to attempt to get the ball in any other way than by the required method.

The dog must now be taught to operate the pedal which releases the ball. To do this the dog must press the foot pedal with one or, more often, two paws. This is simpler than it seems, as dogs have the inherent instinct to use their paws if they cannot achieve the required result with their mouths. Prior to actually teaching the dog to operate the pedal he should be taught a command which means 'use your paw'. Teaching this is quite simple: get your assistant to hold the dog on the lead and restrain him from coming to you. Position yourself a foot or two away, just beyond the dog's reach, and offer him a piece of food or his toy. He will attempt to take it with his mouth at first, but just ensure that he cannot reach it, while still encouraging him to attempt to do so. After a few failed attempts with his mouth he will raise a paw to try to reach his reward. The moment that he does so he should be rewarded, even if the paw was only lifted an inch or two off the ground. Any attempt from the dog to use his paw should be rewarded and, gradually, the dog will realise that using his paw will get him his reward. Once the dog understands this and uses his paw fully, the command 'paws' can be introduced. The dog will soon become confident and will use his paws on command to get the reward.

This command can then be used when teaching the dog to operate the pedal on the Flyball box. Place the dog in the Sit position directly in front of the box, with his feet almost touching the pedal. Make sure that the dog is restrained by holding his collar. Let him see the ball being placed in the box, and get the assistant to encourage him and excite him. Once the dog is excited the command 'paws' can be given, together with the verbal encouragement. Preferably the command should be given by the assistant; however, if the handler gives it this will not be the end of the world. All that is required is that the dog lifts his paw and, if he does so, that the ball should be released, even if the dog did not touch the pedal. Gradually more can be demanded and the ball should only be released if the paw actually touches the pedal. Still later the ball will only be released if the dog uses actual pressure on the pedal and, finally, the dog must actually operate the pedal to release the ball.

This type of training has been called shaping, enticing the dog to perform an act and rewarding him for any approximate attempt to do so, gradually demanding more until the dog performs the act exactly as required. With experience the dog will learn how to operate the pedal to release the ball and will do so without the command. The only drawback with this method is that success relies to a great extent on the insight of the handler, as the dog must be rewarded for any attempt to comply. Inexperienced handlers often lack this insight and fail to reward at the critical moment, thereby confusing the dog. It is

therefore advisable to use an experienced trainer as an assistant. While the dog is being taught this phase of training he can also be taught how to jump the hurdles as a separate exercise.

RETRIEVING THE BALL

This may seem quite logical. However, it would be silly to teach the dog to operate the box if he is going to run off with the ball once he has caught it. In order to teach the dog to bring the ball back once he has caught it, the dog should always be on a flexi-lead, as previously stated. This will give the dog the freedom to run and catch the ball while the handler still retains control. Each time that the dog catches the ball the handler should call his name, while simultaneously giving a tug on the lead to turn the dog, and then run backwards, encouraging the dog to return. All this should be done with lots of praise and reward and should never be attempted off lead until the dog fully understands and is willingly returning at full speed every time.

JUMPING HURDLES

In the UK all hurdles must be 12 inches high, regardless of the size of the dog. Other countries have differing heights which are determined by the smallest dog in the team. However, no countries have hurdle heights that are physically difficult for a dog to jump. The intention is to combine speed and accuracy, and the hurdles are intended as an obstacle rather than a test of jumping ability. It is quite common to see a dog avoiding a seemingly simple hurdle that he could quite easily jump and the dog normally does this for one of two reasons – either he can reach the box faster by going around the hurdle, or he lacks confidence with the hurdles. Both of these problems are training faults and can be avoided by correct training methods.

The simplest way to teach the dog to

TOP: *A good start is essential, but control is all-important.*

ABOVE: *The dog sets off straight, heading in a direct line for the Flyball box.*

LEFT: *As soon as the dog has caught the ball, he turns and heads for home.*

Photos: Carol Ann Johnson.

jump a series of four hurdles is to create a situation whereby the dog cannot avoid jumping the hurdles. To do this a corridor should be erected which is the same width as the upright of the hurdles and contains the four hurdles.

Some instructors advise starting off with only one hurdle and gradually building up to four, and if you feel this will help then I see no disadvantage in doing so. However, I also see no advantage, as the hurdles really are so low and simple that any normal healthy dog of even the smallest stature will be capable of jumping them without much effort.

The corridor should be of a light material such as chicken wire, which is secure enough to prevent the dog escaping, but light enough to avoid the dog feeling trapped and closed in. Later on, as the dog becomes confident, the influence of the corridor can be reduced until, perhaps, it is replaced by one or two strands of light rope. This would never prevent the dog from going around the hurdles if he still had a mind to, but by this phase of training he should be perfectly confident and jumping willingly. Once he has jumped a few times, with only the rope to prevent him not jumping, all restrictions can be removed. However, I advise regular retraining with the corridor in place to avoid bad habits creeping in.

In the United Kingdom the distance from the start/finish line to the first hurdle must be 6 feet and the hurdles must be placed 10 feet apart. The distance from the last hurdle to the box must be 15 feet. This means that the corridor must be at least 51 feet long; however, it is advisable to make it slightly longer so that the dog can be placed a few feet into the corridor when first being taught to jump. Once again an assistant will be needed to help train the dog to jump the hurdles.

Start off by asking the assistant to hold the dog while you run up the corridor, jumping the hurdles and then turning around at the other end and calling the dog to you. Encourage him to come by showing him his ball or offering him a piece of food. The assistant should only release the dog when it is clear that the dog intends to run to the handler. The dog has no choice other than to run up the corridor and, to reach the handler, he must jump the hurdles – which he will manage to do very easily and without any interference from mummy and daddy. Upon arrival the dog should be praised and rewarded and, if the assistant is well known to the dog, turned around so that the roles can be reversed and the assistant calls the dog while the handler holds him by the collar.

Two or three return trips will be enough for the first session. The dog is perfectly capable of doing more, but it is always better to stop training while the dog is full of enthusiasm, as this will make him even more keen at the next session. If the dog is less than willing to return to the assistant then he should not be made to do so. This will just mean that the assistant follows the dog up the corridor to hold the dog at the other end while the handler runs back over the hurdles before calling the dog. Both

methods work equally well, the second just gives the handler more exercise!

Within a reasonably short time the dog will happily run out and jump the hurdles while running up to his handler and the next step can be commenced. This entails the handler *sending* the dog out to retrieve his ball rather than *calling* him over the hurdles. This step merely combines two of the previously taught steps. The dog has already been taught to run out and collect his ball and he has also been taught to jump the hurdles. To combine these two steps the handler should take the dog into the corridor and hold him by the collar. The assistant should position himself at the other end of the corridor and attract the dog's attention by calling his name. Then, once the dog is paying attention, the ball can be thrown into the air – ensuring that it lands in a direct line about ten feet past the last hurdle. The dog is then released and commanded to retrieve his ball and, as the dog picks up the ball, he is called back over the hurdles. If all previously taught steps have been fully understood, this step should be very straightforward and correctly carried out. At this stage the box can be introduced, presuming, of course, that the dog has already been taught to operate the box and is competent at catching the ball as it is released from the box.

RUNNING OUT AND RETURNING AT SPEED
The dog should now be capable of running out to collect the ball thrown by the assistant and returning with it to the handler. The dog is jumping willingly and returning quickly. Therefore the box can be introduced. Start off by placing the box into the corridor and placing the dog in front of the box a few feet away with the flexi-lead attached. Let the dog watch the assistant place the ball in the box and then command the dog to 'get the ball'. As the

dog presses the pedal and catches the ball, give him the return command and back away, at the same time giving the dog a tug on the lead. All this is known to the dog, the only difference is that he is now performing an old act in a new situation i.e. in the corridor. Assuming that there are no problems, and the dog performs as required, he can be taken slightly further away and placed behind the first hurdle. Repeat the previous step with the dog now having to jump one hurdle before operating the box pedal. The flexi-lead is about 25 feet long and therefore the dog can be sent out to the box which is about 15 feet away. Once the dog has proved that the lessons have been well-taught, the lead can be removed and the dog sent out over one hurdle and then two, gradually building up until he will go out and return quickly over all four hurdles.

Bear in mind that he has been taught to catch the ball, operate the box, jump the hurdles, and retrieve the ball all as separate exercises and these steps should constantly be retrained as self-contained exercises throughout his working life. Because Flyball is a speed competition many dogs will realise that they can go around a hurdle faster than they can jump it and will often attempt to do so if the situation allows them to do so. With the use of the corridor this bad habit will never develop.

Teaching a dog to jump four hurdles, operate a pedal, catch a ball and return over four hurdles to the handler is not particularly difficult. However, to get the dog to do this without fault and at top speed in front of yelling people with barking dogs is another story. The next phase of training entails teaching the dog to ignore these distractions.

IGNORING DISTRACTIONS

Flyball is all about speed, and speed is attained by motivation and enthusiasm. If not under control this can create problems.

From the dog's point of view, he has been taught to run out to the box as quickly as possible, catch his ball, and then rush back to his mum. He must also jump obstacles on the way out and on the way back. Suddenly, as he is about to jump the fourth obstacle on the way back, he sees another dog directly in his path. The natural thing to do is run around this other dog, which, without corrective training, almost all dogs will do. As Flyball is a team sport the dogs must be taught to pass each other at a very close distance without reacting in any way. The dogs that have to be passed at such close distance will be members of the same team and therefore should know and recognise each other once they have trained together. However, as often as not, the other team will contain dogs that are strangers and will be running out or returning while your dog is working. To compete in Flyball your dog must be taught to ignore these distractions.

PASSING A TEAM MEMBER

Any dog that is a known fighter, or regularly shows aggression to other dogs, should be excluded from Flyball training. However, even normally placid, friendly dogs can snap at another dog in times of excitement. Training a dog to ignore other team members should be taught before the dogs have become extremely excited at the sight of the Flyball box. Start off by placing two dogs facing each other, about six feet apart and slightly off-centre of each other so that they can pass closely without having to deviate from their line. Preferably one of the dogs should be an experienced Flyball dog. The assistant should hold the new dog while the handler goes off behind the other dog, but slightly to one side so that the dog runs in a straight line past the experienced dog. The handler should attract the dog's attention by the use of a ball and then call the dog while running backwards. At first the dog will, most probably, react to the other dog and circle wide of him. The exercise should be repeated over a period of time until the new dog learns that there is no danger and runs straight past the other dog without reacting. Once this happens another dog can be used, and so on until the new team member ignores all the other dogs in the team.

The next stage is to place the experienced dog just off-centre of the middle line and ten feet or so away from a hurdle. The new dog is held, as before, and then called past the experienced dog to the handler, thereby learning to jump the last hurdle while being able to see the next dog in the team. Up until now the experienced dog has just had to sit still; the next step is to call him just as the new dog has jumped the hurdle. Then the experienced dog should be called as the new dog is about to jump the hurdle. In this way the inexperienced dog will learn to ignore the other team members and concentrate on the job in hand.

As the dog becomes confident the other team members can be lined up, one behind the other, but with each dog slightly to one side of the dog in front, so that the new dog has to pass several dogs without deviating from a straight line. The use of the corridor will obviously prevent the dogs from deviating too far and will ensure that the dogs cannot avoid the jump. But, if a dog is unsure, or even frightened, he may refuse to come back at all if he has to pass another dog in such close proximity. Great care should be taken to avoid all but the most placid dogs until the new dog gains confidence.

COMPETING

Once your dog is working satisfactorily, and has been introduced to the other team members, and is willing to work while ignoring them, then the time has come to train the dog to ignore the other teams. To start off with, the dog should compete against other known dogs from the same group or club, preferably against the experienced dogs. Each team should be in their own corridor, which will prevent interference from the other team. As experience is gained the dogs will learn that the other dogs are no threat and will learn to ignore them as they hold no interest. Once this point is reached the dog should be ready for competition.

CAUTIONARY ADVICE

Flyball was intended to be a fun sport and was developed in that way. Certainly the dogs seem to love the sport, and the amount of training needed to reach competition level is perhaps less than in other competition sports. As it is one of the few team sports for dogs it is obviously a very sociable hobby. Border Collies can make extremely good Flyball dogs and seem to be tireless. However, a certain level of physical fitness is required and, as I have mentioned earlier, the dog must be healthy with a good set of hips. I do have some concern that Border Collies, being excitable dogs, may tend to go OTT in this very fast sport. However, this is, as often as not, caused by bad training rather than by the rules of competition. Expert advice from experienced people with proven ability should avoid this problem. If the dog is trained in a positive way, with the priority being fun as was originally intended, then Flyball is an ideal Border Collie sport.

8 THE WORKING BORDER COLLIE

In this world of high technology it would appear that machines are taking over, doing work which in the past was carried out by either man or animals. Just two examples are the tractor replacing the heavy horse, and computers, which have cut man-power drastically. But, as yet, no machine has been developed to replace the working Border Collie. Certainly, on some lowland farms four-wheeled motorbikes are used to gather sheep, but on high, rugged terrain these quads are of no use. It is in these regions where working dogs are invaluable assets to the shepherd, and I cannot image anything replacing them.

The Border Collie is a thinking dog, for not only does it work to commands, it also uses its own initiative. Working in the hills, often a shepherd will lose sight of his dog. Here the Border Collie must use its head and its own ability to bring the sheep. When they are working stock, these dogs change into completely different animals. They go into a world of their own, with their attention fixed on the animals they are herding. Often they appear completely

The Border Collie has been selectively bred for its herding qualities, and is far removed from the early British guarding dogs.

Photo: Keith Allison.

oblivious to anything else which is taking place around them. It is a very special feeling training your own dog to work sheep well and with confidence. Understanding these animals and their feelings can only be done after a great deal of experience, which can only be achieved by having a go.

ORIGINS OF THE WORKING DOG

It is believed that the working dog may well have descended from the jackal. Prehistoric man is known to have hunted with dogs, and they most probably took in litters of jackal puppies with the intention of domesticating them. Their aims were to become more efficient hunters and also have a means of guarding their stock. The early shepherds first used dogs for guarding their flock against predators. These jackal-blooded animals were relatively small and, to increase their size and aggression, it is thought they were crossed with wolves. Thus they became a larger and more fierce dog capable of fighting off attackers. Indeed, today, these guarding dogs still exist in certain parts of the world, an example being the Maremma dogs of Italy.

Dogs such as these were used at one time in Britain; however, with the disappearance of sheep predators their role became obsolete. A different type of dog was needed, and through careful, selective breeding the working element was introduced. Far removed from the early British guarding dogs, an animal of a much smaller stature and far less aggressive temperament was developed. For generations the Border Collie has been bred with the enhancement of its herding qualities in mind. Going back many, many generations, setters, pointers and hounds are believed to have been crossed with the working sheepdog, all introduced to improve its working ability. Bess, one of my bitches, often stands with one front leg

raised, as she is looking for her sheep, waiting to be sent to gather at a trial. This is the characteristic stance of both the setter and pointer when working.

It is thought that the name "collie" originated from Scotland. The blackface sheep there were referred to as "colleys" which over the years has been adjusted to "collie" for the collie dog. Over three hundred years ago the Border Collie evolved in the Scottish and English borders, where a nimble dog with stamina was needed to work the hills.

THE PACK LEADER

Dogs are pack animals. This can be clearly seen in the behaviour and social structure of wild dogs. Within the pack there is always a pack leader and invariably there are those which will challenge this leadership. To the working Border Collie the pack leader should be its handler. Depending on the dog's temperament, it may challenge this authority, but for a successful working relationship, human leadership must be maintained. Recently I bought Jen, an eleven-month-old bitch. When she was first introduced to my other dogs, initially they were quite hostile towards her. She was a new dog on their ground. Gradually the dogs sorted themselves out and Jen, rather timid in nature, established her place as one of the lower-ranking dogs. It is important however that I retain the highest rank.

The majority of Border Collies have a certain amount of natural ability when it comes to working sheep. Despite this, a young collie is as capable of worrying a sheep as many other breeds of dog, particularly if it is in a group. There is still that primeval instinct of the hunter and the hunted. When the handler and young dog go to the sheep, to the dog they are going as a hunting party. A basic instinct tells the dog to work the sheep to the handler, the pack leader.

Developed from the introduction of the gun dog is the use of "eye". A dog can both hold and move sheep with "eye", a level of concentration which needs to be flexible. There are dogs with too much "eye", where they become transfixed, ignoring everything around them. If the sheep turn and face this type of dog a stalemate situation can arise, with the dog deep in concentration, unmoving and the sheep afraid to move. At the other extreme there are dogs with too little "eye". These dogs tend to have little style; however, they do not pose such a threat and often the sheep move away better for this type of dog. Ideally a dog should have a medium level of "eye", which enables it to concentrate on the sheep yet still respond to the handler. Each dog is an individual, and to develop its working ability correctly requires careful training.

EARLY TRAINING
As with any puppy it is important to spend as much time with it as possible. The puppy needs to develop confidence in its new owner, and this is achieved by plenty of handling. My most recent puppy is Queen; I own her sire and instead of receiving a stud fee, I chose a pup from the litter. From the day she arrived, aged eight weeks, I made a fuss of her, fed her, talked to her and repeatedly called her by her name. When she is in the field and I want her to come to me, I call "Queen" and bending slightly, pat my knees. Mostly she comes dashing towards me and I give her no end of praise. On the occasions when she does not come, it is important to keep patient and under no circumstances should she be reprimanded when finally she does obey.

Once she had settled into her new environment, I started to pop a small collar around her neck, just for an hour or so at a time. Initially she was none too happy and would sit down and scratch away at it, but before long she accepted it being there. The lead was then introduced and soon she learnt that walking along willingly, was more pleasant than being gently dragged. Another early experience for Queen was

EARLY TRAINING
Photos: Keith Allison.

Queen is being taught the command "Lie Down". Elaine has her foot on the chain to keep Queen in position.

Elaine steps back from Queen, repeating the "Lie Down" command, and increasing the distance between them.

"That'll do." Elaine bends down, patting her knee, encouraging Queen to come to her.

Elaine increases her distance from Queen, constantly repeating the "Lie Down" command.

travelling. To start with I just sat her in the back of my vehicle to get her used to it, then I took her for short rides, but not just after she had eaten. She is now thirteen weeks old, she has been fully vaccinated and therefore is allowed outside the perimeter of the smallholding. From now on she will be socialised, meeting different people and facing a variety of situations.

When Queen is about four months old, I will start to teach her "lie down" and "that'll do". When working these are two of the most important commands; obviously the dog must stop when asked and leave the stock when called away. To teach these commands I find that, initially, it is easier to have a collar and lead on the young dog. To make the dog lie down, I hold onto the lead close to the collar with one hand and pull down, while with the other hand I push down on the dog's back. At the same time I say "lie down". I keep the dog in this position for about thirty seconds, repeatedly giving her the "lie down" command. Afterwards I let her get up onto her feet, praise her and then repeat the lesson again. After the second lesson when she gets up, I say "that'll do" and get her to come to me. From this she learns that the lesson is over. I will repeat the lesson perhaps twice a day and, gradually, the dog will become accustomed to lying

down without having to be held. At this stage I take one or two steps away from her, again repeatedly saying "lie down". Slowly she gets used to me moving further away. Sometimes I return to her side, other times I finish by calling her to me with "that'll do". My aim eventually is to get Queen to lie down and to stay in that position regardless of where I am, until I signify that she can move.

Over the weeks I am building a good relationship between myself and the puppy. She is getting to know me and is learning to listen. From the tone of my voice she learns when I am pleased with her and also when I am cross. My method of controlling her is one of quiet authority, for there is nothing to be gained from loud and brash handling. These early lessons are time well spent and the dividends will be reaped throughout the rest of her life.

INTRODUCTION TO SHEEP
People often ask at what age do I start to train my Border Collies. There is no set answer to this, only that I cannot start to train a dog until it is ready to be trained; that is when it is showing interest in stock. This can vary from a dog being only a few months old to being eighteen months to two years old. Provided the dog is showing interest, I normally start training between

INTRODUCTION TO SHEEP
Photos: Keith Allison.

Holly, in the early stages of training, is standing on Elaine's left. She is held steady with the string as she waits for the "Come bye" command to gather a group of sheep standing close by.

Holly runs out to gather the sheep. As she does so, Elaine holds on to one end of the string. The string passes through Holly's collar, and she is released to go to the sheep without any fuss.

Holly reaches the other side of the sheep. She is gently walking up to them, and holding them to Elaine.

ten and twelve months old. At this age I feel the dog will have achieved a certain amount of maturity and it will have developed the stamina and speed to go round and head the sheep.

A small field of either one or two acres is ideal for early training, along with perhaps a dozen quiet sheep. Although the sheep need to be quiet they should not be aggressive, as a young dog's confidence can easily be shaken if it is challenged by a bossy ewe. For the first few training sessions, it is useful to have an older dog present to keep the sheep together and in the middle of the field. If this is not possible then the handler needs to do a little more leg work. Early lessons should be kept reasonably short, as, like a young child, young dogs have limited concentration and it is important not to let the dog lose interest.

Before entering the field I thread a piece of string through the dog's collar; I do not tie the string but keep hold of the two loose ends. With the sheep in the middle of the field, I walk towards them holding the dog on the string. If I want to encourage the dog to run out in a clockwise direction, with my dog at my left-hand side, I approach the sheep from the right. The opposite goes if I want her to run anti-clockwise. When I am about

ten to fifteen feet away, I encourage the dog to run out to the left and hopefully round the sheep by making a 'Shh Shh' sound. At the same time I let the string slide through her collar and release her.

As I have said, hopefully the dog will run round to the far side of the sheep. The idea is to get her to stay at the far side and hold the sheep to me. Unfortunately, this does not always happen. The dog may run straight at the sheep and scatter them, she may run round and round them or sometimes corner the sheep and just hold them up. What is usual is that initially all understanding of "lie down" goes out of her head. Whatever happens, my ultimate aim is still to get the dog behind the sheep and holding them to me. If the dog either scatters the sheep, or continually runs around them, it is important to reinforce the "lie down" command. If the pupil is not running out and round the sheep, I need to position myself between the two, which enables me to push her out. Remember to work with quiet authority, speaking to the dog more gruffly if she is doing wrong.

A point worth stressing here is that to be a successful trainer, a tremendous amount of both time and patience is needed. Without these, little progress will be made. As soon as patience begins to wear thin, the lesson should be stopped and continued later when equilibrium has been regained.

ACHIEVING BALANCE

When the pupil has grasped the ideal of going round to the far side of the sheep, I then start to walk backwards. I move around the field with the youngster holding the sheep to me, varying my directions, which teaches the dog balance.

Imagine a clock – the dog at twelve o'clock, the sheep in the centre and me at 6 o'clock. Here the dog is balancing the sheep to me; if I move to the right she will move to her right to keep the balance. Balance is the position and the distance the dog works from the sheep, enabling her to keep them flowing smoothly and in a straight line. Dogs vary: some can work close to sheep without upsetting them, others control them from a greater distance.

In the early lessons I say little to the dog apart from telling her to "take time" when she is coming on too quickly and "keep back" if she comes too close to the sheep. If I want the dog to move forward and she is not doing so, I ask her to "walk on". Initially I do not insist that the dog always stops, provided she at least slows down; this is done a little later. When I do ask the dog to "lie down", I ask her when she is about to do so naturally; in this way I am preventing the dog from being disobedient.

Once the dog has settled down she is using her instinctive behaviour when she holds the sheep to me. She is also developing a feel for the sheep, using her head and learning to think for herself. This is something she will have to do in her working years, when she goes to gather sheep which are out of my sight.

Often in these early stages a keen young dog is reluctant to leave the stock when the lesson is over. If this is the case, try to lie

the dog down and approach her; if this fails, walk away calling "that'll do", sometimes the dog will follow. Once again, great patience is needed here and, when the dog does come back, remember to praise her, however long it has taken. If she is reprimanded she will be even less likely to come a second time. Sometimes, if I have a real problem persuading a dog to leave stock, I attach a light line of about sixteen feet to her collar. I put myself into a position where I can take hold of the line, then if she refuses to come I have control over her. Once I have caught my dog, I usually do not take her straightaway from the sheep, but put her round them a second or third time. Here she learns that if she returns to me, she is not always taken from the sheep, which makes her more willing to come back. Each time I send her, I put myself between her and the sheep, making her go out and round them, and in that way I am developing a short outrun.

INTRODUCING MORE VERBAL COMMANDS

Gradually I start to introduce the two verbal commands which tell her the direction in which I want her to go. To go round the sheep in a clockwise direction I ask the dog to "come bye"; to go anti-clockwise "away to me". When the dog is balancing the sheep to me, as I move clockwise, so does the dog and I say "come bye"; likewise for anti-clockwise and "away to me". The same goes when I am sending the dog to gather the sheep. If I want her to run out to the left I say "come bye", and "away to me" to run to the right. Try not to direct the dog too often with arm signals as this can lead to the dog watching you and not the sheep. Dogs do vary, some pick these commands up quickly while others take a long time. I am now more insistent that the dog stops when asked and I also introduce the whistle command

RIGHT: Holly taking the "Away to me" command, moving round the sheep anti-clockwise.

BELOW: Jet, who is very keen and fast, is further on in his training than Holly. Here, he is bringing the sheep to Elaine after taking the "Away to me" command.

for this. As I am teaching the two new verbal commands I also teach the dog to flank correctly. When I command the dog to go left or right, I want her to cast off the sheep, not come onto them. In other words, I want her to turn squarely and then go round to the left or right. However, it is important that she does not go too wide and lose contact. If the dog is tending to come forward towards the sheep, I lie her down, walk through the sheep, and send her off again, ensuring she goes with a nice rounded movement. After a short distance, I stop her again and repeat the exercise. Again, all dogs are different, some have a natural flank, others tend to be tight. With the latter much more work is needed to persuade the dog to flank round and not forward. This type of flanking is particularly important if the dog is to be used for trialling.

PROGRESS SO FAR

At the end of this stage, which could have taken a good few months depending on the type of dog and how much time I have spent, my dog will gather the sheep from a short distance and stop; bring the sheep towards me, balancing them when I change direction; her approach will be steady so as not to push the sheep past me – this is where "take time" and "keep back" comes in; she will have learnt her verbal commands for left and right and will flank going round and not forward; she will return to me when called.

MORE ADVANCED TRAINING

Once my dog can gather the sheep correctly over a short distance – that is, go round them allowing enough room to avoid unsettling them – I very gradually increase the length of the outrun. If the dog starts to run tight then I have

WORKING SHEEP
Photos:
Keith Allison.

LEFT: Gem, aged four, ready to be sent out to the left to gather sheep. She is looking down the field for the sheep, and will go as soon as she hears the "Come bye" command.

RIGHT: Bess, who is seven years old, is ready to take the "Away to me" command and gather the sheep right-handed.

probably sent her too far and need to work a little nearer. If she persists in coming in tightly, I stop her, walk up to her and cast her out squarely round me, doing this each time she starts coming in. It also helps to lie the dog down and walk up the field towards the sheep before setting her off. When she is asked to run out she has to run round me and I tell her to "keep out" if she is starting to come in tight.

Initially I have been asking my dog to flank in the direction in which she chooses to go naturally, to keep the sheep balanced. Now I must train her to flank in the direction I wish her to go. Up to now she has been holding the sheep to me, flanking whichever way is needed to do this. I am now going to ask her to flank the opposite way.

To begin with, this can be quite confusing for the dog. When she would naturally want to go anti-clockwise, I stop her and ask her to go clockwise. If she refuses, I take a few steps towards the sheep, putting myself between the two, and ask her again. When she does take the command I let her run round to the 12 o'clock position. Gradually she will learn to go round in the direction I wish, and when she is happy doing this, I start to stop her before she reaches the balance position. At this stage I start to teach my dog to drive.

DRIVING

This is a big step for the young dog; so far she has been using her instinct to hold the sheep to me. I am now going to ask her to take the sheep away from me, which is opposite to everything she has learnt. To start, I let the dog gather the sheep and bring them to me. I ask her to take the sheep round me and I start to walk forward, slightly in front of the dog as she follows them.

Quickly the dog will realise that she is not balancing the sheep to me and will want to head them, i.e. go round to the far side of them. When she does this, I stop her and ask her to drive on. Try to walk a little way before letting the dog head the sheep. Continue working the sheep around the field before trying this again. Over a period of time the dog will become accustomed to walking behind the sheep with me walking slightly ahead and to one side of her. At this stage I drop back slightly. If I want the dog to flank clockwise I ask her to "come bye" and go round behind me, this again is reinforcing the rounded flanking movement. It is important to work on both flanks, as the dog needs to work equally well on both hands. Gradually I start to drop further back, constantly reassuring the dog when she is doing well. As I drop further back I will want her to flank in front of me. I

LEFT: Sue, aged six, walking quietly up to the sheep to lift them after her gather.

BELOW: Sue driving the sheep away. This goes against the dog's natural instinct to bring the sheep to the handler.

BELOW: Sue balancing the sheep to Elaine by going round anti-clockwise. This covers the sheep on the left which is thinking of breaking away from the others.

Gem approaching the sheep, waiting for a gap so he can come though and separate them into two groups. The black sheep are Hebridean. The lighter-coloured sheep are Swaledales.

After a gap has been made, Gem comes through the middle of the two packets of sheep, and is turning on to those on the left, as asked.

If the sheep bunch, human intervention may encourage the sheep to separate.

encourage her to do this but, if she persists in going behind, I back myself up to a wall. With me in this position her only option is to come in front, and soon this will become natural to her. Eventually the dog will learn to drive the sheep further and further away, as well as obeying directional commands.

WHISTLE COMMANDS

Up to now I have been working reasonably close at hand, using mostly verbal commands which the dog now knows well. To work over a distance I need to introduce whistle commands which enable the dog to hear me. She already knows the stop and walk on whistle, now I must teach her the flanking whistles. This is done at hand by giving the verbal "come bye" command followed by the appropriate whistle. Likewise for "away to me". Gradually I drop the spoken commands and the dog learns to be directed by the whistle. The dogs usually pick up the whistle commands quite quickly. Throughout the dog's working life I use both types of commands, normally reverting to verbal at hand, i.e. when the sheep are close by.

SHEDDING AND LOOK BACK

If possible, it is easier to teach the dog to shed using a greater number of sheep, as a group of twelve, once split, tend to try to get back together. To start I have the sheep in front of me, with the dog laid down at the other side of them. I walk towards the sheep and split them into two groups, making a large gap between them. Bending towards my dog I call her to me with "that'll do" and when she comes to me I praise her. Initially I do not worry about the sheep, only that the dog comes straight to me. Once she will do this willingly we move on another step. When she comes through I want her to turn onto one group of sheep. I face the group I want her to turn onto, call "that'll do" and, as she comes, say "this", encouraging her to turn towards them. I then proceed to walk with her as she drives that group away from the others.

After several lessons, normally, the dog will come through and turn onto the sheep without hesitation. I then drop the "that'll do" command and just use "this", the shedding command. Gradually I reduce the size of the gap between the sheep as the dog becomes more confident at coming through a smaller space. Taking one single sheep off a packet comes only after the dog is highly proficient at shedding, as this is much more difficult to do.

Teaching the dog to go back for a

second packet of sheep can be an extension from shedding. Shed the sheep, walking with the dog as she drives them away from the others. I then position myself so that the sheep are between me and the dog, with the second packet behind the dog. I flank my dog to one side of the first packet and ask her to lie down. My next command is "look back" and at the same time I try to direct the dog to go back using a sweeping arm movement. Eventually the dog will realise that I want her attention away from the first group of sheep and she will begin to look around. As soon as she spots the second group, I repeat the "look back" command, followed by the appropriate flanking command. She should gather and bring the second packet to join the first. As she becomes more confident with this manoeuvre I gradually increase the distance between myself and the dog before I ask her to go back. It is important to teach her to look back first and then take the flank given. And it is also important to get her used to going back equally well on both hands.

PENNING

Instead of using a pen I normally teach my young dog to hold sheep up to a wall. Here she learns to hold a sheep if it tries to break away, to flank round and work with quiet, careful movements. Occasionally I do put a pen up in the field for practice; however, the problem with this is that sheep learn very quickly, and after they have been penned several times, they tend to walk straight in.

SUMMARY

Remember, certainly in the early stages of training, to keep lessons short and thereby keep the dog interested. Keeping one's patience is of the utmost importance and as soon as it begins to wear thin, finish for the day. Sometimes during training it is felt that, instead of progressing, things are

Gem walking quietly up to the sheep to move them along the wall.

Gem holds the sheep to the wall and is casting out and round to keep them there. These manoeuvres would be used for penning when the dog must not come in tight on the sheep.

Elaine with the three dogs she uses at demonstrations. Sue (left) is an unusual sable, white and tan colour. She has a very quiet and gentle nature. Bess (middle) is a much stronger dog, meaning she has more push and can move awkward sheep easily. She has a very friendly, out-going nature. Gem is a daughter of Bess. All three have won many prizes in Sheepdog trials, with Gem having the most success.

going backwards. This often happens, and the main thing is to persevere as, gradually, things will improve. All dogs are different and it is important to treat them as individuals, being flexible with your approach. At the end of the day, once you have actually trained your own dog, you will be rewarded with a tremendous feeling of achievement.

TRAINING FOR TRIALS

Exactly the same pattern is followed if you want to train your dog for sheep dog trialling. One of the more important things in competitive work is square flanking, as dogs which are for ever moving forward tend to upset just three sheep, which is the number normally run on. To trial, dogs have to be proficient at driving and this, again, is an area which may need working on. A trial dog needs more polish than a work dog, therefore it needs to respond instantaneously to its commands. Before entering a trial it is as well to give your dog the experience of working away from home, as no dog works as well on unfamiliar ground.

The nursery trials, which are mainly held throughout the winter months, are run to give young dogs the experience of competitive work. Here they learn to work different breeds of sheep over varying types of ground. It is at these trials that the novice handler usually starts their trialling career.

CORRECTING PROBLEMS

Occasionally a dog will show no interest whatsoever in working. The only thing to do here is to try to encourage it to work, taking it to sheep and making them move around. If no interest is shown in sheep, try introducing the dog to poultry; I have had several young dogs which first started to work ducks.

One of the more common problems is a dog refusing to stop. When this happens the handler has to go back to basics and, once again, teach the dog to "lie down" away from stock. It if will not do this, there is little chance of it lying down when there are sheep present.

Sometimes a dog favours one particular hand, wanting to outrun only in one direction and, in consequence, crossing their course. This should have been dealt with during training, as it is important to ensure the dog will work on both hands. If, however, this happens, work the dog on the disliked hand as much as possible. Start the dog again on short outruns, putting yourself between her and the sheep in order to push her out if she starts to come in and, gradually, increase the outrunning distance.

Sometimes a dog is constantly glancing towards its handler, which shows it lacks confidence. To encourage the dog out of this habit, it is important not to distract its attention away from the sheep with your own movements. Try to keep still and not wave your arms about, while giving the dog fewer and quieter commands. A dog that continually grips sheep can be a problem. Here we must teach her not to get hold, and this can only be done close at hand. When the dog is about to grip shout "No" in as aggressive a tone as possible to prevent her from biting. A young dog can sometimes want to head sheep when it is driving, e.g., at a trial on the cross drive the dog may start to bring the sheep back to the handler. Go back to walking alongside your dog while it is driving, then very gradually start to drop back. Practice cross driving at home, paying particular attention to getting the dog to come between you and the sheep.

WORKING OTHER ANIMALS

Border Collies are commonly known as Sheep Dogs and therefore people automatically associated them with sheep. Of course, the majority do work sheep.

WORKING DUCKS
Photos: Keith Allison.

Gem working Khaki Campbell ducks to whistle commands.

Sue and Bess working as a team. Sue is very kind when working ducks, Bess tends to be more boisterous.

LEFT: Sue and Bess working together to bring the ducks to the mouth of the small pen.

RIGHT: Success! the ducks are in the pen and are being held there by Sue and Bess.

Gem, Sue and Bess looking on while the geese decide which way to move. Geese can be very aggressive, especially when sitting on eggs, and at these times the dogs give them a wide berth.

Gem and Bess on the alert.

Gem working up on her feet, driving the geese in a controlled manner.

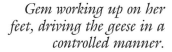

However, many Border Collies are so keen that they will work almost anything that moves.

To a dairy farmer, a dog which will work cattle is a great asset, for it can be sent to bring in the herd for milking. Not all Border Collies will work cattle as, usually, a much harder approach is needed. A dog needs to be fearless to move a cow, as often it needs to go in and nip either its heels or nose. Often dogs can adapt quite easily, changing from the harder approach needed for cattle to the quieter method required for sheep. Suckler cattle with young calves at foot are particularly difficult to work. These cattle are mostly very protective towards their offspring and, in consequence, very aggressive. To avoid injury a dog needs to be extremely alert. Some handlers say it is a crime to use a good dog to work sucklers.

Border Collies often work poultry where, again, a gentle approach is needed. A free-range egg producer, who also keeps sheep, bought a puppy from me about eighteen months ago. Besides working the sheep, her other job is to round up any stray birds which refuse to go into the sheds at dusk. I know of another young dog which was exported to America to work on a farm which keeps 2000 turkeys. Often a young dog will show interest in working poultry before showing any sign of working sheep. Gem, another of my bitches, at just four months old was showing great natural ability and style working ducks. At this age she had no interest in sheep.

I give sheep dog demonstrations at various outdoor events which are held throughout the summer. In the displays my dogs work sheep, geese, ducks and ducklings, showing the general public just how versatile Border Collies can be. Geese take more moving than ducks, particularly as they get older, and with the ducklings the dogs need to be both patient and gentle. Not only are the dogs versatile in the different types of stock they work, but in the different jobs they do. My dogs have to work on the farm, compete in sheep dog trials, give demonstrations and do some corporate work, where other people attempt to work them.

Sometimes sheep dogs are seen chasing cars and this can be a sign of frustration, often caused by the dog being bored, having too little work or exercise. Domesticated Border Collies have even been known to "eye" children, which is another indication of their desire to work.

ADVICE FROM A TOP HANDLER
Thomas Longton farms at Quernmore, near Lancaster in Lancashire. The Longton family have been involved with sheep dogs and trialling for generations, and over the years a great wealth of knowledge and information has been passed down.

The International Sheep Dog Trials are the most prestigious throughout Britain. They always attract a large number of spectators, including many from abroad. A total of sixty dogs compete in these trials, fifteen each from England, Scotland, Wales and Ireland. These dogs qualify to run by being placed at the National Trials of their respective country. The International is a three-day event, and over the first two days the dogs compete in the qualifying trials. Here the points from their individual runs are added together and the highest pointed country gains the team shield. In addition, the fifteen highest pointed dogs go forward into the Supreme Championship, which is held on the final day. To win this award is the absolute pinnacle of any handler's career, and with it comes the recognition that their dog is the best in the country and possibly in the world.

Thomas Longton took this most coveted award in 1986 with a little bitch called Bess. When she won this great honour Bess was approaching the end of her trialling career for she was ten years old. Thomas has trained many good dogs and, although his dogs must be proficient at work, his ultimate aim is to have successful trial dogs. His dogs gain experience doing everyday work on the farm; however, the young ones are started with formal tuition.

I visited Thomas recently and asked about his views and opinions on the working and trialling Border Collie. "I feel," he says, "that there is no substitute for work, as situations which occur naturally can help a weak dog gain confidence and can cool a strong dog down. I prefer a stronger type of dog rather than a weaker, more submissive one. I like a dog which needs to be slowed down as opposed to speeded up, and one with plenty of spirit. Temperament is important, particularly if the dog is to compete, and I want a confident dog with an outgoing nature."

Often when handlers ask about the breeding of a dog, they are mostly concerned with the sire. "I think that the dam is equally, if not more important than the sire," says Thomas, "and that often too little attention is paid to this side of the breeding. With the working Border Collie, breeding is for brains and working ability rather than for looks. It is certainly not a straightforward operation, and finding a pair which breed well together is almost a lottery. It is not always the best that breed the best."

Many handlers have a preference for either dogs or bitches. Thomas has found that he has had more success over the years with bitches. "I find them to be more willing and wanting to help, although they can be more temperamental than dogs. I also feel that it is important to have a dog which suits each individual. A very quiet retiring person would not do well with a very strong and wilful dog."

Thomas was thirty-four years of age when he won the Supreme Championship with Bess. Training a sheep dog to trial standard is a time-consuming job and, with the high standard of competitive work today, to be in the prizes requires an exceptional run. For a young person who is busy working, finding the time both to train to this standard and to compete is difficult, and this is where the older people with more leisure time have an advantage. In the sport it is often found that a large percentage of handlers are retired.

Bess was bred by Thomas's father, Tot, who also took the Supreme title just three years before his son, with Jess. Lionel Pennerather reared Bess up to her being twelve months old, when she returned to Thomas at Lee End Farm, which lies on

Thomas Langton pictured with Bess after winning the Supreme Championship at the International Sheepdog Trials 1986.

the edge of the picturesque Trough of Bowland, North Lancashire. Thomas trained this black, white and tan, rough-coated little bitch on his flock of Swaledale sheep. "She was very courageous and forceful and would never back down to anything. Over a large trial course I believe she was the best dog I have owned. She was an excellent outrunner and at a trial, when I walked to the post, I was always confident that she would gather her sheep well."

Besides being a trial dog of the highest calibre, she was extremely good on the farm, where she helped Thomas shepherd his flock of sheep and work the herd of milk cows. As Thomas farms single-handed now, since his father died, his dogs are vital, in that without them, he would be unable to carry out his work without additional hired help. Bess is one of only fifteen bitches to have won the Supreme Championship since 1906 and this courageous little bitch well deserved the title.

Over the last fifteen years interest in the working Border Collie has grown tremendously throughout the world, particularly in America and Europe. Thomas has travelled to many foreign countries judging trials and giving advice on handling and training. Although he received much guidance from his father, he has developed his own style and training methods. "In the early stages of training," he says, "I find a small circular pen very useful. Initially I put the sheep inside the pen and keep the dog outside it, training the dog to go round the pen. The use of this pen is particularly helpful for beginners, as they have much more control over the situation." He has recently written a book, *Training the Sheep Dog,* which contains a full account of his training methods.

"My advice to new handlers coming into the sport of trialling is to watch and talk to the more experienced handlers and learn from them. For people entering the sport who are not connected with farming, it is important to learn the ways of sheep. The expression is to 'read the sheep', which means trying to assess what the sheep are going to do next. Trialling is very much a matter of timing and judgement, putting your dog in the right place at the right time. Everyone can have a good day and a bad day, even the top competitors. It is a very levelling sport, for the winning dog one day can have a disaster the next. Don't lose heart and be put off. If at the start, things don't go well – persevere."

FINALLY
Training a Border Collie to work stock is hard work and sometimes frustrating. The reward, however, is a great feeling of achievement, a unique bond between yourself and the dog and a greater understanding of this marvellous animal. An emotional relationship is formed where the dog can sense the handler's feelings, be it tension, perhaps at a trial, or a more relaxed mood. To see Border Collies at work and working well is a wonderful sight, and nothing will replace these most remarkable of creatures.

THE WORKING BORDER COLLIE IN THE USA
by Max Caldwell
The USA has a varied and diverse geography and the full range of cultural backgrounds in its population. The Border Collie dog has a wide variation in genetic characteristics. These three factors (geography, population, and dogs) have combined to form endless applications of dog uses. No listing of Border Collie jobs could be complete. There are the obvious general groupings such as house pet, show dog, farm or ranch dogs, and dogs that compete in agility, obedience, flyball, tracking, and trialling. I will discuss the trialling later in this chapter. First, let us investigate some of the farm and ranch jobs these dogs are doing.

SUITING THE DOG TO THE JOB
The body type and temperament of the Border Collie varies with the climate and the job. In the hot and humid South Eastern USA a short-hair coat and a preponderance of white color may be selected. In the wide open desert spaces a lean and rangy body style may be better adapted to the long distances which have to be covered. Farming regions may select a wiry-hair coat to shed weed seeds. If dogs working livestock in pens and lots are to live with the family in the house, a thick undercoat will not clean up easily. A dog working sheep in pastures may have a lot of traditional style and display the piercing stare of the Border Collie "eye".

When gathering wild cattle out of brush and thickets a dog is more likely bred for a hard bite (in some sections the bite is rated by stars, a "five star bite" being the most desirable). In rough, mountainous country it may be useful to have a dog with a bark

124

so you have some idea of where he is. Dogs working cattle tend to work more on their feet and carry their head (and sometimes tail) above their back line. Almost all cattlemen want a dog that will bite if necessary. What is "necessary" varies with the individual cattleman and his livestock handling methods. Most want the dog to exercise self-discipline in deciding when and how hard to bite. It is also desirable to have a dog bite on command. Dogs working hogs tend to be more active than sheep dogs. Hogs seldom respond to "eye" or a slow stalking approach.

To move hogs, a dog may exhibit a confident, powerful approach, displaying a large body stance, or may startle the pigs with sudden, jerky footwork while maintaining a position which exerts positive control. Trial enthusiasts often prefer imported dogs that are extremely stylish and biddable, and have thick bodies and dense coats. Many of the farm and ranch dogs have some recent ancestors that were imported, but their immediate parents and grandparents were selected for specific characteristics peculiar to the breeder's requirements.

BORDER COLLIES AS COWBOYS
Chuck Howard of Altura, California operates a 125 square mile ranch in Nevada which supports 350 cow-calf pairs. This ranch is mostly federal land consisting of open mountains and desert. Desert paths generally lead towards the ranch

Goose and Quill, owned by Robin and Quinn Nufter, working cattle.

Photo: Hope Hanson.

headquarters which may be 12 miles away. Chuck Howard used to spend two weeks gathering his cow herd with a crew of 10 to 12 cowboys. He now loads three or four Border Collies in his airplane and flies to find the cattle. When he sees a group he lands and sends the dogs to gather them. Both the dogs and the cows know to follow the "roads" to the ranch, so Chuck just lands his plane on the appropriate road every few miles to wait for them to catch up. The dogs will work without supervision for one-half to one and one-half hours, depending on how well they know the job. Using this method Chuck Howard can gather his cattle, without cowboys, in three days. He can also use two or three dogs to load a few cattle on a trailer on the open desert, if occasion demands.

Although large bands of sheep graze the large government tracts of land in the

The versatile Border Collie may also be called on to work poultry.

Western United States, I have found only a few examples where dogs are used. Many Latino shepherds have dogs that can be sent to return strays to the grazing flock. Most drives seem to be done by shepherds on horseback or all-terrain sport vehicles (similar to a motorcycle but with four wheels). Chuck Howard is sometimes called on to move neighbor's sheep bands with his dogs. Grazing bands usually number 600 to 700 ewes with their lambs and may be combined to 2500 ewes for major moves. Chuck Howard will use three or four dogs to gather these bands and do a road drive. The dogs can fetch, or drive, or be sent ahead to guard intersections, or to turn the flock. The shepherds and the owners are very impressed with the work his dogs accomplish but have no expectation that they could do the same thing if they had dogs.

Jerry Rowe reports that, in Colorado, Border Collies may be used to tend flocks of 1000 ewes while gleaning harvested vegetable fields. These fields are typically unfenced. The gleaning operation takes only a few days. Again, drives between locations are often done by shepherds without the aid of dogs.

BORDER COLLIES IN CHARGE

Bud Williams relates two stories about shepherding large flocks in the Western United States. One shepherd uses his dogs to get the sheep off the bed-ground and start grazing each morning. He spends the mornings around the camp, then at mid-day finds the flock and turns it back towards camp. He spends the afternoons fishing and by evening the dogs have drifted the band back to camp where he beds them down for the night. The dogs spend the days with the flock without supervision. The other story involves a shepherd who died. When the camp tender found him a week later the dogs had the

sheep under control and in good shape.

In the farming country of the eastern and midwestern states the sheep flocks are small and the pastures are fenced. The sheep are more accustomed to being handled. Many farm flocks are handled with a feed bucket instead of a dog. Those farmers who have Border collies often use them on cattle and pigs as well. These dogs are generally tuned in to the chore routine and may or may not respond to herding commands. One major criterion for selection of these dogs is "I want him to look good sitting in the pickup." This does not mean that these dogs do not work. Their work often involves gathering on hilly and wooded pastures with stream crossings and other obstacles. They usually learn their jobs by applying their instincts rather than by formal training.

CATTLE HERDERS

I have a suspicion that, in the USA, more Border Collies are used on cattle than on sheep. Laura Stimatze of Kansas, and her husband Joe, custom gather cattle out of wheat pastures each spring. There are typically about 150 yearling cattle in each 160 acre pasture. The cattle are not usually accustomed to being handled by dogs. Laura and Joe will send three or four dogs into a pasture to bring the cattle while they saddle horses or set up a portable corral. The dogs will check the cattle from running and turn them in a new direction. After about three repetitions the cattle are ready to respond to the dogs and they are fetched to Joe and Laura. The dogs are not under command until they arrive in the corral or gate area. At this time a fresh dog may assist in penning. The whole process takes ten to 20 minutes on average and is much faster than doing the same job with cowboys and horses. If the cattle are to be driven down the road, one person on horseback leads the cattle with the dogs working behind. Flanking commands are given to a named dog to direct him to guard intersections and driveways.

Joe also has used his dogs to process cattle at a large feedlot. The dog will bite a heel to make a steer stick his head in a catch chute or to make him exit the chute into a dip vat. The dog is expected to lie quietly while each steer is vaccinated, dehorned, etc. but to respond without command when the next steer is ready to be processed. This is a highly automated operation where 60 to 120 cattle may be processed each hour. His dogs are also used to empty pens into alleys, drive to the sorting alley, and to push cattle to the sorting gate in single file. Joe and one dog can sort cattle through a sorting gate.

HANDLING BEEF AND PIGS

For handling a beef cow herd, I routinely use two experienced dogs. If there are no special circumstances I may add a pup in training. Cows are handled daily during the winter feeding season. When they calve in the spring they are more inclined to accept the dog around their newborn calf. For moving a single cow from the herd with her calf only one dog is used and it is under strict command. In this way, the dog moves the cow without getting close enough to cause her to attack. When calves are older, or the whole herd is being worked, multiple dogs are again used and commands are relaxed. In gathering pastures the dogs may be working out of sight without commands for 30 minutes or more. The dogs are expected to bring the cows at a walk and without fighting. In the fall, when the calves are weaned, a single dog will be used to calm the calves. When the dog gently controls their movement around the weaning pen, the calves will stop their panic pacing, forget about their missing mother, and can be lined up at the feed bunk to eat.

Steve and Becky Kerns use their Border Collie on their pure-bred hog farm in Iowa. A dog can easily move a single sow to the boar for breeding. If a person tries to move the same sow, she will freeze in place when touched. If a sow turns the wrong way in a narrow alley, the dog can back her out, whereas a person would have to fight her. The dogs are used in emptying pens of pigs and for many other chores in the modern confinement buildings. Steve and Becky require a dog to have a soft bite that will never puncture the skin of the pigs.

SALE BARN DOGS

For use in sale barns and hog buying stations a dog is expected to quickly establish dominance over pigs who have never seen a dog. When a gate is opened the dog may find a single old boar, a few mature sows, a full pen of fat hogs or a full pen of small feeder pigs. He is expected to go in and empty the pen quickly, using the minimum force necessary. He may decide to use a bold approach, a shouldering away from the fence, a single force bark, a soft nip, or a firm bite. There is no way the handler can advise him which method is called for in the time allowed. It is fascinating to watch an experienced sale barn dog exercise his judgement, and apply differing force to different situations. If the pigs have been introduced to the dog for unloading and penning, they will respond to him well enough so that he can bring them up a wide alley to a sorting gate in single file. Using this approach, one man and his dog can successfully operate a hog buying station without assistance.

TRIALLING IN THE USA

Some of the above described dogs may work all week and go to trials on weekends. Yes, we do train a few of our dogs to obey formal commands! The types of trials are also quite diverse.

The US Border Collie Handlers Association (USBCHA) sanctions trials using International Sheep Dog Society rules. These may be open field trials as in the UK, or may be arena trials held in a smaller fenced enclosure. The course to be negotiated by the livestock is designated the "International Course" and is the one used in the UK. Standard levels of competition are Novice, Pro-Novice, and Open. Classes of Ranch and Open Ranch are sometimes offered, but the qualifications of dog and handler at these levels are not rigidly defined. The livestock used are typically sheep. There are National Finals held at a different location each year. Dogs are qualified for the National Finals at sanctioned trials during the trialling season. The qualified dogs then compete at the Finals for the title of National Champion. There is also a sponsored award given for the cumulative scores achieved at sanctioned trials throughout the year.

The Australian Shepherd Club (ASCA) offers a trialling program open to several breeds (including Border Collies). These trials are held in an arena with obstacles placed around the fence and one center obstacle. The livestock are typically removed from a pen by the competing dog or handler, taken through the obstacles and returned to the pen. In some cases the center obstacle is a free standing pen similar to the pen used in the International Course. In other cases the center obstacle is a chute made of gates with wing gates on this approach. Judging is done against a

standard and qualifiers earn a title. The levels of competition are Started, Open, and Advanced. The livestock used are sheep, ducks and cattle. To receive the most advanced title of Working Trial Champion a dog must have earned all the previous titles on each type of livestock. ABCA also offers the title of Ranch Dog and Ranch Trial Dog for each type of livestock. There is no set course for these titles, but practical ranch work is required.

THE AKC PROGRAM

The American Kennel Club (AKC) started a herding program in 1990 open to 16 breeds of dogs. More recently they recognized the Border Collie as an AKC herding Breed. The AKC herding program is open to those Border Collies that are registered by the AKC. There are three courses offered. The "A" course is an arena with obstacles similar to the Australian Shepherd course above. The "B" course is patterned after the International Course. The "C" course follows the European plan of tending and moving a flock of 20 or more sheep. Courses "A" and "B" may use three or five ducks, sheep or cattle. Each course has levels of competition of Started, Intermediate, and Advanced. Titles are earned by competing to a set of standards. A Herding Champion title is earned by competing against other dogs at the Advanced level. In addition the AKC offers two levels of testing for dogs not ready for the trial competition.

Am. Ch. Darkwind Miles CDX HT.

The American Herding Breed Association (AHBA) offers two levels of testing, three levels of trials, and three levels of ranch dog work. The emphasis is on accomplishment of requirements rather than on competition. Titles are awarded at each level. Titles are specific for the livestock used (sheep, goats, ducks, geese or cattle). A championship title is awarded based on qualifying scores. Fifty-four breeds of dogs with a herding background are eligible to compete. The Trial courses are similar to the International course. At the lower level the handler may accompany the dog through the course. The Intermediate level restricts handler movement somewhat. The Advanced level requires the handler to remain at the post until penning.

LOCAL VARIATIONS
Local and state organizations offer various trial courses. Rules are adjusted to fit local preferences. Timed trials are quite popular. The course may be of any type. All of the livestock must pass each obstacle before attempting the next. Retries are allowed. Style is not important. Biting may or may not be allowed. One type of timed cattle trial features the handler mounted on horseback and, assisted by his dog, sorting marked cattle from a group and penning them. A common trial course for cattle features some open field work followed by assigned tasks in a working corral. This is usually judged instead of timed. For comedy relief some trials offer a "Buddy Brace" class. Any livestock or course may be used. Two handlers, each with one dog, are required to complete the course. Each handler/dog team is responsible only for "his" side and crossovers are penalized.

Trialling has grown in popularity and several trials of each type are offered throughout the year. Of course the warmer climates offer most of the winter trials and fewer of the summer trials. Few trials

attract a large audience of the general public. The news coverage of dog trials is likely to be of the "human interest, 'Isn't this cute'" variety instead of sports coverage. Many of the professional triallers offer teaching clinics for dogs and handlers. Such clinics are well-attended by beginning and intermediate triallers.

In summary, the wide variety of Border Collie types and temperaments makes this a unique breed for fitting a remarkable range of uses. Popularity of the breed is growing rapidly in the USA. The increased interest in trialling and other competitive sports accounts for much of the growth. This is followed by show ring and home pet uses. There is little growth or decline in the use of Border Collies by the livestock industry.

BORDER COLLIES IN SOUTH AFRICA
Border Collies have been in South Africa since the 1920s, but it was only in the 30s that sheep farmers began to take a serious interest in breeding and training them. There were no guidelines for those early farmers. Pioneers such as Ron Philip, now retired and breeding dogs outside Caledon, and Chipper Kingwill, in George, learnt to train their dogs through trial and error. "My first dog taught me more than I taught him," says Philip.

Today, there are 15,000 collies registered with the South African Sheepdog Association (SASDA). The breed minds some 25 million sheep around the country – in market terms more than 61.5 million kilograms of wool and mohair. A top trained Collie can command a price of R6,000 and more. But a good dog is worth every cent, for it can save a farmer hours of labour. Bracken, a dog belonging to Pippa, Ron Philip's daughter-in-law, demonstrated this in a single morning. Working with Pippa, she brought in 700 sheep for dosing – a task that might have taken several men up to two days to complete.

In the best strains, the herding instinct shows early. Often you will see Collie pups of only a couple of months rounding up ducks or chickens. At six to nine months a Collie is ready to start training with sheep. It reaches its peak between the ages of four and eight years, retiring at about ten.

LIVING FOR WORK

The Collie lives for work. Placid around the farmhouse, it becomes quicksilver in the fields, fleet over the roughest ground, long tail a balance as the light body twists and bounds. Muscle and determination give endurance as well as speed. A Collie may cover more than 150 kilometres of gullied, rock-strewn veldt a day. Or it may dig its heels in with intense singleness of purpose.

When a thunderstorm struck the district of Greytown in KwaZulu-Natal one afternoon, Brenda Munitich took her dog Chummy to round up a small herd of cattle. The rain was so heavy that visibility was almost zero, but Chummy brought the nervous cows through a raging stream. Amid crashing thunder and flashes of lightning, Brenda called the dog to follow and turned for home. But Chummy sat down and refused to move. Then he suddenly spun round and dashed back across the stream. Perplexed by his refusal to obey her, Munitich continued to herd the cattle back to the kraal. She glanced back as she reached the kraal to see Chummy running towards her, gently guiding a one-month-old calf which Munitich had completely overlooked in the confusion.

TRIALS EXPERTS AMO AND QUIN

The best place to see a dog's ability is at the various trials and Championships held under the auspices of SASDA. They are both useful pointers to breeding and a

shop window for working Collies. Five times a year sheep farmers and their dogs from all over South Africa gather at rural towns such as Sutherland, Willowmore, Adelaide, Volksrust and Graaff-Reinet to put their dogs through exacting trials. These gatherings are social affairs, where farmers and their families get together for a congenial three days at a selected farm. Braais and boerekos are the order of the day as over 70 dogs are put through their paces.

At the trials outside Sutherland in March this year, I watched Andrew Philip, Ron's son, direct his dogs in the brace event. It is a difficult exercise that involves two dogs competing simultaneously, requiring expert co-ordination. Faced with ten sheep about 400 metres away, the dogs, Amo and Quin, took off at Andrew's command. Making a wide arc so as not to frighten the sheep, one headed left, the other right. Then they converged at the rear and slowly advanced on the flock.

Border Collies work primarily to signals. Andrew kept a tight control of his dogs using a wide range of auditory and physical commands. The most dramatic were the whistled commands, which Amo and Quin obeyed instantly. It was a treat to watch how the short, sharp whistles urged the dogs to move faster, how a low, drawn-out whistle slowed them down. In all, a dog can learn up to a dozen different whistle commands, although these vary in tone and meaning for each handler and his or her dog.

Quickly and steadily, Amo and Quin started to herd the sheep back to where Andrew stood. Suddenly a ewe darted out of the group and made for a patch of grass. In a flash Amo was round the flock and in front of the straying animal. Crouched low and ready to sprint, Amo fixed what farmers call the "eye of control" – which gives the Collie a seemingly extra-sensory command over sheep – on the ewe.

Bernie Strydom and Spot from Grahamstown.

Henry vd Merve with Bimbo: Dog of the Year 1988 and 1989.

Unblinkingly, he willed it back into line.

Such calmness is vital, particularly when a dog is faced with a belligerent ram or a lambing ewe. These so-called "wild" sheep can often test a dog to the limits of its patience. A good sheepdog will not bite a sheep under normal circumstances; if it does so during trials it is automatically disqualified. A young dog may be intimidated and back off, but an experienced dog may well end up giving the recalcitrant sheep a well-placed nip – and that particular animal will think twice about misbehaving again.

Amo's restraint gave the pair extra points. In the next part of the run, the two dogs had to drive the sheep through two narrow gates set up on either side of the field, then pen them neatly into a small enclosed area. Amo and Quin completed the course within the required 25 minutes, winning the event with a final tally of 132 out of 150. "I work with the dogs every day," Andrew Philip told me. "But when they are in top form, like today, I still get a thrill watching them."

9 THE VERSATILE BORDER COLLIE

The versatility of the Border Collie is renowned. Their ability to herd sheep is unsurpassed. They also excel at the varied disciplines of Sheep trialling, Obedience, Conformation, Agility, Flyball and Search work. Their working ability as guide, assistant, search and therapy dogs is probably less known; nevertheless a small number of pure-bred dogs qualify each year within these disciplines.

GUIDE DOGS
In the 1930s, when the Guide Dogs for the Blind Association (GDBA) relied on adult dogs donated by the public, German Shepherd and Border Collies were the breeds offered most often. Pedigree dog breeding declined during the war, resulting in fewer good-quality German Shepherds being offered to the Association, so they turned their attention to other breeds. A variety were tried, including Labradors, Golden, Flat-coated and Curly-coated Retrievers, Keeshonds, Dalmatians, and Airedales as well as Border Collies. Only the Border Collie at that time was judged to have the qualities needed. It seems surprising that the Labrador, which now so dominates the guide dog world, was found to be unsuitable then.

The switch was made to using more Border Collies. There was a plentiful supply from farmers, dealers, breeders and other, more dubious, sources. The quality varied enormously. Unneutered males and bitches were used with obvious consequences. Neutering dogs did not become policy until the early 60s; interestingly, the males were more successful than the bitches at this stage. The dogs were not bred or reared for this specialised work and, looking back, it is amazing any succeeded at all.

Border Collies in training at the the Guide Dog centre in Leamington Spa, 1941.

Fox Photos.

SWEEP AND FLY

One of these remarkable dogs was Sweep, a large Border Collie, that had been sorely neglected before arriving at the Leamington training centre. He had never been off the farm, his only experiences were those of a farm dog. The late Derek Freeman, GDBA Breeding Manager, recalled that whatever situation Sweep was presented with he took in his stride – steps, elevators, pushchairs, traffic, trains, slippery shop floor surfaces and flapping blinds, to name a few. If Sweep ever showed any hesitation, it was momentary.

He progressed through training and qualified with an ex-soldier who had lost his sight fighting the Mau Mau in Kenya. An active man, who was still very keen on walking and climbing, soon after arriving home with Sweep he decided to put the dog to the test. He planned a 33-mile walk from Luton to London. This was nothing to him, but would Sweep cope? They did. It took them 12 hours, only asking for assistance once on the way and that was to cross the junction of two major roads.

Alfred Morgan qualified with his Border Collie guide dog, Fly, and arrived home in Liverpool the day before war broke out. He worked at the docks and described how Fly guided him safely through nine months of regular blitz to and from work 'without the loss of a single hour's work'. Alfred Morgan's working days with Fly were tragically ended in 1942. While crossing the road with Fly, Alfred was seriously injured when hit by a lorry. He described what had happened in a letter to his guide dog trainer. A noisy horse wagon was drowning the other traffic sounds. He was about half-way across the road when he heard a motor coming down the hill from the right. It was travelling at a good pace and the driver did not notice Alfred and Fly until it was too late. Alfred records that Fly did struggle in the harness to move on but, not being sure which was the safest direction to go, Alfred stood his ground. The driver then saw him and tried to stop the vehicle, but it skidded and hit Alfred.

When Alfred awoke some ten minutes later he was being attended to by a doctor, but there was rather a commotion going on in the waiting room. It was Fly, running around, jumping at the door trying to burst in and get to Alfred. He asked them to let her in to him, which they did. She settled immediately once Alfred had put his hand on her head. Alfred survived the accident but sadly had to have his right leg amputated. This did not deter him. Fitted with an artificial limb and once again active, he applied to have Fly back. This was not allowed; Fly was too fast for someone with an artificial leg. A more gentle, quieter dog that did not pull was found, and Alfred was retrained. Fly was found a pet home with the nurse that cared for Alfred during his hospital stay.

CROSS BREEDING

From 1938 to the mid-1950s the Border Collie and German Shepherd, or Alsatian as they were called then, dominated the scene. But as the quality of the Labradors offered improved, it became evident that the sound temperament and steadiness of this breed were more suited to a wider range of blind owners. The Border Collies high hearing level and body sensitivity were making them increasingly more difficult to match. As the demand for more guide dogs grew, so too did the guide dog owners' expectation of the dogs' ability in an increasingly busy environment.

Nowadays only a small number of pure-bred Border Collies qualify each year. Training the Border Collie is not difficult but matching them to a prospective owner is. The Border Collies' speed of response to commands can make them difficult for blind people to cope with. While they are easy to follow, they need the sort of owner who has a brisk walking speed, is light on their feet, swift to react and one who leads an interesting lifestyle to occupy the Border Collie brain.

GDBA decided to cross breed the Border Collie with the Golden Retriever because it was having difficulties in establishing pure-bred lines suitable for guide dog work. The first litter of seven were born in the late 70s and all but one qualified. The Golden Retriever softens the drive of the Border Collie, giving a calmer attitude and greater confidence, and they are not so sound-shy. Out of a working guide dog population of 4,454, there are nine pure-bred Border Collies and 58 Border Collie x Golden Retrievers.

The UK, New Zealand and Austria are the only countries on record to have used the Border Collie as a guide dog. The qualities required of the ideal guide dog are: stability; a pleasing disposition; not neurotic, shy or frightened; reasonably energetic but not hyperactive; non-aggressive but properly apprehensive and protective; a low chasing instinct; an ability to concentrate for long periods; not easily distracted; willing, and responsive to the human voice; confident with and tolerant of children; confident with and tolerant of other animals; not sound-shy; able to show a level of initiative; not too dominant or self-interested; adaptable to change of environment and/or handler; an acceptable level of body sensitivity and as free as possible from hereditary defects.

THE TRAINING PROCESS

The puppy walking scheme for prospective guide dogs has proved to be a major factor in the success rate currently enjoyed by GDBA. As the pioneers of early socialisation, it is now widely recognised as the fundamental issue to ensure the development of acceptable temperamental characteristics. Puppies are placed in homes from the age of six weeks. The aim is to rear a puppy in a family environment and for it to be socialised in a variety of different situations. The puppy must get used to the sights and sounds of a busy town life, it has to learn to walk slightly ahead of the handler and should ignore distractions. They are also housetrained, taught good social behaviour and basic obedience responses. This period of early training lasts, on average, for one year. The puppies are visited and assessed regularly while at walk by a member of GDBA staff.

Between the age of 12 to 14 months the dogs are taken in to one of the regional training centres for assessment and further training. Initially they are taught the straight line procedure, kerb stops, turns (left, right and back), and speed control. Once these skills have been developed they are then taught obstacle avoidance – at first it is solid stationary objects, such as lamp posts and letter boxes, then it is moving objects, namely people.

Speed control in busy crowded areas is an important aspect of training. Border Collies learn the guiding skills very quickly but tend to rush their work and anticipate commands, so the correct approach from the handler is essential to develop a calm, relaxed attitude from the dog. On average it takes nine months to train a guide dog.

In the later stages of training the dog is matched to a suitable blind owner. The needs and circumstances of the client are assessed, as well as their lifestyle, fitness and temperament. It is important to match the capabilities of the client with the ability of the dog. Training the dog with the client can take up to four weeks. The flexibility of the residential course allows for the variety of client ability. The rate of progress will depend on the aptitude of the owner and the dog's acceptance of the change of circumstances.

The new blind owner will be taught how to handle the dog in all the different situations and environments that the dog experienced during training. They are also taught basic dog psychology, feeding, grooming and general care procedures. When the guide dog owner returns home with their new dog, their instructor will visit them to practise the routes they do regularly, e.g. to work, to the shops or to school, to ensure the safety and confidence of the dog and owner in their new role together. All guide dog owners are visited on an annual basis, throughout the dog's working life; more frequent visits will be made if required.

Most guide dog owners who have lived with and worked a Border Collie ask for another one the next time they train with a new dog, so their usefulness in this field continues.

A WORKING RELATIONSHIP
Roger Hall is 49, married, with two boys, one of seven years and one 14 months old, and he is working his second guide dog. His first dog was also a Border Collie, a tri-coloured dog called Andy, who was retired at the age of 11 years. Andy was beginning to slow up and, because Roger preferred to have another Border Collie, he knew he would have to keep Andy going until a new dog could be found. This turned out to be Megan. She was a black and white Border Collie who was in training at the Bolton centre and thought to be suitable for Roger's needs, so she was transferred to the centre closer to Roger's home. She was small, fairly light in weight; she walked at a fast pace and was quick to learn new routes – almost everything to suit Roger's requirements. But, most importantly, would she mind sailing on a boat? Roger's occupation and hobby is the building and sailing of boats.

Registered blind at seventeen, Roger was encouraged to be a machine operator, which he hated; so, after finding limited opportunities in this field, he decided to make a career out of his hobby. He had

Border Collies are still in demand as guide dogs.

been sailing since he was in a carry-cot, he owned his first boat by the age of twelve and, as with any passion, he learnt all there was to know about boats. He now builds new boats to order, and does a lot of restoration work at the Maritime museums in Cardiff and Swansea and repair work as requested.

Roger spends most of his day going between the workshop and the marina. He needed a dog that he could carry up and down ladders and lift on and off boats; one that could learn the different routes around the many marinas he visited in the course of work and, finally, he wanted a bright, quick-witted dog to suit his personality and temperament.

His first impression of Megan, as he put his hand on her head, was how different she was to Andy, smaller and more lady-like. When they went for their first walk together he realised just how much Andy had slowed up. Roger found himself back in top gear again. Adjusting to a new dog takes time but he recalls that it seemed to happen quite quickly with Megan; she soon transferred her allegiances from her

135

trainer to Roger. While in training together Roger was expected to take over full responsibility for the dog's daily needs, the feeding, grooming and free-running. This all helps quickly to form a bond between the two. Training starts in quiet areas and, as the two develop in confidence, they are taken into busier situations. The guide dog owner has to be taught how to use their dog in a variety of environments and situations, including obstacle avoidance and traffic awareness. These skills develop over a period of time but usually within the four-week course they have perfected the basics and are ready to go home and utilise their dog for their specific needs.

Roger knew his home town and regular routes well and Megan picked these up quickly. He was more nervous about taking Megan on her first sailing trip. Roger's guide-dog instructor, Emma, remembers the trip well. Megan was well used to being picked up and carried by now and, as Emma talked Roger through getting Megan on board, she described the visual experience as being a cross between a fireman's lift and Megan using Roger as a human gang plank. Once on board they all went for a sail around the bay. Megan took to it like a duck to water and has been sailing regularly ever since. Megan is now nine years old; she too is beginning to slow up. Roger's name is on the waiting list for a new dog and he hopes for another Border Collie. When Megan retires she will, like Andy did, move next door but one, to live with a good friend and neighbour and enjoy being a lady of leisure.

ASSISTANCE DOGS
Schemes to train dogs to alert people with hearing loss started in the United States and by the early 1980s there were several programmes operating across America, including the American Humane

Association in Colorado. As a result of close co-operation between this organisation and the UK, Hearing Dogs for the Deaf was founded.

Canine Companions for Independence in Santa Rosa, California, has an assistance dog training programme that is divided into three categories: hearing dogs, service dogs and social dogs (companion dogs). Some of the organisations in the USA use a few Border Collie types but there is one school that uses nothing but Border Collies and Collie types as hearing dogs. Hearing dogs in the UK are usually mixed breeds selected from animal shelters, but a few Border Collie cross breeds have been successful.

Hearing dogs are trained to make physical contact by using a paw to alert the owner, then lead them to the source of the sound, such as the doorbell, the telephone, an alarm clock, cooker timer, a smoke alarm or even a crying child. The clients spend time at a training centre in a purpose-built unit that resembles a small home, to learn how to use their dog and care for its needs.

DOGS FOR THE DISABLED
Dogs for the Disabled is a growing organisation set up in 1986 by Francis Hay, herself a disabled lady severely affected by bone cancer. She was also a dog lover who found her own pet dog, Kim, could be trained to carry out tasks that she was finding increasingly more difficult. Opening and closing doors, activating light switches, picking up dropped items and collecting the milk basket and the post are but a few of the commands taught. Sadly Francis died, but the effort she had put into this passionate belief was continued by friends and family, enabling Dogs for the Disabled (DFD) to become a registered charity in 1988.

The organisation trains specially selected dogs to carry out a range of practical tasks

Dogs for the Disabled carry out a wide range of practical tasks.
Photo courtesy: Dogs for the Disabled.

ownership. The feeding, grooming, health checks, first aid, play and free running procedures are taught in detail. Once the dog and owner have achieved an acceptable standard they will qualify as a working unit and return home. Dogs for the Disabled instructors continue to work with and support the partnership in the home environment throughout the dog's working life; these regular visits are made to ensure that everything runs smoothly.

There are now 100 working partnerships in the UK. Two of these are pure-bred Border Collies, a third recently had to retire early and they have one in training. They also have qualified six Border Collie x Golden Retrievers, with one more in training. It is all credit to the versatility of the breed that they are able to excel in another worthy field.

to assist a disabled person, the key benefits being greater independence, an increased sense of security, renewed confidence, improved health and companionship.

DFD is developing with the support and co-operation of the Guide Dogs for the Blind Association, which provides many of their trainee dogs. Adult dogs rejected from the guide dog training programme, usually because they are unable to accept the role of a guide dog in busy conditions, can make a good dog for a disabled person. It is good to see these dogs respond to the requirements of a different role. DFD also accepts adult dogs offered to them by the public, and some rescue dogs, and they now have a few puppies being specifically reared for their purpose.

All dogs are trained to respond to basic obedience commands, and to have good social behaviour and they are then trained to carry out specific tasks as required by their future owner. The new owner then spends up to four weeks at the training centre learning to work with the dog, and the essential elements of good dog

CAROL FLETCHER AND TARN

When Carol Fletcher drew up the guest list for her wedding, there was one name that was certain to be there, right at the top. Dog for the Disabled Tarn has become so much a part of Carol's life over the past two years that arriving at church without such a good friend in attendance was unthinkable. Proudly taking up his position alongside the bridesmaids and page boys, Tarn's presence completed a perfect day which only a few years ago would have been almost impossible for the bride to imagine.

"Tarn has given me back my life. He has made all the difference. The confidence and the companionship I get from him, you can't put a measure on," says Carol, with obvious affection for her two-year-old Border Collie.

It was 12 years ago that 36-year-old Carol was struck down by a brain haemorrhage. Although her speech returned, she remained permanently paralysed along one side of her body, making walking extremely difficult and

ABOVE: Tarn – guest of honour at Carol's wedding.

RIGHT: Tarn gives Carol independence, and she is able to continue her work as a singer.

even the smallest of everyday tasks a struggle. Hobbies, activities, a job, going out with friends – the kind of lifestyle most 24-year-olds take for granted – became further and further beyond reach.

"I spent a lot of time at home, because getting out was so hard," Carol recalls. "You begin to feel lonely and, being so dependent on other people, your confidence soon starts to be sapped. Then it becomes a downward spiral."

The turning point came when a friend who had a guide dog told her about the Dogs for the Disabled organisation. Having enjoyed owning a dog in the past, Carol needed no persuasion to apply: "I went onto a waiting list, and when Dogs for the Disabled thought they had a dog that would be suitable, they got in touch. It can take a while, as they try to match the dog to the owner and disability, though the basic training is the same for all, once a possible match has been decided. The dogs are trained with that particular person in mind, according to the tasks they will need to do. I don't need to be helped out of my wheelchair, for example, but for those people who do, a solid type of dog will be chosen which can pull the person up and is very steady. Being a Border Collie, Tarn is quite lively, of course, and very quick-

thinking, so he wouldn't suit that kind of job, but he is ideal for me.

"The dogs come from all kinds of sources. Many of them began by starting training to become guide dogs for the blind, but weren't suitable for one reason or another. They have to be so perfect to be guide dogs that a lot do not make it, but can often adapt to being assistance dogs or hearing dogs. Tarn was actually donated to the organisation, as his breeder specifically wanted him to become a dog for the disabled."

Tarn's preliminary training taught him obedience, social awareness and hygiene discipline. He learned how to walk alongside a wheelchair, and that he was expected always to walk on the left-hand side of the chair, because Carol was unable to use her right-hand side. As dog and potential owner first met for their fortnight's intensive training together, the Border Collie already knew as much about household chores as most self-respecting housekeepers. Loading and unloading the washing, tidying away, 'retrieving' the post or fetching a ringing mobile phone, opening and closing doors, switching on the light, carrying the shopping – Tarn was the kind of domestic help anyone would like to employ! Now it was time to start to

138

create that crucial working partnership.

"For two weeks you spend every day with the dog," Carol explains. "You go out doing your shopping, going to the doctor and all the places you would normally go, carrying out your usual routine, to get them used to it. Then away you go. The trainers are always ready to help – but essentially you get on with it."

The bond between the two was immediate. "I delayed taking Tarn home for a couple of weeks because we had visitors and I wanted to be able to give him my full attention. I needn't have worried about it taking time for us to gel, as we got on well right from the start."

As the partnership developed, getting used to his changing role occasionally proved confusing for the new recruit. "After Tarn first arrived, he was so used to walking by a wheelchair that when my little niece visited and was scooting about on her tricycle, there he was trotting gently along by her side, following her every turn. That is typical of Tarn – he has to be looking after somebody all of the time."

For Carol, her dog's love of simply 'being with you' is all-important. Essential for any assistance dog, this companionability is a characteristic that makes the Border Collie especially suited to the carer's role.

"Their love of companionship, I believe, is their most important quality. Collies are so faithful and loyal that, put together with their intelligence, it makes them very special. My particular dog absolutely loves everyone, especially children – and yet he knows that he is there for me. Whatever else is going on, he watches every move I make. Even if I go out of the room, I swear he can see through doors! His eyes follow me everywhere I go. It is more than just obedience – it is a bond.

"Tarn is definitely a 'people' dog. It is in his nature to be carer. We recently went on holiday and this time left him behind with friends who have children. Apparently he

spent the whole time rounding up the children! He always knew exactly where each child was. It was as if, because he didn't have me to look after, he had to transfer his allegiance temporarily to someone else that needed his care. I have a cockatiel at home, and if I'm not asking Tarn to do anything particular, he lies there, riveted by it. His powers of concentration are phenomenal."

The Border Collie seems to have an innate need to be useful and gain the all-important approval of his owner. Carol finds that Tarn is never happier than when he is being asked to perform a task. As a Dog for the Disabled, he could hardly have better job satisfaction.

"If Tarn is doing nothing, he is not as happy as when he has got a task to be doing and he knows he is pleasing you," she says. "He will go out to get my post in the morning, gets the washing out of the washing machine and picks up anything that I drop.

"Wherever I go, Tarn goes too. I am a singer, and Tarn goes to all my gigs and lies there listening to the music. I am not sure what he thinks of it, but he hasn't complained yet!

"Tarn loves everyone and gets fuss from everyone and loves his walks with my husband, but in the back of his mind that dog knows I am the one. I think the relationship between us is still building all the time and, even after two years, we are still getting closer.

"He is incredibly sensitive to my moods and feelings. On the rare occasions since I have had Tarn that I have cried, he is so concerned for me it is very moving. Recently, when I received a telephone call telling me that my grandmother had died, I must have sounded upset because, although he could not possibly have understood the conversation, there he was, right on top of me, trying to comfort me. It was quite strange – he so clearly knew that something was not right and he wanted to make it better."

Dogs for the disabled are a 'partnership for life'. There is no doubt that Tarn will still be keeping those faithful eyes on Carol even when he has officially been allowed to collect his retirement papers – just in case he can be of assistance. "Tarn means so much to me, and does so much for me, I cannot put it into words. Remembering all the details is difficult, because to Tarn and I, it is everyday life – to everyone else, he is amazing."

SEARCH DOGS
Border Collies are relative newcomers to the discipline of search dogs. Labradors, German Shepherds and Springer Spaniels are more frequently used but recently the qualities of the Border Collie have been recognised. There is a constant requirement for specialist dogs to carry out searches for large organisations and individuals who have been assessed to be at risk; this requirement is met by the various law enforcement agencies in the UK and the USA.

In the UK the armed forces use a few Border Collies but it is the Police, Customs and Excise and the Prison service who use the Border Collie for search work in surprisingly large numbers. At present there are 37 Border Collies working as drug and explosive detection dogs for the police force. When off duty they live with their handler, at home, as a pet dog, but when on duty they are expected to attend any situation where drugs or explosives may be found.

Rip was the first Border Collie to qualify for the prison service, in 1991. There are now 29 working within this department around the UK, with three more in training. Their main function is to make regular sweeps throughout areas within the prison searching for drugs or firearms, items that have been smuggled in or makeshift guns made on site.

Customs and Excise has six Border Collies working at coastal ports and airports throughout the UK. They have one Border Collie working in a pro-active method; this means that when it is searching it will dig, bite and scratch to find any of the four substances commonly smuggled in or around the country. Their passive search dogs are taught to behave in a controlled manner when searching or making a find. The dogs are working among the public, so it is important they remain calm and that they do not intimidate the public in any way. Good-looking, friendly dogs are used. These departments all rely on adult dogs offered to them by the public as the major source of future working dogs.

There is also a Civilian Commercial Search Dog team in the UK that now uses Border Collies. At present they have two fully-trained working dogs and one young star coming through the ranks. I had a chance to meet these dogs and learn a little about how and why the breed are proving to be so successful at searching for explosives.

All dogs used need to be fit, healthy specimens, well-constructed, hip and eye tested, and have an amenable disposition. Handlers Matt Matulewicz and Maggie Peacock have switched from the proven ability of the German Shepherd to the Border Collie and are complete converts.

The Border Collie is so much easier to motivate, and will concentrate for long periods of time," said Maggie. "Physically they are easier to cope with than the large, heavy and sometimes clumsy German Shepherd, especially when working in small or confined areas. Their obsessive nature is useful, if correctly channelled in training, providing keenness and an ever-ready enthusiasm to work."

Maggie also finds that the inbred shepherding skills can be useful. "The

Border Collie was sent out to find lost sheep, and so it has excellent scent discrimination,," she said. "We also find that they will work more independently than other breeds and are prepared to use their initiative."

Matt and Maggie currently have three working dogs: Passims Seabreeze (Breeze), Arnpriors Spectre(Specy), and Arnpriors Trader (Tay). Maggie is a strong believer that the working dog should still conform to the Breed Standard, and she she shows her working dogs under her Arnpriors kennel name.

TRAINING A SEARCH DOG

Like the German Shepherd the Border Collie is slow to mature mentally, so training progresses gradually, based on basic obedience commands, the retrieve, and play as the reward. Once the retrieve is established they are then taught to be article-conscious. Using a scented dummy they are taught to recognise the different scents associated with the full range of explosives or drugs, depending on which field the dog is going to specialise in. The dogs I met were training to detect explosives; they would have to learn to recognise the five main types of explosive regularly used.

During early training they are taught to search and retrieve, in many different environments and situations. They are encouraged to search with plenty of positive reinforcement from the trainer; when they make a find they are instantly rewarded with a play session.

The next and more difficult stage of the training comes when the dog is searching and makes a find but, because of the dangers involved with explosives detection work, the dog must not pick the article up, so it is important to teach the dog to give a positive signal to indicate a find. This is ultimately displayed as a back step of two paces and a bark; this conditioned response is again instantly rewarded with a play session. The dog's incentive to work is established and then maintained on each training session by always finishing with a find.

It is very much a working partnership. The handler has to assess the environment to be searched, deciding which are the high risk areas and prioritising the order of the search. First the handler will make a visual check, leaving the dog somewhere away from the area to stimulate keenness, hopefully to achieve peak performance. Some large buildings or areas can take a while to search thoroughly because the dog has to be rested regularly. A search is usually broken into forty minute sessions. This gives the dog's dried nasal membranes a chance to recover, which enables the dog to effect a thorough search.

The dog and handler have to be attuned to one another. A slight change in the dog's body language, a flick of an ear or a

ABOVE: Brains and Beauty: Arnpriors Spectre (Speccy) who works as an explosives search dog.

BELOW: Arnpriors Assassin in training to be a drugs search dog.

Photos courtesy: Maggie Peacock.

Passims Seabreeze (Breeze) is an experienced search dog specialising in explosives.

A Search dog must be able to work in different environment, and to concentrate despite outside distractions.

Breeze is prepared to work independently, which is a great asset in this work.
Photo courtesy: Maggie Peacock.

brief glance, could indicate a presence of some sort – sometimes in addition to a find. Matt told me of the time they where carrying out a search. Nothing was found but he felt the dog had definitely reacted to an old stain on the floor and had indicated that there was something in the drawer of an empty desk. Sometime later, after a full investigation, it turned out that a gun had been kept in the desk and some gun oil had been spilt on the floor. The ability of a dog's nose to detect such scents, even stale ones, is amazing.

All the departments mentioned rely on adult dogs offered to them from the public as their main source of supply and will always consider a Border Collie if offered to them. They will look at any dog between the ages of ten and eighteen months, of a bold, enthusiastic, confident nature who shows an interest in retrieving.

COLLIES IN THE SOUTH AFRICAN POLICE

It is for their sometimes uncanny intelligence, as well as their almost paranormal sniffing ability, that Collies have recently become highly prized dogs in the South African Police Services. More than 100 have been trained for work with the stock-theft units, the narcotics division

and in the investigation of suspicious fires. Says Inspector Kim Yates of the Pretoria Dog School: "As far as sniffing and tracking go, the Border Collie is the finest there is." His dog, Tilly, can detect up to 18 flammable liquids. Since 1995 she has visited more than 100 fire scenes and positively detected flammable liquids in 90 per cent of cases.

Even more amazing are the abilities of the Collies used by the Narcotics Unit. Last year, Border Collies were instrumental in sniffing out over 23,000 drug cases leading to the capture of more than two million kilograms of marijuana and almost 300,000 units of heroin, cocaine, mandrax and other illegal substances. As a result, over 20,000 dealers and pushers were arrested.

WATER SEARCH WORK IN GERMANY
by Angela Seidel

The Border Collies I own and train are British imports and German-bred dogs. My first dog is a red and white four-year-old stud dog, Ch. Beagold Red Baron (Dt.J. Ch., Dt. Ch., Dt. Ch./VDH, Beagold Justification ex Jephaniel Scarlet Lightning), bred by Felix Cosme. He has passed his examinations as a search dog (stage three, the highest level). My second dog is the black and white two-year-old, Charouska Rin Tin Tin (Brooksbid Country Classic ex Charouska Border Mist), bred by Mrs Sue Garner. He has passed stage two, second level as a search dog. Both of them are also trained for searching for dead and drowned bodies. The third dog is the black and white stud dog Juvine Stand and Deliver (Dt.J.Ch.) bred by Mrs J. Woodvine-Aldrich. He is the youngest dog in the "gang". He is one-and-a-half years old and also a search dog stage two as well as being trained in the same skills as my other two dogs, but he is lacking some experience, naturally, given his age. All of us are working for the Technisches Hilfswerk (THW). This is a German organisation which is part of Germany's Ministry of Internal Affairs. We are called in to cases of murder, or suspected murder, when the whole body, or parts of the body, are missing. In the last quarter of 1996 we were called to 17 such cases, 13 of them being water searches. Now I had better explain what these are.

Water search is very new in Germany. It was pioneered in America, and I know of one dog there who located a dead person in a lake in a depth of 25 metres. In water search, the dog is working in a boat which takes him across the water. It is very dependent on wind and water conditions. The dog sniffs about just above the surface and shows the handler, by his behaviour, if he has found something.

Every dog I take to water search training is already a completely trained search and rescue dog, which means he has already learned how to locate living victims in disaster areas. I started water training with my dogs because we have many lakes in our neighbourhood and I was often asked by the police if my dogs were able to help in locating drowned victims. I thought they could, so I started to train them.

First of all they had to learn how to behave in a boat. Then they learned that water, too, could contain and carry human scent. For this part of the training you need some divers. They stay under water until the dog is showing interest in the scent that is coming up from them. Then they come to the surface and give the dog his reward, a toy. A properly trained dog will show the location of a dead body too, if he is confronted with one; the only difference is that his alert varies from his usual alert on living beings. All you have

Members of the Technisches Hilfswerk– a German organisation that specialises in water search work.

Photo courtesy: Meike Bockermann.

to do is to praise the dog and encourage his alert.

We train for the alert on drowned victims with special chemicals, which we put into the water under controlled conditions, and we watch the dog's reaction. There always is a reaction, and this has to be encouraged. It works because the dog is already a trained search dog and knows what to do on the command of "Search".

The most spectacular search we made in 1996 was finding a diver who had died in the biggest lake in a part of Germany called Sachsen-Anhalt. The lake's name is Arendsee and it is about 5,400,000 square metres surface, with a depth varying from 30 to 60 metres. When we were called in the diver had been missing for two weeks and already part of the lake had been searched by police divers time and again, but they could find nothing. The police suspected that this was a non-natural death, so it was essential to find the body for the coroner.

The first dog we take out on water search calls is always Charouska Rin Tin Tin because he is a very "noisy" worker. He starts whimpering if he smells anything, so it is easy for us to find the area of the smell very fast. It is a kind of hot and cold work. If the smell gets intense, the dog gets louder. If the smell lessens, the dog is still. In the direct area of the smell the dog is howling very loudly. As second dog we take Jack (Juvine Stand and Deliver), who has a precise alert. We can tell, then, exactly where the smell lies. Our third dog is my very experienced and very professional worker Beagold Red Baron. We take him to make absolutely sure of the point of alert. We have to do this because it is always very expensive and dangerous working divers, and if they go down we must be absolutely sure that there really is something there.

In this case we were lucky because we had the best divers in Germany at hand, 18 marine divers from the Bundeswehr, who really knew what to do in these deep and muddy waters. The divers were able to locate the victim in exactly the area where we told them he would lie. You have to realise, of course, that the place where the dog gives his alert is never where the victim is found – you have to know the water and wind conditions and follow the scent back to its source on the bottom of the lake. In our case the victim was found in a depth of 40 metres, which is the deepest location worldwide that I have heard of for this sort of successful search. By the way, two weeks later Jack was shown on the Bundessiegerschau in Dortmund and won his class and got the title Bundesjugendsieger and his last CAC required for the German Youth Champion.

The Border Collie is extremely suitable for this kind of work because he has a very good nose, has great stamina and is willing to please his master. He can also be trained to work out of sight – and will disobey orders when necessary. For example, when he has found a victim, and is then called off by an inexperienced handler, he should disobey that instruction. The Border Collie is also very sure-footed in disaster areas and is not too heavy, so he is able to walk on unsafe parts of broken-down buildings.

He is able to work for longer than any other breed I know, and recovers very fast after spending a long time searching. It is possible to let a Border Collie work for up to three hours in water search – with suitable breaks, of course – in one day. Compared to the maximum of one hour that other breeds will work, that is a lot! The dogs are able to work until they are eight or nine years old, then they should retire.

THERAPY DOGS
Early in 1974, B.M. Levinson, a professor of psychology from New York, presented a

paper at a symposium held in London. He attempted to forecast how life would be in the year 2000. He predicted that man would become aware of the importance of companion animals as a source of mental health and stability in increasingly strained and unhappy family relationships. He foresaw an animal lending service, available on prescription for the sick and disabled. Little did he know how his ideas would develop.

In the USA pioneering work was started in 1980 by the American Humane Association on the first bibliography of Pet Facilitated Therapy to assist societies with an interest in this new venture. This resulted in the Pet Partner programme, founded by the Delta Society, which now has representatives in 45 states across the USA, and a total of 2,000 Pet Partner teams. Michael McCulloch of Oregon and Sam Corson of Ohio were two of the early influential enthusiasts, expounding the benefits which animals can bring to the lonely or depressed.

The charity Pets As Therapy was started in England in 1983 as an extension to the work already carried out by the charity PRO Dogs. Initially the organisation received a negative reception. Allowing animals, mostly dogs, who were seen as a danger to human health, into environments such as hospices, hospitals, homes for children and the elderly, was actively discouraged. Getting the medical profession to accept dogs within these environments was an uphill struggle. However, medical consultants eventually agreed that the risk of infection to patients was far greater from the humans accompanying the dog than from the dog itself. After several years, attitudes started to change. The charity, which provides the visiting scheme free of charge thanks to willing owners and their dogs, has over 9,000 registered PAT Dogs.

The programme offers dogs who are well-trained and have been carefully tested and found to have a friendly, reliable temperament. Thousands of people now benefit from the comfort and contact they receive from these dogs. There is also a demand for therapy dogs who can help desensitise children and adults to overcome any fear or phobia they have of dogs.

The organisation Canine Concern provides a similar service with their care dogs, visiting the sick, the elderly and the lonely, as well as giving talks at schools to educate children, hopefully to become responsible dog owners of the future.

One of these dogs is Mat, a registered Border Collie who recently won a second prize in a national competition for rescued care dogs. His achievement is all the more remarkable when you consider the dreadful condition he was in when Kim Bendien gave him a home. Kim described the state he was in when she first saw him. She had never before seen such a scrap, his coat was matted and caked with excreta, he had sores and ingrown dewclaws which prevented him from walking normally, he was very underweight, and he shivered and urinated every time you looked at him. Would he ever trust her enough to get him to the vet to have his claws sorted out? It took three months to gain his trust and for Kim to feel he was confident enough to cope with a trip to the vet.

In addition to house-training Mat and teaching him basic obedience commands as well as acceptable social behaviour, Kim had to cope with the problem of Mat being terrified of umbrellas, brooms and garden hoes – anything that resembled a crook. He also went berserk every time he saw a milk float or a bicycle, howling and panicking as they passed. Curing these fears took time; he now ignores bicycles and is slightly more tolerant of milk floats. Kim took Mat to obedience and agility classes and to local dog shows, which he began to enjoy. After three years of

Griselle Kachina UDX OA working as a
therapy dog in the US.

Kim Bendien with her therapy dogs.
Photo courtesy: Evening Argus, Brighton.

training and socialising he won a third
prize in a breed class at an Open show.

Kim was already a regular visitor to the
local hospital and hospice with her Border
Collie Care Dogs, Raksha and Rani.
Gradually she introduced Mat to
accompanying her and Raksha on these
visits. He took to it enthusiastically,
thoroughly enjoying the love and attention
that was lavished on him by the patients.
Barbara was one particular patient with
whom he built up a good relationship. He
visited Barbara once a week for four years.
She was always looking out for Mat long
before he was due to arrive and Mat always
made a mad rush for her bed as soon as he
was in that particular ward. She would say
that a cuddle with Mat was better than any
medicine. One patient who was unable to
speak enjoyed Mat's visits. Although he
was unable to communicate verbally, his
eyes and body language displayed the

pleasure and comfort Mat gave him. The
nurses regularly comment on how much
perkier the patients were on 'dog day'.

These organisations are always looking
for well-behaved dogs and their willing
owners to participate in this form of
therapy, so do not hesitate to contact them
if you are interested – you will never regret
it.

HEROIC DOGS
by Lesley Scott Ordish

It never ceases to amaze us the way dogs
behave in any given situation and we have
all read about heroic accomplishments
being carried out by brave animals of many
different breeds. To celebrate this, the
British Charity PRO Dogs reward dogs
who have given notable service to their
owners or to the community. One such
dog, a Border Collie called Nipper, owned

147

by Mr E.A. Norris, received the PRO Dog of the Year Gold Medal for devotion to duty.

Few people rely more on the assistance of working dogs than farmers and shepherds. Even with the progress of modern technology, the value of these dogs is beyond price. In 1985 Nipper faced death to save his sheep. One day in February that year, when lambing was just about complete on Mr Norris's Ansty Farm in West Sussex, farm workers Jayne and Patrick Leaney had good cause to praise this outstanding Border Collie. Everyone had retired to bed after a busy day on the farm and the flock of some three hundred ewes with their new-born lambs were shut in the barn for the night.

Nipper was the first to smell the smoke coming from the barn, but his early warning barks went unnoticed. The dog was insistent, but by the time Patrick and Jayne were aroused, and had alerted the fire brigade and thrown on some clothes, huge clouds of smoke were coming from the barn. The terrified bleating of the ewes and their lambs was driving Nipper crazy with concern. As soon as the barn door was opened, he did not hesitate to face the smoke and flames, in order to reach the sheep.

Self-preservation is the strongest instinct in any animal and there is no way of ordering a dog, however obedient, to face such a life-threatening situation, unless the animal has a high level of courage. Nipper worked diligently. He brought out as many as he could and, in spite of burnt paws and lungs filled with smoke, returned for more. In the confusion, many ewes had become separated from their lambs; some tried to return to the barn when they heard them bleating. Nipper continued to brave the conditions, returning many times into the thick acrid smoke, until at last nearly every ewe and lamb had been brought to safety. Only ten of the total number of some three hundred sheep died as a result of the ordeal.

Nipper's heroism was not finished yet. There were still cows and calves left at the far end of the burning barn. Nipper was asked to work on. In spite of the pain and injury he was suffering by this time, Nipper responded gallantly. All the cows and calves were driven out. A remarkable achievement by a dog of outstanding courage. Nipper received his medal at the annual PRO Dog award ceremony the following December. The citation of his medal for devotion to duty read: 'For bravery in overcoming the danger and fear of fire to rescue his sheep'.

10 THE BREED STANDARDS

When discussing the Standard for any breed registered at the Kennel Club one must realise that it is only a rough guide as to what the Breed should look like. If you gave the Kennel Club Breed Standard to one hundred different people and asked them to draw the dog that it described, I am sure that you would be presented with one hundred different dogs. It must, therefore, be realised that a Kennel Club Breed Standard is no more than guide for breeders and judges and it gives them an indication of certain points that they should be aiming for or looking for.

Beauty is in the eye of the beholder and everyone is entitled to their point of view as to what they regard as a beautiful dog, in this case the Border Collie. As a Championship Show judge I have my opinion as to what I regard as a good-looking dog but a fellow judge may totally disagree with me, and this is what dog showing is all about. It would be very boring if all judges thought alike and placed the same animals in the same position show after show. In a very short space of time dog shows would not exist.

So, in this chapter, you have my opinion of the Breed Standard which, I hope, gives you a better insight into the various points which are listed in the US, the UK, the New Zealand and the Australian Breed Standards – but always remember that the dog that you own must, to you, look like your own interpretation of the Breed Standard because, at the end of the day, it only has to please your eye and no-one else.

COMPARING THE BORDER COLLIE BREED STANDARDS

GENERAL APPEARANCE

UK: Well proportioned, smooth outline showing quality, gracefulness and perfect balance, combined with sufficient substance to give the impression of endurance. Any tendency to coarseness or weediness is undesirable.

USA: The Border Collie is a well balanced, medium-sized dog of athletic appearance, displaying grace and agility in equal measure with substance and stamina. His hard, muscular body has a smooth outline which conveys the impression of effortless movement and endless endurance – characteristics which have made him the world's premier sheep herding dog. He is energetic, alert and eager. Intelligence is his hallmark.

AUSTRALIA: The general appearance is that of a well proportioned dog, the smooth outline showing quality,

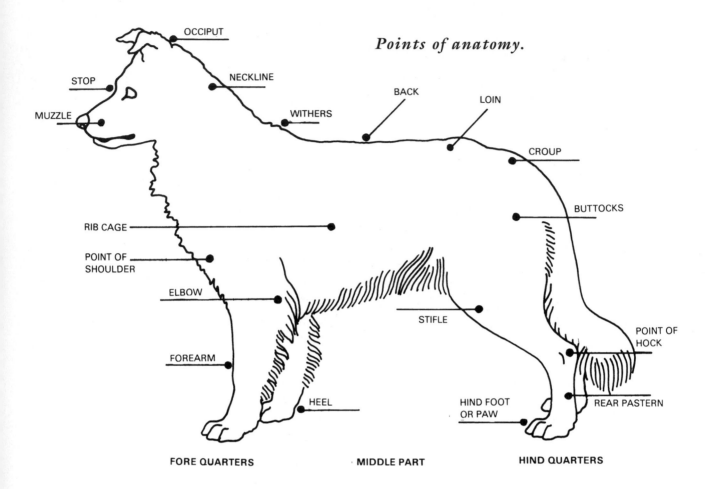

Points of anatomy.

gracefulness and perfect balance, combined with sufficient substance to ensure that it is capable of enduring long periods of active duty in its intended task as a working sheep dog. Any tendency to coarseness or weediness is undesirable.

NZ: The general appearance should be that of a well proportioned dog, the smooth outline showing quality, gracefulness and perfect balance, combined with sufficient substance to convey the impression that it is capable of endurance. Any tendency to coarseness or weediness is undesirable.

In all Standards the dog is described as balanced. This is absolutely essential in a

working dog, and particularly in the Border Collie, who has to twist and turn to counteract the movement of the sometimes wild and erratic sheep that the dog is called upon to herd in its daily working life. As far as the show dog is concerned, Breed Standard balance must take into account height-to-length ratio and the dog should be slightly longer than high. The UK Standard calls for gracefulness and quality, two things which are difficult to define, because what one judge regards as a quality dog, another may not. Gracefulness, I feel, comes under the same heading as balance, as a dog that has perfect balance and construction must be graceful. The UK Standard also asks for substance which, for a working Breed which may be called upon to work all day

The skeleton.

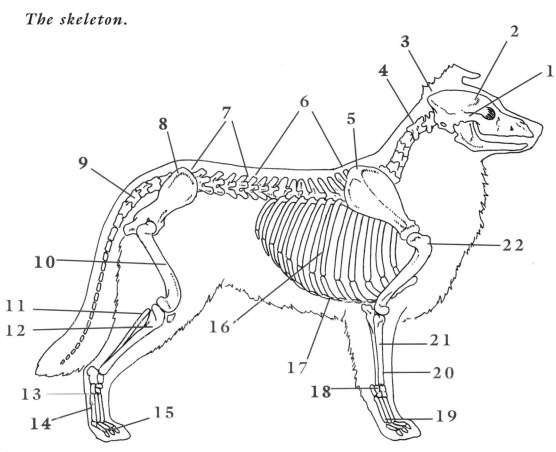

1. Zygomatic Arch
2. Cranium
3. Occipital bone
4. Cervical vertebrae
5. Scapula
6. Thoracic vertebrae
7. Lumbar vertebrae
8. Illium (pelvis)
9. Coccygeal vertebrae
10. Femur
11. Fibula
12. Tibia
13. Tarsal Bones (hock)
14. Metatarsal bones (hind pastern)
15. Phalanges
16. Ribs
17. Sternum
18. Carpal bones
19. Metacarpal bones (pastern)
20. Radius
21. Ulna
22. Humerus

on the hills, is definitely required. Any weediness would cause a serious lack of stamina to show in a hard working environment.

I feel that the American Standard, which asks for a medium-sized animal of athletic appearance, gives the reader a much better description of what is required. It also asks for a hard, muscular body which, again, is absolutely essential to the working sheepdog, and for a smooth outline which conveys the impression of effortless movement and endless endurance, both essential to the working Border Collie but very difficult to judge in the show ring. All Standards should be considered together, to gain a better idea of what is required in the Show Border Collie. The New Zealand Standard is exactly the same as the UK one. The Australian Standard is much the same but mentions active duty as a working sheepdog.

CHARACTERISTICS

UK: Tenacious, hardworking sheepdog of great tractability.

USA: is covered in the General Appearance section of their Breed Standard and states that the Border Collie is energetic, alert and eager. Intelligence is his hallmark.

AUSTRALIA: The Border Collie is highly intelligent, with an instinctive tendency to work and is readily responsive to training. Its keen, alert and eager expression adds to its intelligent appearance, whilst its loyalty and faithful nature demonstrates that it is at all times kindly disposed towards stock. Any aspect of structure or temperament foreign to a working dog is uncharacteristic.

NZ: Should be neither nervous nor aggressive, but keen, alert, responsive and intelligent.

The UK Standard calls for a tenacious dog which, for any judge, is virtually impossible to ascertain in the few minutes available to him. Certainly, in a working Breed, tenacity is a must and particularly in the sheepdog, who needs to be bold and courageous, and capable of standing up to the most stubborn of sheep. The working sheepdog must be tractable, to allow the shepherd the necessary control. The term 'hardworking sheepdog' does give the impression of a hard, fit dog and, obviously, this is a must for the working sheepdog. The dog in the show ring must also exhibit these qualities, because the show Border Collie must be judged as a working dog and not as a pretty show dog. Having said that, however, the show Border Collie usually carries slightly more weight than his working counterpart as, to the eye, this does impart a little more quality.

Both the New Zealand and the Australian Standards include temperament in the above, whereas the UK and US Standards separate it. The New Zealand Standard for characteristics uses the same wording in a slightly different order. The Australian Standard mentions the Border Collie's loyal and faithful nature and also states that any aspect of structure or temperament foreign to a working dog is uncharacteristic.

TEMPERAMENT

UK: Keen, alert, responsive and intelligent, neither nervous nor aggressive.

USA: The Border Collie is intelligent, alert and responsive. Affectionate towards friends, he may be sensibly reserved towards strangers and, therefore, makes an excellent watchdog. An intensive worker while herding, he is eager to learn and to please, and thrives on human companionship. Any tendency towards viciousness or extreme shyness are serious faults.

For the pet owner I would say that if the dog does not have an excellent temperament, then it has nothing. Good temperament for the Border Collie breeder is an absolute essential and there can be no excuse for trying to disguise a faulty temperament in order to win prizes in the show ring. Likewise, the dog should show no signs of aggression. The dog should be keen and show interest in all around him, giving the impression that he is totally alert and aware of everything that is required of him. It is a pleasure to see a dog in the show ring that is on his toes, looking about him and generally giving the impression of enjoying life to the full. The American Standard states that the dog may be reserved towards strangers, but I would point out that 'reserved' is totally different to being nervous or aggressive and certainly these things should never be confused. The American Standard also states that the Border Collie thrives on human companionship which, I think, applies to all Breeds, but Border Collies do make excellent companions and workmates.

HEAD AND SKULL

UK: Skull fairly broad, occiput not pronounced. Cheeks not full or rounded. Muzzle tapering to nose, moderately short and strong. Skull and foreface approximately equal in length. Stop very distinct. Nose black, except in brown or chocolate colour when it may be brown. In blues the nose should be slate colour. Nostrils well developed.

USA: Expression is intelligent, alert, eager and full of interest. Eyes are set well apart, of moderate size, oval in shape. The colour encompasses the full range of brown eyes; dogs having primary body colours other than black may have noticeably lighter eye colour. Lack of eye rim pigmentation is a fault. Blue eyes are a fault except in merles, where one or both eyes, or part of one or both may be blue. Ears are of medium size, set well apart, carried erect and/or semi erect (varying from one quarter to three-quarters of the ear erect). The tips may fall forward or outward to the side. Ears are sensitive and mobile. Skull is broad with occiput not pronounced. Skull and foreface approximately equal in length. Stop moderate but distinct. Muzzle moderately short, strong and blunt, tapering to nose. The underjaw is strong and well-developed. Nose color matches the primary body color. Nostrils are well-developed. A snipy muzzle is a fault.

AUSTRALIA: The skull is broad and flat between the ears, slightly narrowing to the eye, with a pronounced stop, cheeks deep but not prominent. The muzzle, tapering to the nose, is strong and the same length as the skull. The lips are tight and clean and the nose is large with open nostrils. The nose colour shall preferably be black but liver shall not be regarded as a fault in light coloured dogs.

NZ: Skull fairly broad, occiput not pronounced. Cheeks should not be full or rounded. The muzzle, tapering to the nose, should be moderately short and strong, and the skull and foreface should be approximately the same length. Nose black, nostrils well developed. Stop very distinct.

In the male the head should be strong and masculine, there should be no mistaking the male for a female and, likewise, the bitch's head should be feminine without any masculinity. The head on both should be broad, with a good stop and the muzzle should also be strong. As it states in the American Standard, the underjaw should be strong and well-developed. The UK and US Standards differ with regard to the stop, with the American Standard asking for it

Correct, balanced head with good length of muzzle and flat skull.

Incorrect: No stop.

Incorrect: Muzzle too short, domed skull.

Incorrect: Too long in muzzle.

to be 'moderate but distinct', whereas the British Standard asks for a 'very distinct' stop.

The British Standard, when referring to the eyes, states 'set wide apart, oval shaped, of moderate size, brown in colour except in merles where one or both or part of one or both may be blue. Expression, mild, keen, alert and intelligent.'

Although the American Standard states that the full range of brown eyes can be seen in the Border Collie, the British Standard only asks for brown eyes and does not specify any further than that. Most judges seem to prefer a darker brown eye to the lighter one. Obviously in blue and red merles, red and white, blue and white etc. the eye colour will be different to the eye colour in the black and white and the tricolour. As the Standards state, in

the merle blue eyes are permissible but a blue eye in any other colour would be regarded as a serious fault. The American Standard also points out that lack of pigment in the eye rim is a fault, again a relevant point not covered in the British Standard.

The American Standard states that the ears should be 'of medium size, set well apart, carried erect and/or semi erect'. Ears in the Border Collie vary enormously and range anywhere between erect and dropped. Most judges seem to prefer semierect ears but I must admit that, when I am judging, I regard the ear carriage as being insignificant compared to the overall construction of the dog. Far too much emphasis is placed on ear carriage by a few judges to the detriment of other points. Ears are there for one purpose only, solely

Correct: Ears carried erect.   *Correct: Tip ears.*   *Incorrect: Drop ears.*

for the dog to hear, so, providing the ears are of the correct size, the carriage does not really matter.

Again the NZ Standard is virtually the same as the UK Standard and to be fair the UK Standard can only be regarded as a pretty good copy of the NZ one. The Australian Standard differs slightly referring to the lips, which it stipulates should be tight and clean. They also slightly differ on nose colour.

MOUTH
UK: Teeth and jaws strong, with a perfect regular and complete scissor bite, i.e. upper teeth closely overlapping lower teeth and set square to the jaw.

USA: Teeth and jaws are strong, meeting in a scissor bite.

AUSTRALIA: The teeth should be sound, strong and evenly spaced, the lower incisors just behind but touching the upper, that is a scissor bite.

NZ: The teeth should be strong, with perfect regular and complete scissor bite, i.e. the upper teeth closely overlapping the lower teeth and set square to the jaws.

In neither the British nor the American

MOUTH

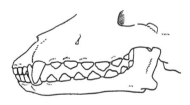

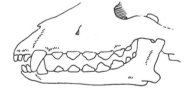

Correct: Scissor bite.   *Incorrect: Overshot.*

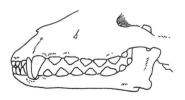

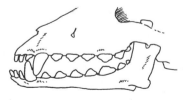

Incorrect: Level bite.   *Incorrect: Undershot.*

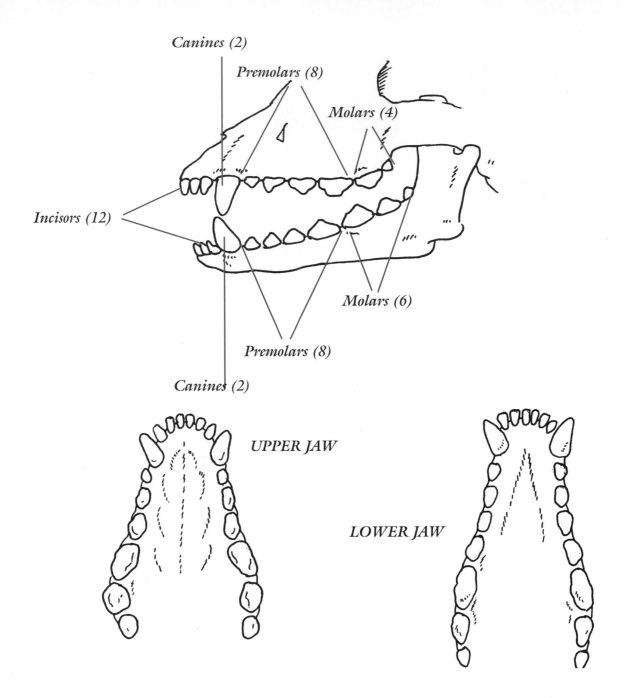

Canines (2)

Premolars (8)

Molars (4)

Incisors (12)

Molars (6)

Premolars (8)

Canines (2)

UPPER JAW

LOWER JAW

Standard does it mention the number of teeth that the dog should have and there are very few judges who check the teeth, apart from looking to see if the dog has a scissor bite. The dog should have a total of 42 teeth, 20 in the upper jaw and 22 in the lower jaw. These teeth are made up of 12 incisors (6 in each jaw), 4 canines (2 in each jaw), 16 premolars (8 in each jaw) and 10 molars (4 in the upper jaw and 6 in

the lower). The teeth should be clean. Several faults can be found with the mouth of a dog from missing teeth, to undershot jaw (bottom jaw protruding in front of upper jaw), overshot (upper jaw protruding in front of lower jaw) and a level bite.

Again the NZ Standard reads virtually the same as the UK and the Australian Standard is self-explanatory. Also, as in both the UK and US Standards, no mention of the number of teeth is made!

NECK

UK: The neck should be of good length, strong and muscular, slightly arched and broadening to the shoulders.

USA: Neck is of good length, strong and muscular, slightly arched and broadening to shoulders.

AUSTRALIA: The neck is of good length, strong and muscular, slightly arched and broadening to the shoulders, without throatiness or coarseness.

NZ: The neck should be of good length, strong and muscular, slightly arched and broadening to the shoulders.

The length of neck is in the eye of the beholder, for one person may think that a particular dog has a good length of neck while another may regard the same dog as lacking in neck. The only method of determining individual points is by looking at the whole dog. Obviously the neck must be strong and muscular to support the head.

Both the NZ and Australian Standards are virtually the same as the UK one. However, the Australian one goes on to say that there should be no throatiness or coarseness.

FOREQUARTERS

UK: Front legs parallel when viewed from the front, pasterns slightly sloping when viewed from the side. Bone strong but not heavy, shoulders well laid back, elbows close to body.

USA: Forelegs well-boned and parallel when viewed from front, pasterns slightly sloping when viewed from side. The shoulders are long and well-angulated to the upper arm. The elbows are neither in nor out. Dewclaws may be removed.

AUSTRALIA: The shoulders are long

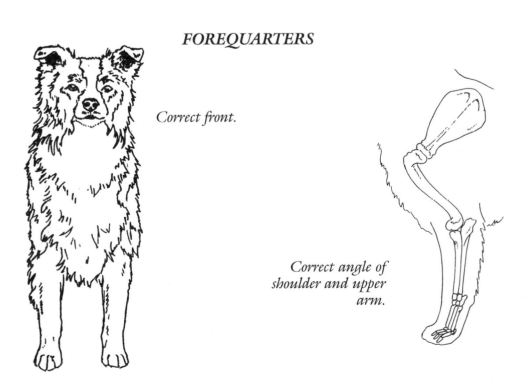

FOREQUARTERS

Correct front.

Correct angle of shoulder and upper arm.

and well angulated to the upper arm, neither in nor out at elbow. The forelegs are well boned, straight and parallel when viewed from the front. Pasterns show flexibility with a slight slope when viewed from the side.

NZ: Front legs parallel when viewed from front, pasterns sloping slightly when viewed from side. Bone should be round and strong but not heavy. Shoulders well laid back, elbows close to the body.

The American Standard states that dewclaws may be removed; this point is not mentioned in the British Standard and I must admit that you do not see many dogs in the British show rings that have had them removed. However, we did purchase a young bitch from Scotland a few years ago who had had the dewclaws removed from her forelegs and the legs did look very clean and neat.

When viewing from the front the elbows should be close to the body because, if they are not, the dog's front action cannot be correct, the front legs cannot be parallel and the pasterns will not face forward. The bone should be strong but certainly not heavy. The British and NZ Standards state 'shoulders well laid back', while the American and Australian Standard state the shoulders are 'long and well angulated to the upper arm' – two statements that I am sure would mean very little to the uninitiated. The shoulder blade, or scapula, should meet the upper arm at an angle of 90 degrees. If this angle is correct and the bones are of the correct length, then the dog will have the correct length of forward reach when moving. There will be no hackneying and no jarring of the front, thus enabling the dog to work for long hours without discomfort, and with ease, with a ground-covering stride.

BODY
UK: Athletic in appearance, ribs well sprung, chest deep and rather broad, loins deep and muscular, but not tucked up. Body slightly longer than height at shoulders.

USA: Topline is level, with slight arch over the loins. Body is athletic in appearance. Chest is deep, moderately broad, showing great lung capacity. Brisket reaching to the point of the elbow. Rib cage well sprung. Loins moderately deep, muscular, slightly arched with no tuck-up. Croup gradually sloped downward.

AUSTRALIA: The body is moderately long with well sprung ribs tapering to a fairly deep and moderately broad chest. The loins are broad, deep, muscular and only slightly arched, flanks deep and not cut up.

NZ: Ribs well sprung, chest deep and rather broad. The back should be broad and strong, and loins deep, muscular and slightly arched. The body should be slightly longer than it is high at the shoulder.

Only in the American Standard is the topline mentioned. I think that this is a major omission from the other Standards. Numerous dogs have been criticised in show critiques for having dippy backs etc. when, in point of fact, there is no guidance in the British, Australian or New Zealand Standards for judges on this point. Judges vary on what backline they think is correct and I feel that the time has arrived for the topline to be included in all the Standards. All standards call for well-sprung ribs; this allows for, as stated in the American Standard, great lung capacity, an absolute must in the working dog. The body should be slightly longer than the height at the shoulder; if the body is too long then this can only lead to weakness. At this present time we are seeing quite a few dogs in the show ring that are far too long and this should be corrected as soon as possible.

HINDQUARTERS

UK: Broad, muscular in profile sloping gracefully to set on of tail. Thighs long, deep and muscular with well turned stifles and strong well let down hocks. From hock to ground, hind legs well boned and parallel when viewed from rear.

USA: The American Standard closely follows the wording of the British one but then states – When viewed from the rear, hind legs are well-boned, straight and parallel or are very slightly cow hocked. Dewclaws may be removed.

AUSTRALIA: The hindquarters are broad and muscular, in profile sloping gracefully to the set on tail. The thighs are long, broad, deep and muscular with well turned stifles and strong hocks, well let down, and when viewed from the rear are straight and parallel.

NZ: The hindquarters should be broad and muscular, in profile sloping gracefully to the set on of the tail. The thighs should be long, broad, deep, muscular with well turned stifles and strong hocks, well let down. From hock to ground the hind legs should be well boned and parallel when viewed from the rear.

I feel that no Breed Standard should accept any weakness as being correct and, personally, I would like to see the reference to cow-hocked removed from the American one. What is slightly cow-hocked for one judge may be regarded as very cow-hocked by another. All standards ask for well turned stifles; good hind angulation is essential in a working Breed, enabling the dog to propel itself forward with thrust from the hind legs.

FEET

UK: Oval in shape, pads deep, strong and sound. Toes arched and close together. Nails short and strong.

USA: Feet are compact, oval in shape, pads deep and strong, toes moderately

HINDQUARTERS

Correct hindquarters.

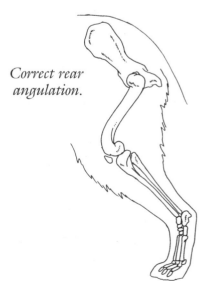

Correct rear angulation.

arched and close together. Nails are short and strong.

AUSTRALIA AND NEW ZEALAND have very similar wording to the UK Standard.

All Standards ask for the same qualities, and the feet are extremely important in a working dog. Just as a horse with poor feet is of little use, so the sheepdog with poor feet would not work for long before becoming lame or injured. Nails should also be checked and trimmed regularly, as a working dog with long nails will soon injure the nail or the nail bed. The feet should be tight and the toes arched. Flat, spread feet are a weakness in the working dog. The dog's feet should be examined at regular intervals and attention to any problem should be immediate.

TAIL
UK: Moderately long, the bone reaching at least to hock. Set on low, well furnished and with an upwards swirl towards the end, completing the graceful contour and balance of the dog. Tail may be raised in excitement but never carried over back.

USA: Tail is set low. It is moderately long, bone reaching at least to the hock. It may have an upward swirl to the tip. While concentrating at a given task, the tail is carried low and used for balance. In excitement it may rise level with the back. A gay tail is a fault.

AUSTRALIA AND NEW ZEALAND have very similar wording to the UK Standard.

The tail in the working Border Collie is used as a rudder to balance the dog as it twists and turns when herding sheep or cattle. The tail should be carried low and, indeed, when working the dog will naturally carry it low. The show dog, however, is a different matter. When moving around the ring the tail should be carried low, as if it is raised it will spoil the outline of the dog and dogs who move with their tail over the back look totally unbalanced. The tail should be of good length for the afore-mentioned reasons.

GAIT/MOVEMENT
UK: Free, smooth and tireless, with minimum lift of feet, conveying the impression of ability to move with great stealth and speed.

USA: The Border Collie is an agile dog, able to suddenly change speed and direction without loss of balance and grace. Endurance is his trademark. His trotting gait is free, smooth and tireless, with minimum lift of feet. The topline does not shift as he conveys an effortless glide. He moves with great stealth, strength and stamina. When viewed from the side, the stride should cover maximum ground, with minimum speed. Viewed from the front, the action is forward and true, without weakness in shoulders, elbows or pasterns. Viewed from behind, the quarters thrust with drive and flexibility, with hocks moving close together but never touching. Any deviation from a sound-moving dog is a fault. In final assessment, gait is an essential factor, confirming physical evaluation.

AUSTRALIA: The movement is free, smooth and tireless, with a minimum lift of the feet, conveying the impression of the ability to move with great stealth. The action, viewed from the front, should be straight forward and true, without weakness at shoulders, elbows or pasterns. Viewed from behind, the

MOVEMENT

LEFT: *Correct movement viewed from the font.*
RIGHT: *Correct movement viewed from behind.*
BELOW: *Correct movement in profile showing how the forward reach and drive from the hindquarters produces the typical ground-covering gait.*

quarters thrust with strength and flexibility with hocks not close nor too far apart. When trotting, the dog's feet tend to come closer together as speed increases, but when the dog comes to rest, he should stand four square.

NZ: The movement should be free, smooth and tireless, with a minimum lift of feet, conveying the impression of the ability to move with great stealth and speed.

There is very little that I can add that has not been covered and explained in the American and Australian Standards which, on this item, are far better than the British or New Zealand Standards. Dogs can be posed by good handlers to disguise many faults and can be made to look superb when standing, but a dog moving on a loose lead will show you the real dog.

COAT
UK: Two varieties: 1) Moderately long. 2) Smooth. In both, topcoat dense and medium textured, undercoat soft and dense giving good weather resistance. In moderately long coated variety, abundant coat forms mane, breeching and brush. On face, ears and forelegs (except for feather), hindlegs from hock to ground, hair should be short and smooth.

USA: Two varieties are permissible, both having soft, dense weather-resistant double coat. In puppies the coat is short, soft, dense and water resistant, becoming the undercoat in adult dogs. The rough coat is medium to long, texture from flat to slightly wavy. Short and smooth coat on face. Forelegs feathered. Rear pasterns may have coat trimmed short. With advancing age, coats may become very wavy and are not faulted. The smooth coat is short over entire body. May have feathering on forelegs and fuller coat on chest.

AUSTRALIA: Double coated, with a moderately long, dense, medium textured topcoat while the undercoat is

161

black and white.

Tri-colour.

Blue merle.

Red and white (tri).

Sable and white.

Blue and white.

short, soft and dense, making a weather resisting protection, with abundant coat to form mane, breeching and brush. On face, ear tips, forelegs (except for feather), hindlegs from hock to ground, the hair is short and smooth.

NZ: There are two varieties of coat, one moderately long, the other smooth. In both, the topcoat should be dense and medium textured, the undercoat short, soft and dense to give good weather resistance. In the moderately long coated variety, there should be abundant coat to form a mane, breeching and brush. On face, ears, forelegs (except for feather), hindlegs from hock to ground, the hair should be short and smooth.

The Standards describe the different coats of the Border Collie. The coat of the Border Collie is most important as it is a working Breed, out in all weather, rain, hail and snow. The coat must therefore be weather-resistant, otherwise the dog would find great difficulty working in such conditions. We see very few smooth-coated Border Collies in the show ring and, when they do appear, they are very rarely placed in competition with their rough-coated opposition. However, it is a different story at Sheepdog Trials where very many smooth-coated dogs appear, as many if not more than rough-coated dogs. Nothing shows off the construction and muscle structure better than watching a smooth-coated Border Collie working sheep.

COLOUR
UK: Variety of colours permissible, white should never predominate.

USA: The Border Collie appears in many colors, with various combinations of patterns and markings. The most common color is black with or without the traditional white blaze, collar, stockings and tail tip, with or without tan points. However, a variety of primary body colors is permissible, the sole exception being all white. Solid color, bi-colour, tri-color, merle and sable dogs are judged equally with dogs having traditional markings. Color and markings are always secondary to physical evaluation and gait.

AUSTRALIA: Black and white, blue and white, chocolate and white, red and white and the tri-colour black, tan and

white. In each case the basic body colour must predominate and be the background colour of the dog.

NZ: The wording is the same as the UK Standard.

The American and Australian Standards are far more detailed than the British Standard with regard to colour variety, although the Australian Standard does not mention the merle colour, but I think that the British and New Zealand Standards cover everything; remember always that a good dog cannot be a bad colour. A dog with half-white face or mismarking on the body should not be penalised as long as white is not the main colour of the dog.

SIZE
UK: Ideal height, dogs 53 cms. (21 inches), bitches slightly less.

USA: The height at the withers varies from 19 inches to 22 inches for males, 18 inches to 21 inches for females.

AUSTRALIA: The height at the withers should be: dogs 48 to 53cm (approx. 19 to 21 inches), bitches 46 to 51cm (approx. 18 to 20 inches).

NZ: Ideal height: Dogs about 53 cm (21 inches). Bitches slightly less.

There is not a lot to choose between the Standards and, within reason, size should not really matter too much. Many working dogs are quite small and others quite big and, for a shepherd, the size does not matter as long as the dog can do the job required of it. Contrary to popular belief, the NZ Standard reads exactly the same as the UK Standard but the Australian Standard states 19 to 21 inches for males and 18 to 20 inches for females.

FAULTS

UK: Any departure from the foregoing points should be considered a fault, and the seriousness with which the fault should be regarded should be in exact proportion to its degree.

USA: Any deviation from the foregoing should be considered a fault, the seriousness of the fault depending upon the extent of the deviation.

AUSTRALIA AND NEW ZEALAND have very similar wording to the UK Standard.

The Standards state basically the same, but every fault should be considered against the whole dog. It would be a great pity if an otherwise excellent dog was excluded from the prize list because of one fault; there is, after all, no dog born who cannot be faulted by someone. The error is to simply judge a dog by its faults. Judges must evaluate the whole dog and then make a considered judgement.

NOTE

UK: Male animals should have apparently normal testicles fully descended into the scrotum.

AUSTRALIA AND NEW ZEALAND have the same wording as the UK Standard.

There is no mention of this in the American Standard but it is a disqualification under Amereican Kennel Club rules for any male to be missing a testicle. Although the Kennel Club does allow dogs without two testicles to be shown, it is rare to find any in show entries and, when judging, I have only ever judged one adult male with a missing testicle.

11 *THE JUDGE'S VIEW*

When you have been involved in the dog showing world for a number of years, you may well feel ready to take on the task of judging. It may be that you have enjoyed a considerable degree of success, and you feel you have something to contribute. Or perhaps you have not been as lucky as you think you should have been, and you see judging as a way of redressing the balance. Whatever your reasons for wanting to judge, you will soon find out that it is not as easy as it looks! It is all too easy to criticise the judge's placings, it is quite another matter to stand in the centre of a busy ring and make calm, rational decisions, based on an in-depth knowledge of the breed, and, most importantly, the ability to make a clear interpretation of the Breed Standard when assessing living specimens.

JUDGING IN THE USA

In the USA, becoming an AKC licensed judge for any breed is a lengthy process. The AKC is constantly changing its stipulated requirements, seeking to improve the selection of judges with the implied intent of improving the quality of new judges.

An aspiring judge applying to the AKC for the first time must meet the following minimum prerequisites: (1) have ten years' documented experience in the sport; (2)

have owned or exhibited several dogs of the initial breed(s) requested; (3) have bred or raised at least four litters in any one breed; (4) have produced two champions out of a minimum of four litters; (5) have five stewarding assignments at AKC Member or Licensed Shows; (6) have judged six Sanctioned matches, Sweepstakes or Futurities; (7) must meet the occupational eligibility requirements under AKC Rules; (8) must pass a comprehensive 'open book' examination demonstrating understanding of AKC Rules, Policies and Judging Procedures; (9) must pass a test on the Standard of each breed requested; (10) must be interviewed; (11) must provide two references. To satisfy these and additional requirements requires time, effort, and money on the part of the would-be judge. It is unnecessary to detail further all the convoluted arrangements whereby an applicant is finally approved to judge initially on a Provisional basis, and, after a specified number of assignments, to become a Regular Judge.

The American Kennel Club publishes Guidelines for Dog Show Judges which details, in general terms, the required judging procedures. All judges must physically examine each dog, i.e. must open the dog's mouth (or have the handler do so) to check dentition and bite and must check that every male has two

American show scene: Am. Ch. Wizaland Daily Double At Darkwind (imp UK) bred by Sue Large, owned by Robyn L. Powley handled at Westminster 1997 by Andy Linton and received an Award of Merit. Top winning Border Collie bitch 1997, and nationally ranked by Pedigree and All breed systems.

normally descended testicles. He/she must go over the dog to determine soundness of back, hocks and coat condition. Some judges do an extensive 'hands on' examination, while others do as little as possible. The judge is required to individually gait each dog to determine soundness, always using the same ring pattern to ensure impartiality.

The interpretation of the Standard is the sole responsibility of the judge. A judge can adjudicate only those dogs which are presented in the conformation ring on a particular day.

JUDGING IN THE UK

In Britain, the Kennel Club does not give rules and regulations regarding an individual's qualifications to judge. It is a matter of acquiring experience in a breed, achieving success in the show ring and in a breeding programme, and generally serving an apprenticeship in the breed. The Kennel Club has a list of approved Championship judges, which is based on levels of previous judging experience.

In most cases, the would-be judge will serve an apprenticeship of around five years, during which time they should be reasonably successful at Championship Shows, and their home-bred litters should display soundness and type. During this pre-judging period, the aspiring judge should learn as much as possible about the breed, reading books and attending seminars, and also studying the Breed Standard in great detail, working on a personal interpretation of it. It is a useful exercise to watch leading judges at work in the ring, studying their methods and working out why certain selections have been made.

Ring stewarding is a useful way to start a judging career, as this gives experience of organising a ring. The next step is to start judging at Matches and Exemption Shows, and then gradually work towards bigger shows. It is essential to keep accurate records of all judging appointments, and when a judge officiates at Championship level, this is required by the Kennel Club.

A JUDGING EXERCISE

All Border Collies must be judged by the Breed Standard which has been adopted in the country where the breed is being judged. This is the guide that all judges must follow, regardless of whether the type varies from country to country.

As an academic exercise, three breed specialists: Bruce Kilsby (UK), Robyn Powley (USA) and Judy Vos (New Zealand) were asked to assess six Border Collies – three dogs and three bitches – from a series of photographs, showing head, profile, forequarters, and hindquarters. The dogs were not named, the experts were merely told their ages.

Clearly, it is impossible to make an accurate evaluation of a dog from photographs alone, as the essential areas of temperament and movement cannot be brought into the balance. Robyn Powley (USA) comments: The American Standard emphasizes movement when evaluating the breed. It states: "In final assessment gait is an essential factor, confirming physical evaluation." As a consequence, evaluating exhibits solely on the basis of their photographs puts some real limits on this exercise. I must assume the pictured dogs are all medium-sized, as specified by the Standard, that the bites are scissor, that tails reach the hock, and that temperaments are sound. In addition, photographs do not allow me the chance to test the exhibits, hearing – a critical ability in this breed.

"Finally, markings can present interesting optical illusions in photographs, illusions that would be discovered upon physical exam. Having made the required leap of faith, there are some interesting observations one can make regarding the six pictured Border Collies

"However, all six are recognizably Border Collies, much closer in type than is often the case in the USA. All look clean and well groomed – an important aspect for the judge's initial assessment. In my opinion, all six would be of sufficient quality to finish in the USA."

Judy Vos (New Zealand) makes the following points: "The basic requirements to look for can be summarised in the following order of importance:
• BREED TYPE i.e. a dog exhibiting and embodying all the essential and physical and mental characteristics of the breed as laid down by the standard.
• BALANCE i.e. the balanced relationship of one part to another, and of all parts to the whole, in the desired proportions laid down by the Standard of the breed.
• SOUNDNESS i.e. structure, gait and temperament, as laid down by the Standard.

Many of the basic requirements cannot be judged by photographs, and are only obvious with the physical examination and presence of the dog. These points include:
TEMPERAMENT: Various descriptions of temperament and characteristics, as laid down in the Standard of the breed, such as willingness to please, keenness, responsiveness to training, and stability cannot be judged by photographs.
FOREQUARTERS: It is difficult to measure the value of forequarter angulation when neither the bones nor the angles can be seen. Markings can play a deceptive part, especially of the forequarter area, in making a shoulder appear straighter, or better angulated than it actually is. Without physically measuring the angles of the forequarter by running your hands over a dog, it is difficult to assess a dog's angulation. In action, dogs conforming to the basic principles of forequarter angulation, when observed from the side, move correctly (assuming of course that the rear assembly is also correctly put together).
MOVEMENT: The movement of the Border Collie is of utmost importance, next to type, balance, soundness and temperament. However, a well-balanced, and well-proportioned dog (a combination of all the correct points of conformation), should therefore move as desired – but not always so!"

Bruce Kilsby (UK) concludes: "To judge dogs from photographs is obviously not the ideal way of evaluating them, as so much about their overall construction can be revealed when observing them moving. However, this is an interesting exercise, and, within limits, assessments can be made."

A JUDGING EXERCISE
Photos: Lynn Kipps.

BORDER COLLIE A.
Bitch: Three years.

HEAD STUDY

Bruce Kilsby (UK): *Very pretty, feminine, alert expression. The ears are set well apart with excellent carriage. The eyes are oval-shaped and set well apart, but I would prefer a darker colour. A nice broad skull with good head markings. From the photograph, she appears to lack underjaw.*

Robyn Powley (USA): *Feminine features, obviously mobile, with well-set and well-carried ears. Lighter, though acceptable eye color. Nice pigment. A slightly harsh expression.*

Judy Vos (NZ): *Nice strong head with sufficient stop. Eyes a little light for my liking giving a harsh expression. Good width between the ears which are well set and carried well.*

PROFILE

Bruce Kilsby (UK): *A smooth outline, good length of neck, correct shoulder and upper arm assembly. Good forechest and depth of body. Good underline, correct backline, and the croup appears to be of correct length and lay. Excellent hind angulation. Excellent length to height ratio. Good pasterns with correct slope. From the hock joint to ground, the length is correct.*

Robyn Powley (USA): *Very athletic in appearance, certainly graceful. Well-balanced in height, length and bone. Well-angulated rear, with nice turn of stifle. Well let down hocks. Good forechest.*

Judy Vos (NZ): *The profile shows this dog is overall well-balanced with good angulation in both front and rear. Particularly impressive is her nice long stifle which is well-turned and excellent short hocks which are well laid down. The hindquarter of this bitch would be close to my ideal as far as her angles are concerned. Sufficient reach of neck with nice length of back and good topline. Overall an excellent type of bitch.*

FOREQUARTERS

Bruce Kilsby (UK): *Good width of chest, this bitch stands correctly in front, with forelegs parallel. Good depth of chest, elbows are tight to body. The front feet appear to be slightly open.*

Robyn Powley (USA): *Legs parallel but narrow in front. Nice depth of chest.*

Judy Vos (NZ): *Nice, clean front with good bone and feet. I would like to see more depth of chest on a three-year-old.*

HINDQUARTERS

Bruce Kilsby (UK): *Good width to hindquarters, and the tail appears to be of correct length. She is standing with her left hindleg in the correct position, but the right hindleg is turning in slightly.*

Robyn Powley (USA): *Wide, slightly cow-hocked. Right foot toeing out.*

Judy Vos (NZ): *The hocks not as straight from this back view as I would like. However, I would like to see her going away from me on the move to make further judgement. Often, this slight cow-hocking (on the stance) can be associated with over-angulation in the hindquarters, as this bitch does have extremely well-angulated stifles. If she was straight from behind when moving away, I would not penalise this. The tail appears to be of sufficient length.*

A JUDGING EXERCISE
Photos: Lynn Kipps.

BORDER COLLIE B.
Bitch 18 months.

170

HEAD STUDY

Bruce Kilsby (UK): *A feminine head with a very appealing expression. Correct shaped dark eye. Good head markings, nice broad skull. I would prefer her with a higher ear carriage. Good strong muzzle, and strength of underjaw.*

Robyn Powley (USA): *Stronger headed, though still obviously a bitch. Very dark-eyed. Nice under-jaw. Good dark pigment. Friendly, open and intelligent expression.*

Judy Vos (NZ): *Nicely shaped head with lovely dark eye. Expression marred by slight almond-shaped eye. Good stop and nice length of muzzle. Although the ears are correctly set on the head, I would like to see a better lift and shape to them.*

PROFILE

Bruce Kilsby (UK): *This bitch is slightly long, with a slight dip in her backline. She appears to lack depth in body but no more than one would expect from a female of her age. Good slope of pasterns, her forehand angles appear okay, but she is standing with her front legs slightly too far forward. She could do with more hind angulation; her croup appears slightly steep.*

Robyn Powley (USA): *Another balanced bitch, though she appears less compact than Border Collie A. Her topline is not quite level, perhaps due more to immaturity than incorrect assembly. Good forechest but lacking the depth of brisket, again perhaps an aspect of age.*

Judy Vos (NZ): *This bitch, although still young, needs time to mature and develop in body. At present she appears long in back which is making her topline look weak. I like her forequarter angulation, and I think she would make an excellent brood bitch. Sufficient reach of neck and nice length of stifle. A little longer in hock than desired. A nice type of bitch.*

FOREQUARTERS

Bruce Kilsby (UK): *Good width of chest, but needs to develop more depth as she is standing slightly narrow in front. The front legs are parallel and she has nice, tight feet.*

Robyn Powley (USA): *The front legs parallel, but depth of chest is lacking.*

Judy Vos (NZ): *Due to her age, the chest needs to develop and drop slightly. Excellent tight feet and sufficient bone. I like her straight front which is to be expected from such a nicely angled forequarter.*

HINDQUARTERS

Bruce Kilsby (UK): *Good width of hindquarters with correct length of tail. She is standing slightly cow-hocked, and her leg length from hock to ground is too long.*

Robyn Powley (USA): *The hocks appear to turn inwards, and she appears to be too long in the hock.*

Judy Vos (NZ): *I would prefer a cleaner hindquarter, however she is not well let down in hock and this is extremely noticeable from this angle. Excellent length of tail.*

A JUDGING EXERCISE
Photos: Lynn Kipps.

BORDER COLLIE C.
Bitch: Three years.

HEAD STUDY

Bruce Kilsby (UK): Keen expression, with nice, dark eyes set well apart. She is folding her ears back so it is not possible to judge the ear carriage. Good strength to underjaw.

Robyn Powley (USA): Perhaps due to the angle of the photo, the top of her head appears rounded rather than flat. Asymmetrical face markings, though perfectly acceptable, slightly distort the shape of the face. Eye very nicely set and correctly shaped, and a pleasing shade of brown. Expression eager and alert. I found this bitch's head actually more pleasing in shape in the profile shot.

Judy Vos (NZ): The uneven facial markings on this bitch should not be a distraction to what is a nicely shaped muzzle with good stop. Although her skull is broad, I would prefer to see a more level plane between the ears. Eye colour is acceptable; however, my preference is for a slightly darker eye.

PROFILE

Bruce Kilsby (UK): A very well-balanced female who could do with slightly more length of neck. Good depth of chest and body. Excellent backline. Croup appears to be slightly steep, good hind angulation. She is standing with front feet forward and is leaning back slightly. If the front legs were in the correct position, it would give her slightly more height at the withers. Her forehand angles appear correct. The length of hind legs from hock to ground is correct. She is standing with her tail tucked between her hind legs which make her appear apprehensive.

Robyn Powley (USA): She appears unbalanced, being heavy in the front, with a short neck and lacking well-laid back shoulders. Short-coupled.

Judy Vos (NZ): The profile of this bitch shows a smooth outline, well balanced, with good height to length ratio. I would prefer more reach of neck and due to her propping slightly in front, I would believe (subject to physically going over this bitch's forequarter) that she is short in the upper arm. Sloping topline drops off too severely in croup. The hocks are a little long in comparison to length of stifle. However, the stifle is moderately angled.

FOREQUARTERS

Bruce Kilsby (UK): Good width and depth of chest, legs parallel, elbows tight to body, she is turning her pasterns out slightly and her feet are slightly open.

Robyn Powley (USA): Wide in front, unbalanced stance with left foot toeing out.

Judy Vos (NZ): Nice depth of chest showing well-boned forelegs. Feet too splayed and not in sound condition – the feet are the working end of the running gear. Pasterns bending in, which results in the feet toeing out. I would prefer her forelegs to be straighter and parallel.

HINDQUARTERS

Bruce Kilsby (UK): Good width to hindquarters, tail of good length. She is standing cow-hocked.

Robyn Powley (USA): Wide, unbalanced stance, with left leg toeing out.

Judy Vos (NZ): Nice length and set-on of tail. The hocks are not as straight and parallel when viewed from behind as one would desire.

A JUDGING EXERCISE
Photos: Lynn Kipps.

BORDER COLLIE D.
Dog: 18 months.

174

HEAD STUDY

Bruce Kilsby (UK): *A good masculine head. The ears are set well apart but could be carried higher. Nice, dark eyes set well apart. Good head markings. Good expression.*

Robyn Powley (USA): *The top of the head appears rounded, not flat. Beautiful dark-brown eyes, though they appear set somewhat close together. Very pleasing symmetrical marking on a broad head. Very dark pigment. Expression is eager and full of interest. Ears lower set – certainly acceptable.*

Judy Vos (NZ): *A very masculine head of good type. Strong muzzle and lovely eye shape and colour. Typical Border Collie expression. Slightly doomed skull. Ears correctly set on head; however, they could have better lift to them.*

PROFILE

Bruce Kilsby (UK): *Appears from the photograph to be slightly long and stands overbuilt at rear. Lacks strength to underjaw, could do with just a little more length of neck. Croup appears to be long and flat. Good depth of chest. Forehand appears to be okay. Good slope to pasterns, lacks hind angulation and tail appears to he high set.*

Robyn Powley (USA): *Height to length ratio looks good. Bone is in proportion. However, the topline is very uneven, suggesting a roach back. The tail set appears higher than I'd like, giving a squared appearance. Somewhat straight in stifle. Lacking the smooth outline called for in the USA Standard.*

Judy Vos (NZ): *A dog of medium bone, with sufficient layback of shoulder. Shorter in stifle and longer in hock than I prefer. I would like to see a better length of neck (which grooming could improve). Coat texture appears correct.*

FOREQUARTERS

Bruce Kilsby (UK): *Good width and depth of chest, front legs parallel, elbows tight to body, good feet.*

Robyn Powley (USA): *Straight legs and nicely shaped feet.*

Judy Vos (NZ): *The front view seems to show that this dog's forechest has not yet fully matured. Straight front legs with sufficient layback of shoulder.*

HINDQUARTERS

Bruce Kilsby (UK): *Good width of hindquarters with good tail length. The length of hind legs from hock to ground is too long. To be very critical, he appears to be turning his hind feet out very slightly.*

Robyn Powley (USA): *Correctly placed with legs parallel. No obvious exaggerations or faults.*

Judy Vos (NZ): *Hocks weak, but with a longer stifle and shorter hock this would improve the dog's hindquarters tremendously. Correct compact feet and good length of tail.*

A JUDGING EXERCISE

Photos: Lynn Kipps.

BORDER COLLIE E.
Dog: Two years.

HEAD STUDY

Bruce Kilsby (UK): *A masculine head, although I would prefer a higher ear carriage. Good broad skull. Nice dark eye, good head markings. Good strong muzzle.*

Robyn Powley (USA): *I am struck by the melting expression, so full of intelligence. Beautiful dark eye. Obviously masculine head, strong but not coarse. Ear-set and carriage acceptable.*

Judy Vos (NZ): *Nice, strong head with good stop. Nice underjaw; however, gives the impression of looseness in flews. Eyes medium brown with typical alert and keen expression. Good width between ears and nice flat skull. I would prefer better lift from the base of the ears.*

PROFILE

Bruce Kilsby (UK): *A little long in body and a little stuffy in neck. Very good forechest and forehand angulation. Backline dips slightly, croup appears correct. Good slope to pasterns, front feet appear to be a little long and flat. Lacks a little in hind angulation.*

Robyn Powley (USA): *Appears very square in shape, rather than slightly longer in body. Strong bone without excess. Good depth of brisket. Appears short in neck and upright in shoulder.*

Judy Vos (NZ): *The profile shows this dog is short in neck which often relates to insufficient forequarter angulation. Slightly 'cut up' in appearance, but still a young dog who has some maturing to do yet. Good turn of stifle. Sufficient height to length of body ratio.*

FOREQUARTERS

Bruce Kilsby (UK): *Good width of chest, elbows out slightly. Weak in pasterns which are turning out, and he is standing with his feet in the 10-to-2 position.*

Robyn Powley (USA): *Legs slope inward with feet turned outward, indicating weak pasterns.*

Judy Vos (NZ): *This dog has good bone with nice depth of chest. Not a good front - the feet turning out as "east-west" is often associated with insufficient forequarter angulation. Feet appear very down in pastern.*

HINDQUARTERS

Bruce Kilsby (UK): *Good width of hindquarters, stands soundly, hock to ground long, good length of tail.*

Robyn Powley (USA): *Slightly wide rear stance, with left hind foot toeing out somewhat. Appears longer in hock, but this could be due to the angle of the photo.*

Judy Vos (NZ): *Hocks straight; however, hind does not appear muscled. Nicely marked hocks. Tail length appears marginal.*

A JUDGING EXERCISE
Photos: Lynn Kipps.

BORDER COLLIE E.
Dog: Five years.

HEAD STUDY

Bruce Kilsby (UK): *A keen, masculine expression. Very good ear carriage, nice broad skull with ears set well apart. Good head markings. I would prefer a much darker eye.*

Robyn Powley (USA): *Well set, obviously mobile ears. Correctly shaped and set eye; though light in color, this paler eye color falls within the acceptable range of brown described in the American Standard. Nice dark nose and lip pigment. Alert expression.*

Judy Vos (NZ): *The lightness in eye of this dog immediately conveys a harsh or offensive expression which is not desirable. Lovely semi-erect ears, although the eyes have it ... the expression comes from the eye and not the ears! Good stop, although the profile shot would indicate he has a slight "roman" nose.*

PROFILE

Bruce Kilsby (UK): *Good length to height ratio, he appears to be very immature for his age and his lack of body depth makes him look long in body. Good length of neck, good backline, croup appears to be of correct length but flat. Lacks a little hind angulation. Tucked up in loin. Standing with front legs too far forward which, if in correct position, would give him more wither height and improve his forehand.*

Robyn Powley (USA): *A very pleasing, correct outline, with level topline flowing into a nicely sloped croup with correct set of tail. Good turn of stifle. Nice length of neck. The length and wispy nature of coat makes it difficult to evaluate brisket and forechest. I would prefer more bone, especially in a male; however, the overall balance and clean lines of this dog outweigh other considerations.*

Judy Vos (NZ): *Not a good stance as the dog is propping, making his front appear straighter than it actually may be. I would prefer slightly more bone for size. Good length of body in comparison to height. Coat texture appears correct, with nice feathering and fall.*

FOREQUARTERS

Bruce Kilsby (UK): *Appears a little wide in chest and stands wide in front. Feet appear to be slightly open.*

Robyn Powley (USA): *Nice straight front. Forelegs parallel.*

Judy Vos (NZ): *Nice clean, straight front. I would prefer more depth of chest in a mature dog of his age, and more layback in shoulder.*

HINDQUARTERS

Bruce Kilsby (UK): *Good width of hindquarters, good tail length. When standing, he turns his right hind leg out.*

Robyn Powley (USA): *Slightly cow-hocked – certainly acceptable under the American standard.*

Judy Vos (NZ): *Not as clean from the back view, although uneven hock markings do not help and give the appearance he is slightly cow-hocked. Length of tail appears satisfactory.*

12

THE SHOW
BORDER COLLIE

hoosing a puppy for the show ring can be a very daunting task for the experienced breeder and the novice exhibitor alike. This chapter aims to cover all aspects, from picking a puppy in its early stages to following it through to training and handling it in the show ring. Through my own experiences in breeding litters and raising youngsters for the show ring, I can give anyone who is thinking of buying a show puppy an insight into what to look for and what is expected from a show dog.

There are many factors which will govern how a litter will turn out – these include your own bitch's qualities and failings, your choice of stud dog, the rearing and socialising of pups and, of course, genetics. From my own personal experience I start to evaluate my pups straightaway, as soon as the litter is born. I do not believe that anyone can pick a show pup at this early stage and I am sure if they have, it's a fluke! However, you can assess markings and, perhaps, head shape. I am not pedantic about classical markings but I do like to see new-born pups with nice short, blocky muzzles and broad, square skulls. This gives you a good indication of how your puppy's head will eventually turn out. About two to four days old is a good age for early assessment, as by this time your litter should be well-fed and content and tending to fill out a bit.

ASSESSING THE LITTER
At about three weeks old your puppies will be up on their feet. They will have opened their eyes and should be starting to feed – with a little help from you, of course. As they reach this stage of crawling about the whelping box I start to look at them a bit more thoroughly. I get a secure table and place a towel over it. I then start to put the pups on it individually and stack them up as if it was a judge assessing them. You will obviously have to give them a bit of support. This now gives me an indication of angulation both in the fore and in the hind quarters. I am still keeping an eye on head shape and, by now, looking to see how the stop is developing; it should be steep and well-defined, even at this early stage. Ears are still pretty small but I should hope for them to be on top of the back skull if their carriage is going to be correct.

I keep assessing the puppies like this every few days and, by the time they are about five to six weeks old, they should be standing on your table long enough for you to have a good look at them. By this time I will have made up my mind which puppies are constructed well enough for me to consider them good enough for the ring or, at least, showing potential. During these early weeks I use a soft brush on each puppy's coat and brush them perhaps twice a day. This is a good time for your puppies

ASSESSING A PUPPY

Bekkis Piper at eight weeks of age (handled by Alison Hornsby and Jenny Jefferson).
Photos: Amanda Bulbeck.

LEFT: Head: Look for a wide flat skull,, short muzzle, high ear-set, sufficient stop, scissor bite, and almond-shaped eyes.

RIGHT: Front: The legs should be straight, with well-formed feet and good bone. the elbows should be close to the body. Check for width between the legs – it should be neither too narrow nor too wide. The pasterns should not be too short or too long and neither upright nor weak.

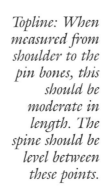

Topline: When measured from shoulder to the pin bones, this should be moderate in length. The spine should be level between these points.

Upper arm: Check for good length and correct angle.

Layback of shoulder: Check for length and angle.

LEFT: Length of loin: The length of the body should come from the ribbing, not from the loin.

RIGHT: Length of croup: Puppies tend to have flat croups. Feel for some angulation from the pin bones to the tail-set, with proportional length.

LEFT: *Hindquarters: When viewed from behind, the tail should be low, the rear pasterns should be short and the entire leg should appear straight, turning neither in nor out.*

CENTRE: *Check the length of bone within the tail: it should reach at least to the point of hock.*

RIGHT: *Assess the overall impression: Bekkis Piper is showing good potential for his age, with plenty of type, balance, style and character.*

to get used to being handled and this helps in character building. It is also a prime time to assess the nature of your pups – those that seem quite laid back and those with a bit more spirit.

At seven weeks old I have all my litters eye-tested and, from then on, will allow those that are booked as pets to go to join their new owners – puppy packs and all necessary information included. Those that I feel have show potential I will grade as I would a breed class, although this can change slightly from day to day, as the puppies are developing so rapidly and can change so quickly. By eight to ten weeks you can more or less assess your puppy as you do an adult dog. Most areas of the Border Collie will grow at the same rate, so look at your puppy critically but fairly. Remember that the perfect dog has yet to be bred, so do not be too harsh in your assessment.

I would say that areas such as front and hind angulation, length of neck, tail length and body proportions will not alter that much from puppy through to adulthood. What this does mean is that a puppy with no angulation at ten weeks will not miraculously get it by the time it is six months old. To get a balanced specimen of our breed I think you should be looking at everything in moderation. Other areas such as head, stop, eye shape and colour, ear

and tail set/carriage are factors that will change, and this can be from day to day, as you will no doubt find out. Movement at this age can be all over the place, but you should be able to see glimpses of the ground-covering, driving movement so typical of our breed. I find the best time to see this is when the pups are out in the garden playing; watching from the window can be a real eye-opener for you.

So now that you have either bred your puppy or bought it from a reputable breeder, you have to prepare it for the show ring. Between eight weeks and six months your puppy will undergo the most dramatic changes in its life and you have an important role to play in it, not only in the training aspect but, more importantly, in rearing. In my opinion, you only 'get out what you put in' and I don't just mean the nutritional aspects. A balanced diet does play a major part, but the time and effort put into socialising and training, or having fun with your puppy, is as important. The time spent here will pay its just rewards.

EVERYDAY EXPERIENCES
Socialising your puppy from about eight weeks onwards may entail you carrying him about in your arms for six weeks or so until the inoculation course is complete but, by being taken out at this age, babies

tend to accept situations more readily and without much reservation. This early exposure will ease any situations that, perhaps, would have occurred at the three-and-a-half month stage. Border Collie intelligence is one of the breed's major attributes but it can prove to be a hindrance when they take a dislike to certain situations.

By the time your puppy is twelve-and-a-half weeks old it should be well used to many everyday experiences such as traffic, pavements, other humans etc. However, care is still needed when introducing the puppy to new situations on a lead and, more importantly, at ground level. I find this situation can be eased a little if you

take a well-socialised adult dog with you – the puppies' mum perhaps. This helps to build up confidence and it should not be too long before they get into the swing of things and are quite happy and confident to go out on their own.

LEARNING THE STAND

As your puppy gets older, training should be maintained at all times. Practising every other day is a good way to train your puppy and it will not be too long before he learns what is expected of him. You will only need the most basic of equipment to start off with – a thin training collar and a light nylon woven lead are what I would recommend. Start off by stacking him the

SHOW TRAINING: THE FREE STAND
Bekkis Osbeckia at five months, handled by Jenny Jefferson.

1. At five months, Bekkis Osbeckia is at a very raw stage – puppies of this age can often appear disappointing. Do not panic!

2. With some bait in the right hand, walk backwards to encourage the puppy into the correct position.

3. Continue walking backwards until the correct position is achieved with the puppy standing foursquare.

4. Having achieved the correct position block any forward movement with the hand containing bait. Give a command, e.g. "Stand", and reward the puppy.

Maintaining attention should be taught as a separate lesson from free-standing. Hold the bait in your right hand and offer it to the pup.

Having gained the pup's attention, move the bait further away.

Praise the puppy for use of ears and focused attention. Use a command, e.g. "Watch", and reward.

same way as you did when assessing him as a baby. Make sure his front legs are completely underneath his chest and are at right angles to the ground; the same should be done with his hind quarters. This time his hocks should be straight and at right angles to the ground. His topline should be level and his tail down between the back legs. These early lessons should be kept very short so as not to bore him. As he stands there, talk to him at all times, assuring him he is good. You should always make your training fun and always finish on a good note and preferably with a tidbit or treat. I find liver to be the best for this.

Gradually build up this time until he will stand for a few minutes without struggling. Maintain his attention by using your liver treat and try to get him to look up at you, using his ears if possible. Praise him all the time but correct his stand position should he move his legs out of place. Practise moving him on the lead. He will not like it at first, but will soon get

used to it when he realises there is a reward at the end of each lesson. He should preferably move at your side or out in front. If he moves out in front never correct him and pull back, let him go out on the lead and, should he need more, let him have the full lead extension. Telling him to 'walk on' is a good way of letting him know what is expected. Keep the lead and treats for training purposes only – he will soon learn that when he puts his show lead on then he has to behave and show.

Along with this training you should be continuing to groom him daily. This is a good way of building up a relationship between the two of you. It is also getting him used to brushing, which will increase as his coat grows.

SHOW TRAINING
By the time he is about 14 weeks old he will be able to attend your local ring-training classes. These are usually advertised in your local library. These classes are very good for socialising your

puppy with other people and, more importantly, other dogs. For the first few nights you attend I would advise you to just sit with your puppy at the side of the hall and let him see what is going on. If he seems quite confident after a couple of outings, try him up with the trainer. A good instructor should inform you about what is expected. Attending Breed Club shows, and other shows where the breed is scheduled, is a good way of seeing what is expected of you and the dog. It is a good idea to watch those dogs and handlers that are winning, as you may well pick up a few tips on handling and presentation. If you have any questions – ask! Do not be afraid to go up and ask, as I am sure everyone remembers what it was like when they first started in the show ring, and they will be only too happy to pass on experiences.

PREPARING FOR THE SHOW

By the time your puppy is six months old he should be ready to enter the show ring. If you have both done your homework it should not be too much of a traumatic experience!

It is very important that you show your dog to its best advantage and in the quickest possible time. In the big breed classes seen at today's Championship shows you will be lucky if the judge looks at your dog for any more than a few minutes, so it is in these few minutes that you have to make such an impression, both dog and handler, that it warrants a placing (first, hopefully). Teamwork should ensure that both you and the dog are presenting the best overall picture possible. Choose smart, comfortable clothes that best show off your dog. Make sure you bath him, preferably the night before the show, and that he is well groomed. There is no excuse for exhibiting a dirty dog and to do so is an insult to the judge and other exhibitors if you wish him to be placed.

Using a shower-head for bathing makes

With plenty of practice, an adult dog should be able to stand foursquare looking naturally balanced and alert. Attention is maintained with intermittent vocal praise and a tasty reward.

life a lot easier. I use a recommended dog shampoo on our dogs. Only bath and shampoo the white bits, but do all the legs and tail. Make sure you rinse out the shampoo thoroughly, as any left in can cause irritation to the skin. Before finishing, rinse the water over the top of the black coat but do not shampoo. This should remove any dirt or grease on the coat. Dry thoroughly but, while the coat is still a bit damp, I put baby talc on the white bits to bring them up cleaner. By the time you get to the show the next day the coat should have dried and the powder will be easily brushed out of the coat. Take a damp cloth over the black coat just to remove any of the loose talc. Use a water spray (one of the type that is used to spray plants) and damp down the coat. Brush the coat up the wrong way and then back the right way. A good-quality dog brush is

STACKING
Demonstrated by Bekkis Genesis, handled by Jenny Jefferson.
This style of handling is commonly used in the USA.

LEFT: The lift: Gently support the head with the right hand. The left hand lifts the dog under the chest, taking the front legs back, so when slowly lowered to the ground the legs will be placed directly under the dog's withers.

RIGHT: Position when lowered.

Still holding the head, run your left hand along the ribcage and down the thigh.

Gently but firmly take hold of the hock and lift upwards

Place the hindleg down straight, with the point of hock just behind the tail-set.

Place the head looking forwards. If the hands are placed at the base of the skull, it will hold the overall position.

ideal for this and, although initially expensive, should last you a lifetime. This spraying and brushing should just add a little bit of body to the coat just before you go into the ring.

Border Collies require very little cosmetic trimming but, a few days before the show, I will trim around the feet and up the pasterns with a sharp pair of scissors. This applies also to the hind feet and hocks. If there is any dead coat around the ears, take it off with a stripping blade or use the 'finger and thumb' method favoured by terrier breeders. No other area of the coat should need any form of trimming.

THE DAY OF THE SHOW
Now for the day of the show. You should always give yourselves plenty of time to get to the show. As soon as you arrive, let your dog out to exercise and make sure he does his toilet. Give him a run-through of the show ring procedure just to let him know what is going to be expected of him. If it is his first show, or if your dog needs a bit of settling, take him around the ring when it is quiet and let him get used to his new surroundings and all the noises and bustle. Once he has been for a walk, put him onto his bench, if it is a benched show, or into his crate, if you use one. Let him have a good rest now. This is the time for you to get prepared to show him. Take him back to the ring about ten minutes before your class is in and put the finishing touches to his coat. Make sure you have your liver treats with you for his reward.

THE JUDGING
When you are called into the ring, make sure you give yourself plenty of space between you and the dog in front. If it is your first show, let someone else go first and this will give you time to steady your pup and your nerves. The judge will probably ask you all to move around the

The handler stands behind the dog maintaining control of the natural position through light tension on the lead, while the dog is attracted by someone or something from around or within the show ring.

ring. He will want to see you move at a steady pace so he can assess the dog's movement. This first gait is often the time when the judge is picking out the dogs that he is most interested in and will be keen to have a further look at. Leave plenty of room so as not to run into the dog in front. This not only puts your dog off but may also upset the handler of the dog in front.

Now the judge will go over your dog, just like the trainer at ring-training classes. Each individual dog will be examined and then the exhibitor is asked to move them. A 'triangle' and 'straight up and down' are the most common gaiting patterns. This allows the judge to assess front and rear movement, side gait and overall soundness. Be sure to move in straight lines and try, at all times, to keep your eye on the judge to see what he is doing. When you get back to the judge he will probably want you to show how alert and animated your exhibit is, so it is a good idea to have a piece of your liver treat handy at this point and use it to get your dog's attention.

Once the judge has assessed your exhibit you will return to the end of the line-up. Always keep an eye out for the last exhibit to be assessed; as the judge is going over this dog you should be setting your exhibit up to be ready for the final appraisal. I would expect most judges to cut the class down to perhaps about five dogs for final appraisal. He may ask you to take your

dog out and back for one last look, so try to be ready and keep the dog alert at all times. The judge will now choose his first-place dog and the others after this. At Championship shows critiques are usually done on the first and second places, at Open shows first only – so this means you will have to stay in the ring for an extra couple of minutes while the judge jots down a few notes.

If you have not won first place I find it is always courteous to congratulate the winner as you leave the ring – and not forgetting a big pat for your own exhibit. It does not really matter whether the judge places your dog or not; if he has behaved

MOVEMENT

LEFT: Front movement should be straight, neither too wide nor too narrow. Slight pinning, as seen in the photo, is correct.

RIGHT: Movement when viewed from behind should be sound and parallel.

Bekkis Genesis showing good side movement that appears effortless – a long, low action with minimum lift of the feet. The head position is correct, the topline is level, there is good forward reach with plenty of drive from behind, and excellent tail carriage.

himself, shown well and moved well, he has done everything you have asked him to and that should be reward enough. Remember that it is only the judge's opinion and there will be plenty more shows. You will learn from experience your dog's capabilities, and your own for that matter, so put it down to experience and try another show.

STUDYING TECHNIQUES

After showing your dog it is always a good idea to go and watch the rest of the judging. Study the handlers and exhibits and watch to see how their legs are placed, how they are moved and what type of leads they use. I tend to single out a particular handler and watch how they do a particular thing, for example how they hold up their dog's ears. After the show I would go to the park, or to the ring-training class, and practise this until I got it right. It is a learning game between you and your dog and, as you gain more experience, you will realise that not all dogs can be handled in the same manner. A good handler will realise this and be able to adapt to suit the dog, and not vice versa, if he wishes to get the best from him. There are many common faults in handling, but practice is the best way of ironing them out. If you do have problems, smaller open shows are really good training grounds for both dog and handler. Get someone with more experience to watch you in the ring and, once you have finished, get them to pin-point the areas in which you fail.

There are a few good handlers and even fewer great handlers but, speaking as a judge, it is so good to see a dog and handler working as a team, both well presented and turned out, and this, in some cases, can mean the difference between a placing and going away empty-handed. Dog showing at Championship shows, in my opinion, is becoming a sport of the rich and, with spiralling costs and long distances travelled, you want to give yourself and your dog the best possible chance of gaining that coveted first prize and Challenge certificate or those Championship points: this means putting in the homework beforehand.

In the UK there are very few professional handlers, people who handle dogs for a living. They tend to be found in the Terrier and Utility breeds. On the other hand, in the USA there are many more professional handlers and you need only turn to the back of the glossy dog magazines to see the list of many handlers and their advertisements. With the Border Collie only recently gaining Championship status, the breed is in its early stages of showing, but early indications suggest to me that these "professionals" are becoming a necessity if you wish your exhibit to win, especially at Group level, with its added prestige. I do know that there are those breeders who also handle and, hopefully, this trend will continue.

Do not let us forget that, no matter whether we win or lose, it is still the same dog we came into the ring with and the one we will go home with. We love him not only for his good looks but for his charm and character that draws so many people to our wonderful breed.

13 BREEDING BORDER COLLIES

My personal approach to breeding has been to carefully line breed and, in some cases, almost to "inbreed" in order to establish type. After establishing type, however, it is essential then to go to an outcross to ensure that you do not breed too closely, which would result in disaster. I believe most strongly that line breeding and inbreeding should only be done by experts. If novices wish to attempt this type of breeding, it should only be undertaken under the supervision of a dedicated specialist. Inexperienced line breeding and inbreeding can cause many genetic problems, deformities and, in some cases, progressive "fading" which eventually results in death, sometimes not until the dog reaches puberty. I have even known dogs to die suddenly up to the age of two years, although on reaching this age I consider them to be past the "danger point". In the case of my breeding lines, losses of this sort seem to happen more in the male offspring.

BREEDING PROGRAMMES

In planning a breeding programme, consideration must also be given to any evidence, or previous history, of fits in the family line, for example epilepsy. While I do not personally believe that all cases of fits are due to breeding, I do accept that many instances are genetically related.

Another of the major considerations to be borne in mind when breeding is temperament. This can be a major failing with too close breeding, using the line and inbreeding method. Again, I find this mainly relates to one sex more than the other – in this case to bitches more than dogs. On the positive side for sensible breeding, in my opinion the best breeding

When planning a breeding programme, family histories must be researched.

Photo: Carol Ann Johnson.

approach is a grandfather-granddaughter mating, providing that either the grandfather or granddaughter is dominant in the type they produce, with good temperaments and basic good construction. Thus, by mating Trav, who is very dominant, to one of his granddaughters, I can always rely on proven, consistent type with sound temperaments. In addition, litters produced in this way tend to contain evenly-matched puppies, with no extreme diversity of type or size other than what would be normal in dog and bitch puppies.

On the other side of the coin, a well line-bred dog mated to an outcrossed bitch of a similar type can also produce an even litter. This is probably due to the good line breeding of the parents which is, in turn, dominant enough to stamp their mark on to the resulting puppies.

It should also be borne in mind that a mating by two quality dogs, of different variations in type, can result in a litter of very diverse puppies. Even though each individual puppy may be healthy and may even have a successful show career, the litter, as a whole, is not a product of consistent type and temperament. Rather, every one of the puppies is completely different, some big and rangy, some compact, some strong-boned and some light. Even in the most sophisticated line breeding programme, there comes a point at which it is necessary to bring in new blood. In the case of a complete outcross it is wise not to finally select the puppy you wish to keep until it reaches six to eight weeks of age. By then you should be able to assess if it is the typical Border Collie you wish to have in your kennel. In many cases an outcross mating is a bit of a gamble and even the most experienced breeders have to hope and pray that it will work.

For the inexperienced bitch owner a word of warning. Do not be persuaded into breeding from your bitch just because you are told it will be good for her. There are many potential problems which can occur in unspayed bitches, such as pyometra, false pregnancies, etc. The relatively routine operation involved in having a bitch neutered can often be the best course of action. It will prevent any disease of the womb, the inconvenience of your pet coming into season every six months (assuming she has a regular cycle) and the danger of her wanting to escape to go looking for a mate. I would always recommend that the owner of a pet bitch should consider carefully their course of action before allowing her to have puppies. It is a much more complicated business than it may seem and can be fraught with difficulty.

COLOUR BREEDING

I have been asked to pass on some of my thoughts in connection with the genetic passing on of colour. Although my main man, Sh. Ch. Viber Travelling Matt from Corinlea, has never directly sired anything other than pure black and white, I am firmly of the opinion that he carries a colour gene which seems to skip a generation. His immediate offspring have produced a wide variety of colours, including tricolour, blue, slate (thankfully not that sludgy, washed-out colour, but a true clear slate colour) and white. I myself have only ever directly bred three tricolours in 13 years. However, I did once breed a very unsuccessful litter of four blue puppies, all of which subsequently died, with the exception of one. She has since gone on to produce some superb puppies for her owner, including a Challenge Certificate winner. This litter was bred through slightly different lines from my own dogs and, because of this tragedy, I have never attempted to breed blues again.

I do not claim to understand the genetic implications of colour, because I have had so many seemingly unexpected occurrences – for example two black and whites producing all tricolours at birth, many of which later ended up being black and white but one of which remained a true tricolour for life. Could this be the result of a recessive gene? And does it only come down through the male dog?

Some one-generation-removed colour varieties which have come down through the Trav line include tricolour and blue puppies in litters produced from two black and white parents, which have been bred from black and white dogs for more than three generations.

Before I close on this very complex subject, I would like to refer to observations made by other Collie experts who have published on this topic, that the colour blue may merely be a result of a dilution of black. This is an opinion which I share and I have often observed that many blue puppies look alike, often slightly different from the rest, which makes me think that it might almost be a "mutant colour" influence.

I am aware, however, that many breeders are committed to this colour and there are a number of very attractive blue dogs winning successfully in the show ring today.

Finally, although I have expressed my views that Trav seems to carry some latent colour genes, I can confirm that his great-great-grandmother was produced in a mixed colour litter, containing both merle and tricolour puppies.

INHERITED CONDITIONS

While I do not intend to go into detail here on possible inherited conditions, as these are covered elsewhere in this book, there are a number of known issues to be aware of. I have referred above to instances of epilepsy, which have unfortunately been widespread for years, even in the working Border Collie and working Sheepdogs.

Various eye problems can occur, including hereditary cataract. Other more serious conditions include Collie Eye Anomaly (CEA) and Progressive Retinal Atrophy (PRA). CEA is present from birth and can be tested for from six to seven weeks of age. This is the ideal age at which eye specialists recommend testing, as it becomes more difficult to detect after this. Some older, or adult dogs subsequently tested may appear to "go normal". This may not be a true indication as to whether the dog is either affected or unaffected. Unlike PRA, which is progressive, the degree of the CEA condition at birth will remain with the dog throughout its life. PRA tends to become more of an issue as the dog grows older. This means that the ideal situation would be to have the dog tested every 12 months by an eye specialist

A 6-7 month old blue and white puppy. Although a total outcross, both parents were line-bred and had excellent pedigrees.

A 12-month-old dog, totally inbred to a dominant line.

vet. This will then ensure that any incidence or progression can be monitored.

Hip dysplasia is measured in a dog by means of X-rays resulting in a hip score on each side. X-rays can be carried out by your local vet, ideally after the dog is over 12 months old. There is a wide disparity of hip scores around in the breed today but in general HD is less of a problem in the Border Collie than in some other popular breeds.

Osteochondritis Dissecans (OCD) can be hereditary but can also be worsened by allowing a puppy to become overweight, by over-exercise, or by providing too high levels of protein and calcium at the crucial stage of a puppy's growth. Basically this is a shoulder problem which becomes obvious at a very young age.

Bad mouths in a puppy can be either overshot or undershot, or have a level bite. This means the bite is incorrect. Usually, if a four to six week old Border Collie puppy has a bad mouth (once its baby teeth are through) this will not improve. However, when puppies begin changing their teeth (at around four to six months) and their jaws are at different stages of development, mouths can temporarily become either over or undershot. This will normally have corrected itself by the time the puppy is eight months old.

CHOOSING BREEDING STOCK
This is a difficult subject. I, personally, have had two beautiful Champion bitches who have not produced any show-quality puppies. Their puppies have, however, made ideal pets. Conversely, I have had two mediocre bitches who have produced outstanding stock in both show and working environments. Their offspring included a Champion bitch, numerous Challenge Certificate winners, Junior Warrant winners and Best Puppy winners; also puppies which have later excelled in a wide variety of working disciplines, as Police search dogs, at working sheepdog trials, and in Obedience and Agility tests.

Everyone chooses their breeding stock in a different way. I prefer to first look at the pedigree when considering dogs as parents. This enables me to consider the dogs which have contributed to the pedigree, as ancestors. It also allows me to consider what other dogs those ancestors have produced and those of their siblings. In this way I can see what quality of stock has been produced to a wide range of varying bloodlines. Most importantly, as I have already stated, I put greatest emphasis on resultant temperament and breed type.

After I have studied the pedigree to see that the lines will tie in with my own dogs (for line breeding) I then look at the dog itself. The attributes of the male should compensate for any failings of the female, and vice versa. For example, I had a very well-bred bitch which I allowed to go out to a friend on breeding terms. The quality of this bitch was exceptional, but she was small, fine and quite dark in colour. Her shape and movement, however, were outstanding. What I wanted for this bitch was a bigger, stronger male, again of good type, with more glamour. Therefore, the bitch, Sh. Ch. Sacul Highland Mist from Corinlea, was mated to the dog (Sh. Ch. Cluff of Mobella), with the result that she produced three show Champions in her first litter. A definite success story! Not only did this mating produce precisely what I wanted it to produce – all the quality and refinement from the mother and the strength and glamour from the father – but I was due the pick of the dog puppies from this litter. The one I chose became Sh. Ch. Viber Travelling Matt from Corinlea, who went on to become the breed record holder for a considerable number of years, with 30 Challenge Certificates to his credit, 20 with Best of Breed and Group 2. Trav is now fully retired at 11+ years of age after finally taking the Border Collie Club of Great Britain's Grand Veteran of the Year Award this year (1997). At this time, he is the only sire to have produced two sons to pass the working test for show Border Collies, one in Scotland and the other in Holland. Both these males have been closely line bred.

It must be borne in mind, when looking at stud dogs, that it is not always necessary to look at just the top winning dogs in the breed, but also to study pedigrees, lines and previously produced progeny. Type-to-type matings can often work as well as using proven show winners. Another factor to take into consideration when selecting breeding stock is whether there has been any evidence of either monorchidism or cryptorchidism in the males (a condition where either one or both testicles are not fully descended into the scrotum).

For the inexperienced trying to select future breeding stock, I would strongly recommend that they visit as many reputable breeders and kennels as possible, to allow them to see the dogs in their home environments. In this way, they should then be able to discuss, and even see, the results of various matings and establish whether any problems have arisen from combinations of bloodlines. In this way inexperienced or novice persons can eventually draw their own conclusions in deciding what type they wish to choose.

THE MATING
For the uninitiated the mating might be otherwise known as doggy SEX! Seriously, though once you have chosen the lines you wish to pursue (or purchased a suitable bitch with the lines you wish to pursue) and have taken into consideration your selected stud dog, it is best to approach the owner of the stud dog to ensure that they are prepared to allow his use on your bitch. The owner of the dog is likely to ask for details of the bitch's pedigree, whether she is eye-tested or hip-scored, if she is a maiden (not previously mated), and when her season is due, and they will also advise you of the stud fee for the dog's services. Stud fees are due for the service of the dog and are not dependent upon a resulting litter. Most owners of stud dogs, however, will allow one free repeat mating should the bitch not conceive (known as having "missed"). The Stud Fee will normally be in line with the price paid for a puppy, although in some situations the owner of the dog may request a puppy back from the litter in lieu of the stud fee. This is only likely to be requested if the bitch is from particular lines which the owner of the stud dog would like to acquire.

Bitches will usually come into season on a regular cycle. Depending on the bitch, this cycle may be anything from every six months to once every 14 months and the season can last for as long as 28 days. I, personally, have had some bitches who go as much as two years between seasons. It is advisable to contact the owner of the stud dog from the first day the bitch comes into season, because some bitches may be ready to be mated as early as seven days later, while others may not be receptive until as late as 17 days.

Generally most bitches are ready between the 11th and 14th day. Certain characteristics the bitch displays will tell you when she is ready for mating – she will become more affectionate and flirtatious and she will present you with her rear end. If tickled around the top of her tail, she will lift it in no uncertain terms and push herself against you. This is a sure sign that mating should take place immediately. It is normal practice for the bitch to be taken to the dog and not the other way round.

To carry out the mating act, I always prefer to introduce the dog to the bitch, and allow them to play and flirt with each other for a short while. This allows the dog to relax the bitch before conducting the final act of mating. At this final stage, it is wise to hold the bitch steady while the dog climbs onto her back. This can be a little off putting for a maiden bitch so it is advisable to talk quietly and calmly to her while the dog achieves penetration.

Once the dog penetrates the bitch two things will happen; he will ejaculate and swell up and the bitch will use her muscles to hold onto the dog. In common terms this is referred to as 'the tie'. Once tied, it is usual for the dog to try to turn himself to stand back-to-back with the bitch. However, some stud dogs do prefer just to stand at the side. The stud dog owner will normally be your guide in this aspect. As the tie can last from as little as ten minutes up to as long as one hour, be well prepared and make both the dogs and yourselves comfortable. Once tied, nothing will cause the dogs to separate until the bitch is ready to let the dog go – despite the old wives' tales about buckets of cold water!

When the tie finally breaks, the stud dog will be taken away to rest while the bitch will probably still want to 'show off'. You may wish to have a repeat mating carried

out either the next day or within 48 hours to ensure conception, as ovulation can be delayed by as much as three to four days. However, this has to be agreed with the stud dog owner.

CARE OF THE IN-WHELP BITCH
From day one, I normally confine my bitches to quarters, although some other breeders do initially carry on with the bitch's normal routine. However, I like to keep my bitches very quiet for 36-48 hours after mating to allow the best possible chances for conception. At this time bitches can be particularly susceptible to infection and, in order to ensure a healthy litter, I always choose to err on the side of caution. It should also be remembered that the bitch may also still be receptive to other males. Care should be taken, therefore, to ensure that she cannot be accessed by other males.

In connection with the worming of in-whelp bitches, different people have different ideas. Some do not believe in worming when a bitch is in whelp but prefer to worm well before she comes into season. This is all very well if the bitch comes into season regularly on a frequent basis. However, the alternative is to choose a wormer specifically designed for use with pregnant bitches, such as a 2.5 per cent liquid wormer which can be administered from day 40 of pregnancy to two days post-whelping (a period of approximately 25 days). The dosage depends upon the weight of the bitch, but most suitable worming products will be accompanied by instructions for the recommended dose.

With regard to feeding patterns, I do nothing differently with my bitches until they are four weeks in whelp. During this time, however, and throughout their pregnancy, I do like them to have gentle exercise, as the muscles must be kept supple and flexible ready for the birth of the puppies. The total gestation period is generally around 63 days (nine weeks) although healthy puppies can be born as early as 57 days or as late as 70 days after mating.

From four weeks into the pregnancy, I start to provide a higher protein content in the bitch's food. Together with this increase, I also reduce the quantity and provide two smaller feeds per day, rather than one larger meal. This is further increased at six weeks into the pregnancy to three meals per day, two of which contain slightly larger portions, and one of which includes extra nourishment – for example, milk, eggs, fish, rice pudding, etc. I also give a small amount of boiled liver once a week to provide additional iron and vitamins. I am a great believer in a basic, proper, balanced diet to provide all necessary nutrients, rather than giving added supplements. There are a number of extremely good complete nutritional feeds on the market today which are specifically designed to take account of the needs of the in-whelp bitch.

A few days before the bitch is due to whelp she may go off her food. This is a sure sign that whelping is imminent. If left to her own devices, she is likely at this stage to keep herself quiet and go off into dark corners. She will also start to 'build a nest' by shredding and tearing up anything which comes to hand. In order to protect both her and your furniture, about two weeks beforehand it is advisable to encourage her to settle in a warm and safe place where you want her to have her puppies, giving her plenty of newspapers to shred and nest-build. Ideally, this should be a whelping box placed in a quiet room, where she can have peace and privacy for the task ahead.

When you have a bitch due to whelp I would always recommend that you inform your vet of the impending event, in case you need veterinary assistance.

THE WHELPING

Some time before whelping commences the bitch will become restless. At this time her temperature will also drop to around 36 degrees C (97 degrees F). She will begin panting and generally become very agitated and seemingly uncomfortable. She will continually lick at herself, often standing up, turning round and then lying down again, together with renewed, frantic scratching and bed-making (newspaper-ripping). She will also feel the need for more toilet calls, due to the pressure of the puppies coming down into the birth canal. During this stage, it is advisable, if the bitch goes out, that you keep a close watch on her, as it has been known for a puppy to be born in the garden.

Labour can last for several hours before a puppy is eventually born. The first puppy is likely to be the most difficult, especially for a first-time mum who does not really know what to expect. However, instinct does take over and soon she will seem to know precisely what to do. She ought to be encouraged and given a lot of praise and support with each new arrival. As labour progresses, if it becomes apparent that the bitch is panting excessively, and straining and if she appears distressed in any way with no resulting puppy, you should inform your vet immediately.

One vital word of warning. If, either during the pregnancy or the whelping, any unnatural discharge should appear, possibly accompanied by an unpleasant and distinctive smell, something is seriously wrong. Again, you must take the bitch to the vet immediately.

I always have plenty of clean towels over the side of the whelping box, together with a bottle of antiseptic/disinfectant and a pair of sharp scissors at the ready. These would only be used in the case of mum needing some help in breaking the bag (the membrane sac which surrounds each puppy). It is important to ensure that the puppy's airway is cleared as soon as possible. This I do by helping the bitch to remove the covering from the puppy's head to allow it to breath freely.

Some bitches can become over-enthusiastic in their efforts to clean up their puppy. Care must be taken that the puppy is not accidentally damaged in the process. In this connection, if I feel that mum needs some additional help with the breaking of the umbilical cord, I tend to take hold of it, nip the end to ensure the blood is kept towards the puppy's tummy, and tear the cord approximately six inches from the stomach. This must be done gently in order to avoid an umbilical hernia. Bitches will normally try to eat the placentas, which do contain some nutrients which are advantageous to the bitch. I normally take the first two placentas away, because I think in this way she concentrates more on the puppies. It is a good idea to count that the number of afterbirths equals the number of puppies born. If either an afterbirth, or an unborn puppy, is retained inside the bitch, this will require veterinary assistance.

The towels are kept handy in case a puppy needs a bit of reviving. Perhaps two puppies may arrive at the same time – or perhaps one may have been in the birth canal too long. When this happens, I usually wrap the puppy up in a warm towel and rub vigorously, while keeping the puppy upside down. Once I know the puppy's colour has returned to normal (from a blue to a healthy pink) the pup can be returned to its mother for her administrations.

Do not be too concerned if the bitch seems to be giving the pups fairly rough treatment. This is quite normal. In this way, by rolling them around, she helps to stimulate them and their bodily functions. She will also nudge and encourage them to head for her teats for that initial feed of colostrum. Colostrum is present in the

Make sure that all the puppies are feeding from the bitch.

milk for the first 48 hours and provides the puppies with maternal immunity. This early suckling is most essential for a puppy's survival and wellbeing.

I also keep a hot-water bottle at body temperature wrapped in a towel so that, when one puppy has been born and washed clean by its mum and the next is on its way, the first pup can be kept warm and dry while mum concentrates on the rest of the arrivals.

A sure sign that the bitch has finished whelping is when she settles down with her puppies, peace reigns and the puppies are lying quiet and content. At this stage I usually offer my bitches a drink of glucose and water. She may also wish to go out to relieve herself but will be reluctant to leave her new family. If so, I usually put on a light collar and lead and give her plenty of encouragement and reassurance to leave her new babies for a few minutes. This also provides someone with the opportunity to remove all soiled and wet newspapers, to wipe out the whelping box with a suitable antiseptic and to provide new, warm bedding, The new puppies should now settle down quietly with their mother.

THE DEVELOPING PUPPIES

Depending on the weight at birth (8oz to 16oz per puppy depending upon the size of the litter), Border Collie puppies should gain an average of two ounces per day. After the first few days this will be noticeable, as they will fill out before your eyes. Their little tummies should be full and round. It is wise, particularly during the first few critical days to make sure that if there is a smaller-sized puppy, it is not pushed out by a stronger one. This can be remedied by ensuring a smaller puppy suckles on the back teats which generally contain the ample milk flow.

Do not be surprised that your newly-born puppies do not seem to resemble adult Border Collies. Rather, they are little black and white blobs, initially more like little guinea pigs! As they begin to grow, they will get little fat, wrinkly legs and their heads begin to change. British-bred Border Collie puppies' heads will then become more round, almost like those of kittens, with the ears seemingly 'inside out'. From ten days onwards, puppies begin to 'grow' their eyes. By this we mean that little slits will appear, with the eye beginning to peep through. From this time it varies with each individual puppy as to when the eyes will be fully opened.

Although the eyes are now open, puppies still rely mainly on smell. Once the eyes are open, the ears should also be coming forward but rarely can they see or hear fully at this age. The senses seem to develop by the time they are three weeks old, by which stage puppies should be able to lift their head and are trying out their legs – usually with little success. Do not be surprised to find them falling over regularly and rolling around like little balls of fluff. Also, around this age, puppies will learn to growl and practise their first 'bark'. They will also now enjoy mouthing games with their brothers and sisters and they will begin to look more like real dogs.

While the puppies are solely reliant on their mother's milk, the bitch will continually clean up after her 'babies'. She will also continue to stimulate the puppies' bowel and bladder movements. However, as weaning progresses, she will become less likely to continue with this practice and this is where the breeder will need to have a good stock of newspapers available. Many kennel-reared puppies may also have sawdust in their play area. If you are using sawdust with young puppies, do take care to check eyes, ears and any other little creased areas. Stray sawdust particles can sometimes cause irritation.

BELOW: Two days old: the puppies are blind and their ears are closed.

RIGHT: The puppies' eyes open from about ten days.
Photos: Carol Ann Johnson.

Soon the puppies will be feeding independently.

WEANING AND WORMING

I usually wean and worm at the same time, at between two-and-a-half to three weeks, depending upon the size of the litter. Many people believe puppies should first be taught to lap, but in my experience this is not necessarily so. I merely select a good brand of puppy food and mix it to the consistency of porridge. Once they have been introduced to this soft, easily digested mixture, I find they both lap and eat at the same time. We humans often derive as much enjoyment from this first feed as do the puppies, who generally fall on the meal with great relish, with much spluttering, snuffling and general attempts to 'swim in it'. Beware – use plenty of newspapers at this time or make sure that the puppies are fed where the floor can be easily washed and scrubbed! To the serious, hygiene must, of course, be paramount at this time, as the mother's immunity levels in the puppies could now be falling, albeit at a slow pace.

For the first few days, I feed only one meal a day, making sure that the puppies still have full access to their mother. Two or three days later the meals are increased to twice daily until the puppies reach between four and five weeks of age, when they should be on four meals per day, with only intermittent visits by the mother. Once again, a word of warning if using sawdust. This has an inevitable ability to get everywhere – including into the

puppies' dinner dish! Some bitches are difficult to take away from their puppies. These bitches are often quite happy to continue to feed and play with their puppies up until they are ready to leave at around eight weeks of age. Other bitches are only too pleased to be away from their puppies, once they are fully weaned. In general, I leave it up to the bitch, but my bitches are not allowed away from their puppies totally, either day or night, until the puppies are at least four weeks of age. They do, however, have the option to get away from them for some peace and quiet from time to time.

Earlier in this chapter, I referred to a method of worming using a liquid wormer. I start my worming programme at the same time as weaning, from two-and-a-half to three weeks old, and then at five weeks of age and again at seven weeks. I find a liquid wormer is easier to administer to puppies. There are also tablets and worming pastes, but it is essential to ensure that each puppy gets its requisite dosage. Some puppies are more susceptible to worms than others, but this may not be so obvious if an in-whelp worming programme has been given to the bitch.

Perhaps it is worth mentioning here that many of the modern-day wormers will actually dissolve the worms, so that you will not necessarily see the milk-white worms (roundworm) being passed in the puppies' motions. I must point out, however, that it is very necessary to carry out a full worming programme. If in any doubt whatsoever, consult your veterinary practitioner. Regular worming should continue throughout the puppies' life and into adulthood. I worm my dogs every month, up to the age of six months, and thereafter as necessary, but in any event not less than twice a year.

EARLY SOCIALISATION

Everybody has their own ideas on puppy socialisation. It is, however, the early socialisation which is crucial in order that the puppy learns its place both within the 'pack' and in society. Here I must remind everyone, once again, of the possible risks of infection. Puppies should not be taken out of their own environment until they have been fully inoculated. Nor should they be picked up and handled by strangers who might inadvertently be carrying some viral or bacterial infection. Similarly, puppies should not be allowed to go up to strange dogs, cats or any other household pet, all of which can carry germs. In the above paragraph, I made reference to the puppy's place in the 'pack'. This is not necessarily its place just with its siblings but also with humans. Indeed, in the case of a single pet puppy, the 'pack' may be its human family. It is absolutely essential that the puppy must be made aware, at an early age, that it comes well down in the pecking order – below even the youngest child of your family. However, this also means that even the youngest child must be taught to respect the puppy and treat it gently and with kindness.

While I do allow visitors, in general I discourage anyone from seeing my puppies before they are four weeks of age. If people do wish to handle the puppies, which is sometimes necessary with a view to selling puppies, I insist visitors use a bacterial handwash and that they come in clean clothes. I also use a special spray that is designed to destroy certain bacteria to which puppies are particularly susceptible. This light spray is directly applied on to both clothing and, more so, to footwear.

On an individual basis, I carry puppies to view the outside world by first introducing them around their own immediate environment. If possible, this should include seeing cars and buses going by. I also bring the puppies into the kitchen and put them in a pen where they can see – and hear – the general hustle and bustle of life, including the washing machine, vacuum cleaner, microwave, television, radio, etc.

Once the new puppy goes to its new home, it should again be kept within the confines of its own garden until fully inoculated. Thereafter, the puppy can be taken out and about in the car or carried to the shops, for example to collect the daily newspaper. In this way, he or she becomes accustomed to the noise of traffic, to meeting different people and to visiting different places.

It is essential for the puppy to become accustomed to travelling. This should be done in short journeys on a regular basis, always accompanied by talking to the puppy, giving plenty of encouragement and ensuring that there is something pleasurable at the end of each journey.

You may find in your area there are puppy training classes, or puppy play groups, where your puppy will learn to fit in with the social pack. At my local ring-training class, I allow my puppies off the lead, where they can then play and mix together. I let them have a few minutes play when we arrive and do the same again at the end of the ringcraft session just before we go home. In this way the puppies have fun at the beginning, before they need to settle down, and some more games just before they go home. Another advantage of this type of approach is that it teaches older dogs to have tolerance with puppies and teaches the puppy how far it can go with the older dogs. Many ring-training and dog training classes provide this type of facility for the youngster.

SELLING THE PUPPIES

Selling the puppies is probably the major worry for any caring breeder. Most reputable breeders will have puppies booked well in advance of even a mating taking place, but nobody can guarantee the number of puppies which may result. I have found that even the owner of the stud dog may pass on interested would-be purchasers. If you have used a well-known stud dog, several enquiries will generally be passed on to you. If you are a member of a breed club, the secretary will keep a puppy list and be only too happy to add your name, providing you have met the necessary criteria, i.e. eye and hip-tested parents.

There are a number of quality publications, including weekly dog papers and monthly magazines which carry advertisments. In my opinion these are among the most reputable sources through which the more genuine and caring puppy owner will seek a well-bred Border Collie puppy.

When a potential new puppy owner comes to visit you they must be thoroughly 'vetted'. In this way you can ensure that your puppies are being matched to the right owners – for example, is there someone at home to care for the puppy all day, or at least for most of the day? Are they going to be able to pay any unexpected veterinary fees which may arise? Is there ready access to an exercise area for the puppy, such as a well-fenced garden with no escape routes? What will be the intentions of the new owners with regard to arrangements for the puppy should they go on holiday?

Although I stated in an earlier section that you should not be persuaded into

A job well done – a beautifully reared puppy ready to leave for his new home.

breeding from your bitch just because it is said to be good for her, I feel most strongly that this is worth repeating. It is a huge responsibility bringing new puppies into the world, both in terms of ensuring their health and guaranteeing their on-going physical wellbeing. While you might take the greatest care in selecting your puppies' new owners, people's circumstances can change. Often this results in the puppy needing a new home. This may mean that you, as the breeder, are again approached and you will be expected to take responsibility to ensure the dog's welfare is given top priority. In some instances, this may involve you taking the puppy back.

In all the years that I have owned and bred Border Collies, I can think of nothing in life which has brought me more pleasure. While I cannot imagine life without my Border Collies, and the companionship and loyalty which they give, one must not underestimate the work and responsibility involved. It is a rewarding way of life but also a full time job – no-one wants to go out walking in searing heat, pouring rain or six-foot snow drifts – except, perhaps, the dogs!

14 BEST OF BRITISH

In the August 1976 issue of the *Kennel Gazette* came the announcement that the Kennel Club had approved the interim Standard of the Border Collie. They were now eligible for the show ring. Many of the dogs came from farm working lines and some from the Obedience section. Some of the original breeders had experience with other breeds so they were able to use their knowledge of line breeding to bring the Border Collie forward to its present status. It is now a very popular show dog. In 1981 came the news that the breed had been given Challenge Certificates, eight sets per year, the first to be awarded at Crufts 1982. The breed now has 32 sets and regularly sees entries of 150 plus.

Many breeders have made a valuable contribution to the success of this breed and some of the earliest breeders still continue today, while others have gone on to other things. Their dedicated work has undoubtedly been worthwhile as we now have over a hundred show Champions. Featured here are some of the noteworthy kennels that have played a part in the establishment of the show Border Collie.

ALTRICIA

The Altricia kennel is owned by Patricia Wilkinson. The affix was registered in 1967 using the initial letters of Patricia's husband Alan and the latter part of her own name. Previous to this they had two farm-bred Border Collies as family pets. Their affix was used for their Rough Collies and Shetland Sheepdogs which were shown successfully. Once the Border Collies were recognised for the show ring they acquired their ISDS foundation bitch, Border Queen of Altricia, who, when mated to Sh. Ch. Melodor Flint at Dykebar produced Sh. Ch. Altricia Gael. When she was mated to Sh. Ch. Fieldbank Professional she produced the kennel's most successful brood bitch, Altricia First Love. She is the dam of five show Champions and RCC winners.

The most influential sire of this kennel is her son, Sh. Ch. Altricia Kev, who has sired six show Champions and many CC and RCC winners. He was *Our Dogs* top sire for 1987 and 1990. His stock also do well in other aspects of the breed. His son, Sh. Ch. Altricia Merc, has also sired show Champions. Merc's dam was Liberty Lass of Altricia, one of their foundation bitches. Altricia First Love, when mated to Sh. Ch. Asoka Navajho of Firelynx, produced Altricia Lizette, who went onto produce the kennel's other excellent dog, Altricia Bob, who is the sire of the latest show Champion, Altricia Gift Wrapped, and of Champions abroad.

The kennel decided, after much success

ABOVE: Sh. Ch. Altricia Gift Wrapped.

TOP LEFT: Altricia First Love: Dam of five Show Champions.

LEFT: Sh. Ch. Altricia Kev: Border Collie of the Year 1990.   *Photo: Russell Fine Art.*

in the show ring, to spend some time introducing the merle colour into their line. This they did with some success, after a phone call from Alan Gray in South Africa to say Altricia Blue Mac had become the first blue merle champion and also had passed his working test for sheep. Undoubtedly the kennel's most worthy achievement was when Sh. Ch. Altricia Kev became the first Border Collie of the Year (1990) and his grand-daughter Altrica Mercedes was best bitch. A very proud moment for the kennel was when Kev's son, Sh. Ch. Altricia Rosco of Terverley, went Best of Breed at Crufts in 1995 and when Sh. Ch. Altricia Wish Me Luck gained her American title. Having bred twelve show Champions, of which five still remain at home, this kennel was the *Our Dogs* Top Breeder for 1988, 1989 and 1990. This achievement speaks for itself. The kennel continues to make a big impact upon the show scene.

BEAGOLD

Joyce Collis first established the Beagold kennels in 1959. This came about when she showed Beagles and Golden Retrievers and joined the first letters of each of these breeds to create her prefix, Beagold. Felix Cosme, after his experiences in handling and showing German Shepherds in America, returned to England and joined the Beagold kennels. Having established Bearded Collies into the kennels, Felix campaigned several to their titles.

At this time, in 1976, Joyce was keen to introduce Border Collies into their kennels. Felix, however, was reluctant to include another breed as they were so successful with their Beardies. Eventually, Joyce introduced their first Border Collie as a birthday gift to Felix – it was Tilehouse Cassius, bred by Iris Combe. His achievements were many, before CCs were available, and led to an invitation to the Contest of Champions, were he won through to the last eight out of the top

ABOVE: *Sh. Ch. Beagold Mr Lennox: The breed's youngest Champion.*

RIGHT: *Sh. Ch. Clan-Abby Silver Kiwi At Beagold JW: Breed recordholder with a total of 34 CCs.*

thirty-two of the country. 1982 saw the late Mrs Catherine Sutton awarding CCs for the first time at Crufts, where Cassius won the CC and BOB. His second CC was won under Mrs Mary Gascoigne; his third, and title, was won under the late Mr Bill Findlay. He won a total of five CCs.

In 1989 Joyce went over to New Zealand and Australia to judge and was impressed with the New Zealand Border Collies, which led them to import Clan-Abby Silver Kiwi at Beagold. Their initial plan was to combine the breeding of Cassius to the New Zealand import. This has been very successful for their kennel, which has many top winners all over the world. Kiwi went on to gain a total of 34 CCs to date, making him the Breed record holder. In 1996 Felix campaigned their young dog, Sh. Ch. Beagold Mr Lennox (six CCs and one RCC). He is currently the breed's youngest show champion.

Felix has had many memorable moments while exhibiting their dogs, but one that stands out above the rest was when Ken Bullock awarded Sh. Ch. Beagold Louis his third CC and the title, thus making him the breed's youngest male show Champion

at the time. Louis is now 13 years old. Joyce's most memorable moment was judging Border Collies at Crufts in 1983, the first breed specialist to be given that honour. The Beagold kennels continue to produce and show dogs at a top level. Mrs Collis and Mr Cosme are both well-known and respected judges all over the world.

BEESTING
The Beesting kennel was founded by Jean and Jimmy Entwistle in 1978. From a list submitted to the kennel club the Beesting prefix was accepted. At a later date they discovered that beesting is actually the first and the most nourishing milk of the cow, produced when it has calved. Their original stock were working dogs from farms. This initial period of breeding and showing proved to be lots of fun for the Beesting kennels but without much success in the show ring. In an attempt to improve and re-evaluate their lines, they introduced New Zealand stock by using Wizaland Newz Sensation on Beesting Fleck, which produced Sh. Ch. Beesting Warrior, owned by Mr and Mrs Stacey. They carried on this line by using Warrior on their own New

Wizaland Newz Sensation: Introduced new blood to the Beesting kennel.

Zealand-bred bitch, which produced Beesting The Little Wigginer and Beesting The Little Big Man at Pennygate, both RCC winners.

They continued to establish their lines from working stock by having a litter with their ISDS-bred bitch Komargo's Ryans Daughter mated to Sh. Ch. Altricia Kev. This produced, as they had hoped, sound results with Sh. Ch. Beesting Twiglette (nine CCs, three RCCs and five BIS at Breed Club Shows), and Beesting Thomas of Rogansrock (one CC and one RCC). These two lines formed the basis of their continued success in their breeding programme. Their greatest accolade came in 1993 when they achieved the Top

Breeder award. The Beesting prefix still makes its mark in the show ring.

CARISTAN

The Caristan kennel is owned by Harry and Carolyn Ward. The Border Collie first entered the Caristan Kennels in 1982 with the purchase of a dog for Obedience. Up until then they had German Shepherd Dogs. In 1984 they purchased two bitches, Emma and Bijou, who were shown quite successfully. They also purchased a dog, Mizanne The Perno, known as Perry. It was with these dogs that the Caristan Border Collies became established. From their first litter, with Emma mated to Perry, came Caristan Sparkling Sapphire (two

CCs, one RCC), and Caristan Forever Amber (red and white, one CC). This combination went on to produce Caristan Lady in Red, the first red and white to win at Crufts, and Sh. Ch. Caristan Champers who himself has sired show winners.

In 1985 Mobella Promise, who was by Sh. Ch. Cluff of Mobella, joined the Caristan kennel. Promise, mated to Sh. Ch. Rosehurst the George, produced Caristan Captain, who was the first-ever Border Collie puppy to win a Spillers Puppy stakes, and who went on to be their first Caristan Show Champion. Sadly, this dog died at the age of seven. Some years later, in 1990, the Caristan kennel decided to gamble on using the newly imported dog from New Zealand, NZ Ch. Clan Abby Blue Aberdoone, on Caristan Bramble. This was the first litter sired in the UK by this dog and it gave them their most successful show dog to date, Sh. Ch. Caristan Bruce's Choice (ten CCs, 23 RCs). In more recent years the kennel has had much success in achieving the *Our Dogs*/Pedigree Chum Top Puppy with Caristan Scotch Mist and, in 1996, the Caristan kennels were *Our Dogs*/Pedigree Chum Top Breeders. The Wards own five home-bred show Champions. A highly successful kennel.

CORINLEA

A small kennel owned by Karen Dalglish was started 25 years ago with working stock as a pet. Her interest spread into the world of Obedience. Some years later, when the Border Collie was recognised by the Kennel Club, the Corinlea show line came into being with Karen's favourite foundation bitch, Whenway Gypsy at Corinlea. A great character and a superb brood bitch, she gave the kennel its first home-bred Champion, now aged 13, Sh. Ch. Corinlea Rona. From her established breed lines came Sh. Ch. Viber Travelling Matt from Corinlea (JW) bred by Mrs

Sh. Ch. Viber Travelling Matt From Corinlea: Sire of ten Champions.

Vicki Gray, who went on to be one of the greatest influences as a stud dog in this breed. He is the sire of ten Champions, including Karen's own Sh. Ch. Corinlea Canti (JW) and the breed's first and only full Champion, Mrs Heather Turner's Champion Lochiel Look North.

Trav gained his title at 20 months of age; his greatest moment was being invited to the Contest of Champions, the second Border Collie to receive this honour, the first being his great-grandsire, Sh. Ch. Tilehouse Cassius of Beagold. Karen's greatest achievement and fulfilled ambition came at the Border Collie Club of GB, under specialist judge Mr John Ritchie, who awarded Canti her third CC and who, together with his co-judge, the late Mrs Hazel Monk, went on to award her Best In Show. Her sire, Trav, had also won the CC that day. This kennel has made its mark in the show ring, having owned a total of six show Champions, and continues to be successful.

DYKEBAR

The Dykebar kennel, founded in 1981, is owned by John and Lorraine Ritchie. Their first Border Collie, Sh. Ch. Melodor Flint at Dykebar, was bought from Mrs Chris McLean of Melodor Border Collies. Flint had a successful puppy career and went on to gain his first CC at 20 months of age. By the end of his active show career he had become the breed record holder with 13 CCs, and had numerous group short listings. This was no mean achievement at a time when Borders had only a limited number of CCs on offer and were barely being recognised at Group level. Some of his most notable wins included the day he gained his third CC at Three Counties under the late Mr David Samuel. On the same day John handled the bitch CC winner, Flint's sister, Sh. Ch. Melodor Flurry, who went BOB. Flint's most prestigious win must be at the Border Collie Club of GB's first Championship show, under the late Mr Tom Horner, taking the CC and beating his sister this time for BIS. Flint went on to become a successful sire, siring seven show Champions, and he can be found in many pedigrees of the show Border Collie today.

John's most successful home-bred Border Collie is the world-famous Sh. Ch. Dykebar Future Glory, Sky to her friends. Her dam, a Flint daughter, Sh. Ch. Altricia Pandora at Dykebar, was also a successful show winner; she was Top Border Collie Puppy 1989 and gained her first CC as a puppy. Her sire is Sh. Ch. Clan-Abby Blue Aberdoone. Sky must go down in the history of the breed as the most influential show Border Collie to date. Following in her mother's footsteps she was Top Border Collie Puppy 1992, on the way picking up four RCCs and her first CC at nine months of age. The most memorable win was at Crufts 1993 when she took the bitch CC for the second year running, under Mrs Monica Boggia-Black. She then

Sh. Ch. Dykebar Future Glory winning the Working Group at Crufts 1994. She went on to be Reserve Best in Show.

Photo: Carol Ann Johnson.

went on to win the working group under Mr Albert Wight and then reserve BIS under Mr Ken Bullock. After amassing 33 CCs, numerous Groups and a couple more BIS, Sky finally took the top spot at Darlington in 1995, a first for the breed at this level.

The first Dykebar brood bitch was Melodor Shooting Star into Dykebar. Her sire was Flint's brother Sh. Ch. Melodor Robbie and her dam Black Nip at Melodor. Shooting Star was mated to Sh. Ch. Altricia Kev, a Flint son, resulting in Dykebar Firegem at Lydeardlea, who became the foundation line for Mr B. Welsh and Mrs P. Griffiths – an influential brood bitch, producing two show Champion daughters. John and Lorraine now own her daughter, Lydeardlea Lady Jane, in partnership with Mrs Davis to carry on their line. The Dykebar kennels are not big but produce successful puppies all over the world.

FIELDBANK

The Fieldbank kennel is owned by Kathy Burnell (her maiden name is Lister).

ABOVE: Sh. Ch. Fieldbank Professional: Winner of five CCs and six BIS.

LEFT: Fieldbank Midnight Melody: Border Collie of the Year 1991.

Kathy's interest started with Obedience as her father was actively involved in this area. Her first dog, Lady Fleck, was given to her as a ten-month-old puppy, and she became the foundation of Kathy's highly successful breed showing career. Kathy started her judging career at the age of fourteen and continued to work her way through the Obedience classes. After the Border Collies were recognised by the Kennel Club for show purposes she became involved in the breed ring, although her first love was still Obedience. In 1977 she became a qualified Championship Obedience judge and gave her first ticket in 1978 – the youngest person to judge at that level.

In 1979 the time was right for Kathy to breed her first litter, so she had to choose a prefix. The first six names chosen were turned down by the Kennel Club, followed by more names, all turned down. She was running out of ideas when, while watching television one night, a news report mentioned a place called Bank Field. Knowing the Kennel Club was not keen on place names, she changed it round to read Fieldbank. Three months later the Fieldbank prefix had arrived.

On 29th September 1979 Fleck's litter was born. Out of this Kathy kept a tri-colour dog who turned out to be Sh. Ch. Fieldbank Professional (Bodie). He and his mother both had successful show careers; they won every brace class they were entered in. In 1981, at the Birmingham Championship Show, Fleck was Best Bitch and Bodie was Best Dog and there they won the brace class and went on through to the final six of the Working Group brace. Bodie went on to win five CCs, all with BOB, and six BIS, two of them at the Border Collie Club of GB Championship Shows. Bodie proved his worth by siring one show Champion and three Obedience Champions and his blood lines are still sought after for show and Obedience today.

In 1982 Kathy bought a farm-bred bitch who became Sh. Ch. Fieldbank Merry Meg, who went on to produce Sh. Ch. Fieldbank Independence (Herbie), and Fieldbank Midnight Melody, who won a CC and was The Border Collie of the Year in 1991. Both Melody and Meg have produced winners in the show ring here and abroad. Since 1992, due to ill health, Kathy has not been actively involved in the show ring but the Fieldbank prefix remains and, hopefully, will return at some point.

MERRYBROOK

The Merrybrook kennel is owned by David and Jean Hoare. Their affix was granted in 1967 when, at that time, they bred Labradors. In the late 1960s their first Border Collie came to the kennel, Merrybrook Apache. She was an outstanding bitch who, after retiring from Obedience, began a show career, taking the bitch CC and BOB at SKC, at the age of thirteen-and-a-half. Apache was never bred from.

The Hoares' foundation bitch was Meg of Merrybrook, born in 1977. In the early days the task of breeding towards the type

Merrybrook Apache: Aged 12 – this bitch won a CC when she was 13 years old.

Merrybrook Angel (Aust. Ch. Nahrof No Comment – Merrybrook Bluebell).

desired was an uphill struggle but eventually, due to line breeding, they reached the desired quality. In 1981 a granddaughter of Meg was born, Merrybrook Sophie, who, after being mated to Sh. Ch. Melodor Flint of Dykebar, went to live in New Zealand in the Van Den Heuvels Kennel. After winning a NZ CC, she returned in whelp to NZ Ch. Aberdeenboy of Clan-Abby and produced her litter in British quarantine, the first down-under blood to arrive on to our show scene.

The year 1984 saw the birth of all-British Sh. Ch. Merrybrook Lisa, (Sh. Ch. Melodor Flint at Dykebar ex Merrybrook Sarah), who was awarded her first CC at the age of eight months and who gained a total of seven CCs. Out of the quarantine litter came Merrybrook Laura, who is the foundation bitch of the Merrybrook Anglo-Australasian line. Laura has produced Sh. Ch. Merrybrook Joanne and Merrybrook Bluebell and several other winning dogs. In 1995 the Merrybrook kennel imported Australian Ch. Nahrof No Comment to continue their breeding programme. To date the Hoares have bred seven Champions in the UK and abroad and continue to make their mark in the show ring.

MOBELLA

This kennel, owned by Pam and the late Alan Harris, was started in 1969. Once again Obedience was their initial interest. 'Mobella' originated from watching a film about Africa in which a wild-life sanctuary was called Mobella, which means 'free spirit'. They worked German Sherpherd Dogs and Golden Retrievers until their first Border Collie arrived, and this then became their main breed. They bred some very good Obedience dogs, including OB Ch. Mobella Ryley, owned by Terry Hannam, and Mobella Jez (one OB CC and two RCCs), owned by the late Neville

Sh. Ch. Cluff of Mobella (right), his daughter Mobella Purdy (middle) and his grandson Mobella Midnight Cowboy JW.

Photo: Russell Fine Art.

Johnson. Pam and Alan enjoyed the breed ring, showing Tibetan Spaniels and Bernese Mountain Dogs, so when Border Collies were recognised they began to show them. Mobella Quiz won several BB in Breed Awards before CCs were on offer and also won a first at Crufts when CCs were first awarded. At that time the dogs were Obedience-bred, so Pam and Alan decided to introduce some new blood and acquired Cluff of Mobella from Jeanette Hastie.

This proved to be an invaluable dog for this kennel. He became a show Champion, gaining his third CC under Karen Holliday, which was a very special moment for Pam. Cluff was mated to Sh. Ch. Sacul Highland Mist from Corinlea, which proved to be a most successful mating. Repeated three times, it produced these four Champions: Sh. Ch. Viber Travelling Matt from Corinlea, Sh. Ch. Viber Aiming High at Mobella, Sh. Ch. Viber Lover's Tiff and Sh. Ch. Viber Poetry in Motion at Juvine. Cluff also sired three other CC winners and many show, Obedience and working trial winners. Sadly, at the age of seven Cluff died, but he left a big impact on the show scene.

The New Zealand influence was introduced with Wizaland Newz Speculation at Mobella (Ralph) and it proved to match well with Cluff's offspring, producing excellent puppies for the show ring. Ralph has sired a show Champion and other CC and RCC winners. The kennel's most memorable moments were winning novice dog with Mobella Blaze, class B bitch with Mobella Flair and second A Bitch with Mobella Kilty at Epsom Obedience Championship Show and, in the show ring, winning their first CC with Sh. Ch. Viber Aiming High at Mobella at Blackpool, with her brother Travelling Matt winning the dog CC. The Mobella dogs continue to take top honours in the show ring today.

MUIREND

Owned by Mrs Nan Simpson, the Muirend kennel came into being in 1965, and was named after the cottage she then lived in. She first bred Dobermanns, Westies, Cairns and Whippets, but as her first dog, at the age of twelve, was a Border Collie, when that breed was recognised she brought two bitches into her kennels. Sh. Ch. Muirend Border Dream was the first and best Muirend winner. At six months and two days old she was BB at Manchester Championship Show 1980. Before the introduction of CCs she won 11 BB awards and was the only Border Collie to win a JW. In 1982, the first year that CCs were on offer, she won five out of the eight allocated, and became the first show Champion Border Collie bitch the same day as the first dog was made up. She was the top winning bitch for that year. She won, in all, 11 CCs and five RCCs. Dream

Sh. Ch. Whenway Royal Highlander, pictured at two years of age. Photo: Heidi Poschacher.

NZ Ch & Sh. Ch. Clan-Abby Blue Aberdoone. Photo: Russell Fine Art.

came out of retirement for the veteran class at Crufts 1988 and won BOB and was short-listed in the Group. In the five shows she attended between then and Crufts 1989 she won all five CCs, each with BOB. She was the bitch CC record holder from 1982 to 1993, when she was overtaken by Sh. Ch. Dykebar Future Glory, who is a grand-daughter of Muirend Border Reiver. Dream proved her worth, being the mother of Sh. Ch. Border Gypsy and Sh. Ch. Muirend Border Blessing. Without doubt she was one of the most outstanding Border Collies ever to grace the show ring.

Muirend Border Reiver was born three years before CCs were granted but he did his fair share of winning. However, most of the time he was left at home as the bitches were being campaigned. He was a super dog with a great character and was a natural at working various livestock. He was *Dog World* Top Stud Dog 1982, '83 and '84, was the sire of four show Champions, and is behind many of the show Champions of today. From 1991 to 1994 the Muirend kennel did not show or breed but, having bought in a bitch puppy out of a Muirend bitch, it became active in the show ring again. The future of the Muirend kennel lies with the young stock that comes from their original lines.

WHENWAY

The Whenway kennel was established by Bruce and Sheena Kilsby when they were first working Obedience with their German Shepherd Dogs and Miniature Poodles. In 1976, while on holiday in Anglesey, they purchased two Border Collies from Margaret Crispen. Gelert of Gawne and Rhos of Rushmead, both ISDS and KC registered, were shown when possible but also worked Obedience. Gelert unfortunately died at the age of four-and-a-half, but not before siring a litter to their Andersley Demelza from Whenway, which produced the outstanding bitch Sh. Ch. and Ob. Ch. Whenway Mist of Wizaland, owned by Sue Large. She is the breed's only Dual Champion to date. The Kilsbys went on to acquire, from the late Fred Thomas, a puppy who became the well-known Sh. Ch. Tork of Whenway (Skeets), a dog who is behind so many of the top winners of today and who helped to establish many show kennels for other people. Skeets went on to win five CCs and BOB at Crufts, he sired five show Champions and was the Border Collie Club of GB's Stud Dog Trophy winner 1985, 86 and 88. Sadly, he died at the age of seven-and-a-half.

This kennel has not bred a great number of litters but one that stands out was the litter which resulted when Wisp from Whenway was mated to Sh. Ch. Asoka

Bekkis Kitemark: Top winning puppy.

Navajho of Firelynx, which produced show Champion Whenway Rhys of Mizanne and Sh. Ch. Whenway Janita of Monksfield and Whenway Bryn CD EX, ED EX, WD EX, TD EX and one WTC. The Whenway kennel imported New Zealand Ch. Clan-Abby Blue Aberdoone from Judy Vos, which became the first NZ and British Champion, winning eight CCs in each country, and was the first Border Collie ever to win a Championship show Working Group – only to be equalled by his illustrious daughter, Sh. Ch. Dykebar Future Glory. Blue has sired six show Champions and was the top winning Border Collie, jointly with his son Sh. Ch. Clan-Abby Silver Kiwi at Beagold, in 1990, and has gone on to be the Border Collie Club of GB's Top Stud Dog from 1991 through to 1996. In 1995 Blue was *Dog World's* Reserve Top Stud Dog All Breeds, a remarkable achievement. As well as siring many show winners both at home and abroad, Blue is the sire of Ma Biche of Whenway, who has achieved the great accolade of being Registered on Merit at the International Sheepdog Society, the only Kennel Club-registered show-bred Border Collie to achieve this. In addition,

Blue also has other trialling progeny and, when mated to Altricia Zoe, produced a guide dog for the blind. These are achievements the Whenway kennel is very proud of.

OTHER LEADING KENNELS
MELODOR, owned by Chris McLean, the breeder of three show Champions.
MIZANNE, owned by Mr and Mrs Lewin, the breeder of three show Champions.
ROSEHURST, owned by Eric Broadhurst the breeder of five show Champions. Eric owned the first bitch to win a CC, Sh. Ch. Tracelyn Gal.
VIBER, owned by Mrs V. Gray, the breeder of four show Champions.
WIZALAND, owned by Mrs S. Large, the breeder of four show Champions.
  In more recent times the following kennels have made an impact on the show ring.
BEKKIS, owned by Mrs Hornsby and Mrs Jefferson.
GINNYLANDS, owned by Mr and Mrs Charlesworth.
SHELTYSHAM, owned by Miss P. Forster-Cooper.

15 BORDER COLLIES IN NORTH AMERICA

The show Border Collie is a recent development in the USA. The breed was not fully recognized by the American Kennel Club until December 1994. Prior to that time, in fact since 1955, the breed had been in the Miscellaneous Class, which allowed Border Collies to compete in Obedience and Tracking events only. As in other countries, there were many who opposed recognition, fearing that the breed would be bred for beauty and not for herding instinct. Within the AKC there were also officials who did not want to see the breed recognised, mainly because they had doubts as to the breed's integrity as a pure-bred dog.

While all the controversy has not yet subsided, the AKC has accepted the Border Collier as its 140th breed. The Official Standard of the Breed approved by the AKC has its roots in the Standards of other countries, while allowing more leeway in matters of height and size and placing greater emphasis on gait in the evaluation process.

The breed made its debut in the show ring on October 1st 1995. To mark this special occasion, the American Border Collie Club hosted a National Specialty show in Lubbock, Texas, inviting breed specialist Judy Vos of New Zealand to judge. In the three days leading up to the

SHOW DOG, SHEEPDOG: Dual-purpose Border Collie Sheltysham Ladysman, imported from the UK, owned by Scott A. Wilhelm.

Am. Ch. Borerbreeze Barnstormer From Darkwind, imported from the UK.

Photo: Kohler.

THE SHOW SYSTEM

The AKC system of showing dogs is really quite different from that of other countries. To become a Champion, a dog must acquire 15 points. Part of the total must come in two "major" wins of three, four or five points, under two different judges. The maximum a dog can win at one day's show is five points. Dogs competing for points do so in various classes, including puppy, novice, bred-by-exhibitor, American-bred and Open. All dogs and bitches competing for points are known as "class dogs". The winners of each dog class will compete for Winners Dog and, with it, the available points. After the male class dogs have been judged, the process is repeated for bitches, ending in a selection of Winners Bitch. Champions of Record who are competing for Best of Breed are only judged after both the dog and bitch classes have been judged. Male and female Champions, called Specials, compete with the Winners Dog and Winners Bitch. From this group, the judge will select Best of Breed, Best of Opposite Sex (to Best of Breed), and Best of Winners (from either Winners Dog or Winners Bitch). When a dog has accumulated the necessary fifteen points, it is said to have "finished".

debut show, ABCC members showcased the versatility of the breed by hosting agility, flyball and Obedience demonstrations. Mrs Vos found her Best of Breed in an export from her own kennel, Kiwi Envoy from Clan-Abby, owned by Debby Wood. Mickey, as he is called, went on to make breed history when he received a standing ovation and was placed fourth in the Herding Group under judge Norman Herbel. Mr Herbel happens to be the only Herding Group and Herding Trial judge in the AKC and is very knowledgeable about the breed in its role as a working dog.

Unlike the situation in Britain, New Zealand and Australia, the Border Collie in the US is not generally known in its role as a sheep-herding dog – a fact that is not too surprising considering the sheep industry has never assumed the importance in the USA that it did elsewhere. Many AKC judges have never seen a Border Collie in the field and are unfamiliar with the important and unique aspects of the breed. Currently, there are no Border Collie breeder-judges licensed by the AKC, a situation that will hopefully be rectified in the very near future.

The Best of Breed winner will go on to compete against all the other Herding Breeds in the Group competition. At AKC shows, Group judges select first, second, third, and fourth placings. Only the first in Group goes on to compete with other Group winners for Best in Show.

In the USA, there are Champions and then there are *Champions*. Many people exhibit their Border Collies in the classes until they are finished. It is often said that if people will spend enough money on handlers, then, given enough time, any dog can become a Champion. These dogs are rarely seen in the breed ring again, but most go on to successful careers in Obedience, Agility, Tracking or Herding.

Many finished bitches are simply retired to begin a second career in the whelping box. A very few Champions go on to be "specialled". Specialling a Champion means showing the dog regularly, generally in order to achieve a national ranking. A dog can achieve this by becoming the top winning dog in a region, defeating the same dogs over and over. Occasionally, a dog is campaigned. A campaigned dog will compete around the country, on the theory that a truly great dog should win anywhere, against all competitors. These dogs are the rare treasures. More about campaigning later.

When a new breed is accepted by the American Kennel Club, it has the minimum requirement for points: two males in the classes equal one point, three males equal two points, and so on, until the maximum of five points is reached, with an entry of six or more dogs in the classes. The point scale is the same for bitches. After the breed has been shown for a period of approximately two years, the American Kennel Club re evaluates the scale of points. In regions where many Border Collies became Champions of Record, and where there was a plethora of major points on offer, the scale of points will be raised – but that hasn't happened yet.

Am. Ch. Darkwind Chartop Blue Thunder (NZ Ch/Sh. Ch. Clan-Abby Blue Aberdoone – Ch. Chartop May Queen) – import UK in utero. The breed's second blue and white Champion, number 1 Border Collie in Texas, nationally ranked, Pedigree system 1997. Co-owned and co-bred by Robyn L. Powley and Mrs R.C. Ecob.   Allen Photography.

CLUSTERS OF SHOWS
There are no Championship shows as found in the United Kingdom. American dog shows are actually more comparable to the British Open shows, with total entries that range from 800 dogs to 2500 dogs. Often, local kennel clubs band together to hold a 'cluster' of shows, covering three or four days of showing, all in the same location. In some areas there will be successive clusters within a few hundred miles of each other, and these are known as 'circuits.' One of the most famous circuits is the Florida circuit held every January,

which draws enormous entries from the colder areas in the northern United States.

The very first Border Collie Champion in America finished as Winners Bitch and Best Opposite Sex with three five-point majors over one weekend of shows in Tulsa, Oklahoma, on the 3rd, 4th, and 5th November 1995. This was Ch. Clan-Abby To-Hell-And-Back, known as Helen, a New Zealand Champion bitch imported by Robyn Powley. The second US Champion, Kiwi Envoy From Clan-Abby (Mickey), was finished immediately after Helen by going Best of Breed over her. Three days later in this Oklahoma circuit, Clan-Abby Too Much Tartan (Johnny) became the third Border Collie Champion in America.

THE WESTMINSTER SHOW
These three Clan-Abby pioneers were the only Border Collies finished in time to qualify for the prestigious 1996 Westminster Kennel Club show. Known among the fancy as 'The Garden', the Westminster KC show has been an annual

Am. Ch. Terbo Color Me Badd CD, bred, owned, handled by Terry Wise Hammon. The breed's first chocolate and white Champion.

event for over 120 years. This most prestigious of dog shows has a limited entry of 2500 exhibits, all of which must be Champions of Record. The Champions in each breed compete for Best of Breed only – there are no points on offer and no class dogs allowed. This benched two-day show is held at Madison Square Garden in the heart of mid-town Manhattan in New York City.

At Westminster, besides the usual awards of Best of Breed and Best of Opposite Sex, each judge may bestow Awards of Merit to those Champions deemed worthy. When the first three Champion Border Collies were shown at Westminster in 1996, Ch. Clan-Abby Too Much Tartan was Best of Breed, Ch. Clan-Abby To-Hell-And-Back was Best of Opposite Sex, and Ch. Kiwi Envoy from Clan-Abby CD received an Award of Merit.

TOP WINNING DOGS

Also unique to the American show system are the two different systems of rating top winning dogs. The Pedigree System is concerned with competition in individual breeds. Every time a dog is declared Best of Breed, each dog defeated is counted as one point. There is a cumulative score that runs from January 1st through to December 31st each year. At the end of each year the dog in each individual breed

with the most points is declared the Pedigree Dog for that breed. Pedigree Dog Foods hosts an annual banquet to honor the Pedigree winning dogs and their breeders. The first Pedigree Border Collie of the Year (1995) was Ch. Kiwi Envoy From Clan-Abby CD.

The second rating system is the All-Breeds System. To be ranked in this system requires success in the Group ring, and is generally the purpose behind specialling a Champion. Each time the Best of Breed winner is placed in the Group he receives one point for every dog in every herding breed he defeated. A Best in Show win gives the exhibit the total number of entries in the show, minus one (the winning dog himself). These points are also accumulated on an annual basis. The 1995 All-Breeds System number one Border Collie was Ch. Nahrof Highland Gecko, an import from Australia.

Dogs who appear in the top ten of either ranking system are said to be nationally ranked. Because America is such a vast country, there are generally many shows held simultaneously in different locations. It is not at all unusual for nationally ranked dogs to appear at a show in Dallas on Saturday, and on Sunday be shown in Los Angeles.

CAMPAIGNING

The quest for top honors and national recognition has resulted in a practice known as campaigning. In the United States hundreds of thousands of dollars may be spent campaigning a dog. A campaign generally includes hiring a top professional handler, advertising, and travelling across country. Sometimes backers are found to help in the expenses. Backers are wealthy individuals who have the means to finance a campaign, and enjoy the glory of co-owning a dog that achieves national acclaim for its success.

Professional handlers are just that –

people who make their living exhibiting dogs. The skill level of these professionals can be quite varied. Top handlers are generally members of the Dog Handlers Guild Inc., the Professional Handlers Association, or are Board Certified Professional Handlers. Their services do not come cheap. Besides a handling fee of $50 to $100 every time they exhibit a dog, these professionals will charge Group bonuses, grooming fees, boarding fees, training fees, airport pick-up or delivery charges, and a portion of the costs of travel, including lodging, meals, and airfare.

Advertising is another incredible expense, but unavoidable if one is aiming for top honors. Full page color ads can run to well over $1000, and many dogs are featured in the different dog show magazines such as *Dog News*, *Show Site*, or *Canine Chronicle* at least once a month.

THE WINNING FORMULA

One of the most successful and highly regarded professional handlers, Andy Linton, has said that the formula for winning in the AKC show ring is:
1. Obvious quality of the dog.
2. Condition of the dog (including physical conditioning and grooming).
3. Presentation.

The quality of the dog is the responsibility of the breeders. However, no matter how good the dog is from a conformation viewpoint, he must have a confident attitude and charisma to win top honors.

When it comes to condition, the owner must take a good hard look at his animal. The Border Collie Standard requires an "athletic appearance". No matter how great the quality of the dog, an overweight exhibit is going to be penalized by the judge. Exhibitors should also remember that a dog carrying excess weight will not move as well as the dog that is trim and

NZ Ch/Ch. Clan Abby To-Hell-And-Back (imp. N.Z.). The breed's first Champion, Best Opposite Sex Westminster KC 1996, dam of six Champions. Photo: Don Petrulis.

muscled; however, for show purposes the dog should not look emaciated, and the ribs should not show.

When it comes to grooming, a whole new realm is entered. Though most books say the breed is presented naturally, with the dogs being bathed and having rear hocks trimmed and feet shaped, success in the AKC show rings requires quite a bit more. A visit to a show site reveals large areas set aside for grooming.

SHOW GROOMING

At a show site, many exhibitors construct elaborate set-ups with grooming tables, hair-dryers, and a wide array of grooming utensils and products. Most dogs are bathed on the morning of the show and blown dry. Dogs with long coats may be towelled to prevent frizziness or a fly-away appearance. The hair on the ears will be shaped to maximize mobility. Much goes on in the way of shaping and scissoring. Fur may be trimmed underneath a dog that is shorter in leg to give the exhibit the appearance of adequate length of leg. A dip in the back that spoils a topline may be disguised by teasing hair above the dip. Neck hair may be trimmed to give an illusion of greater length of neck. Teeth are cleaned.

Am. Ch. Darkwind Jessica the Newzmaker NZ/Aust Ch. Loch-N-Legacy To Clan-Abby – NZ/Am Ch. Clan-Abby To-Hell-And-Back): Second highest ranking bitch 1997 Pedigree System, bred by, co-owned and handled by Robyn L. Powley. Family pet, agility dog, herding started and successful show dog. Co-owned by Steve Stapleton.
Photo: Joe Rinehart.

Dogs may have their white areas bleached to a snowy white using hydrogen peroxide. At the very least, whitening mousses are used, and the dog is then chalked and powdered. Groomers can create the illusion of more or less bone by skilful application of these substances. Areas lacking pigment may be filled in with various markers. Bodifyers are used to create an illusion of greater coat where shedding has occurred or nature has not endowed sufficiently. Hair sprays are used. Lastly, the black parts will be given some sort of spray with a substance for shine.

The most important part of this entire process is the finishing touches. Powder and chalk are removed, usually with a blow dryer. Any coloring materials are wiped clean. There must be no oily residue. The judge must be able to examine the dog without feeling any substances in the coat or having any matter wipe off. This is what is known as "groomed to perfection". In October of 1996, we spent three hours grooming Ch. Borderbreeze Barnstormer From Darkwind (import UK) who was so out of coat his skin showed. The dog went

Best of Breed from a very large entry that day and went on to achieve a Group 4th!

PROFESSIONAL HANDLING
The final ingredient to a successful show career is presentation. There are many people who elect to show their own dogs and who do it superbly. There is even The Owner Handler Association of America Inc., which was created expressly to support those who wish to show their dogs themselves. However, the use of professional handlers is very common, and there are many reasons why this proves so fruitful.

First of all, the professional is just that – very skilled technically, eliciting performances from their exhibits that are breathtaking. Secondly, they generally are expert groomers. Thirdly, the judges know and respect the professionals.

This public recognition can pay off. As an example, when I began to show my blue and white import Charttop Shadow, I encountered lots of resistance from judges who were unfamiliar with, and doubtful of, her color. Though a beautiful mover, we kept being awarded the reserves. However, once I enlisted the aid of top handler C.L. Eudy, Shadow became the first blue and white champion is just a few short weeks. It is my belief that Mr Eudy's reputation as an excellent handler, who presents first-rate specimens, made the difference by lessening the resistance to her color.

RECENT SUCCESSES
The first Border Collie to win the herding group was Ch. Clan-Abby The Wizard Of Oz, owned and presented by professional handlers Carol and Warren Rice. This dog later became the 1996 Pedigree Dog.

In the fall of 1996 Anne Marie Silverton, a top Obedience trainer, imported Australian Champion Nahrof First Edition, from Lauren Somers. Placed in the hands of one of America's foremost professional handlers, Bruce Schultz, Jarrah received a Group 1 the first weekend he was shown.

At Westminster KC 1997, Jarrah was Best of Breed and electrified the audience by placing second in the Herding Group – an incredible feat for the breed's second appearance at The Garden. He was also the 1996 All-Breeds System top-ranked Border Collie, following in the footsteps of his son, Gecko.

On March 23, 1997 in Tucson, Arizona, Jarrah made history by becoming the first Border Collie in America to go Best in Show, under judge Keke Kahn. From new breed to Best in Show in less than eighteen months!

The youngest Champion is Ch. Korella A Star Is Born (imported from Australia, bred by Sigrid Mathew) who finished at the age of eight-and-a-half months, with three five-point majors in one weekend, and who was nationally ranked in 1996.

The first American-born Border Collie to win the Herding Group is Ch. Darkwind Charttop Blue Thunder, who is also the first Border Collie to win the group who is not black and white. He is blue and white.

THE BORDER COLLIE'S FUTURE

What's left for the future? Plenty. Time will show which of today's winners will go on to be top producers for the breed. Who will emerge as top breeders? The initial successes belong mainly to imports, but soon we will incorporate these lines to produce something uniquely American, a combination of the best of Great Britain, New Zealand and Australia and the best of the established, and beloved, US Obedience and herding lines.

There is an active community of Border Collie fanciers who are knowledgeable and committed to the breed. No matter how much we may disagree with each other, no matter how heated the competition, we are, as a whole, determined to keep the

Am. Ch. Korella A Star Is Born: Thebreed's youngest Champion at eight and a half months, finishing with three majors in one weekend.

intelligence and the herding ability – traits that are the hallmarks of the Border Collie.

The Border Collie Society of America, the AKC parent club, has taken a very active stance to ensure we keep the brains as we develop the beauty of the breed. The first planned National Specialty is scheduled for October 8th to 12th 1997, with an AKC Herding Trial, Obedience Trial, Agility Trial, and of course conformation show. The BCSA has also instituted a Versatility Awards program that recognizes those dogs who are accomplished in diverse activities.

For many breed devotees, more important than being the first Best in Show winner is the competition to have the first AKC conformation and herding Champion. There is a strong desire to prevent this breed from developing into a generic show dog, winning because of traditional, black and white markings, tip-tilted ears, and a glamorous long coat.

At the time of this writing there are more than eighty breed Champions in the USA. We have traditional black and white, tri-color, blue merle, chocolate, red, and blue Champions. The first Dual Champion was the Obedience Trials Champion Wynsota's Horizon. There are Champions with herding, agility, and tracking accomplishments to their credit. Though there is a preponderance of foreign show lines in 60 per cent of the Champions, Ch. Nick is of all-American herding lines. Best of Opposite Sex at Westminster 1997 was Ch. Tasmanian Bandit, a beautiful bitch also of herding stock.

BUYING A SHOW PUPPY

The complexity of showing in the AKC can easily lead to confusion for anyone considering the purchase of a puppy to show. Each potential buyer should prioritize their desires before contacting breeders. Many breeders can produce a dog nice enough to finish – few can produce specials or a dog worthy of campaigning. A successful breeder-owner-handler will obviously be better equipped to assist the novice handler. Aspiring breeders should go straight to those who specialize in breeding, versus those whose fortes are in other areas but who once in a while breed a litter. If one's main interest is in an area of performance, go to those who specialize in that area. And remember, the top breeders will be very selective in placing their puppies.

Many people wish to purchase bitches first so they can eventually breed, but often males make the better show dogs. Not only do males carry more coat, they may be blessed with very out-going, show-off personalities, and of course, they do not experience the heat cycles that make showing a bitch more difficult. Though it is an American characteristic to want overnight stardom, success in the dog world often takes a lifetime.

16 BORDER COLLIES IN AUSTRALASIA

Most Border Collies in New Zealand and Australia can be traced back to Adam Telfer's Old Hemp, or Hemp no. 8, who was born in Northumberland in 1894. New Zealand was fortunate in having rich farmers who could buy the International Supreme Sheep Dog Trial Winners. Several of the early winners went to New Zealand and many followed on to Australia, or the progeny of these winners ventured to Australia.

James Lilico, a Scotsman who shepherded in Northern Ireland and migrated to New Zealand in 1894, is synonymous with New Zealand sheep dogs. Lilico left his top working dog, Captain, in Ireland when he went to New Zealand. However, during his first two years there, he found himself desperately in need of a good working dog and finally he sent for Captain. In Lilico's book *Sheepdog*

Sweep 21: Exported to New Zealand and later on to Australia.

Memoirs he claims that Captain had a great influence on sheep dog breeding in New Zealand. I understand Lilico's books were some of the earliest on the breed.

Lilico was responsible for the arrival in New Zealand and Australia of the first of the new Border Collie strain of carefully selected top sheepdogs which later were interbred with the local stock in New Zealand and Australia. Hindhope Jed (born in 1895) was the first bitch Lilico imported from a Scottish farmer. Having no work for Jed at the time, Lilico sent her out to his friend in the Marlborough province a few weeks after her arrival. Then, while Mr A. E. McLeod of New South Wales, Australia, who was a well-known breeder and trialler of Kelpies, was on a visit to New Zealand in 1901, he bought Hindhope Jed, who was in whelp to Captain. Thus Hindhope Jed became the first Border Collie dog to arrive in Australia. McLeod was so taken with Jed that he designated Lilico to buy the bitch pups out of her and Captain.

A daughter of Adam Telfer's Old Hemp, H.T. Little's Maudie, was imported in the year following the arrival of Hindhope Jed. Maudie was a top working bitch. However, Lilico considered that Jed was the better-looking of the two. Over a quarter of a century after Jed and Maudie arrived in New Zealand, Lilico still

believed that those two bitches would hold their own on any contemporary trial ground in the Southern Hemisphere. He stated that his opinion would be backed by those who had seen Jed and Maudie at work.

Several years after importing Jed and Maudie, Lilico bought William Wallace's dog Moss 22 who, when exported, became known as Border Boss. He won the International in 1907 and, possibly, had the most influence on the breed in New Zealand. Lilico declared him to be the greatest stud dog he ever had and one of the most perfect workers ever seen south of the Equator.

Other winners who went to New Zealand were the 1910 and 1912 winner Sweep 21 and Don 17, the 1911 and 1914 winner (Armstrong's invincible pair), who were bought by Lilico and later sold to Arthur Collins of South Australia. Also sent to Lilico was Lad 19, the 1913 winner, a litter brother to Lammermoor Dan. The importation of these great Sheepdogs had a enormous influence on the Border Collies in New Zealand and Australia.

DEVELOPMENT OF THE SHOW BORDER COLLIE

Hindhope Jed had been shown at bench shows in New Zealand prior to her departure to Australia in 1901. However, it is believed that it was in 1907 that Border Collies were benched for the first time at a breed show in Australia.

It is understandable that, with the introduction of these top imported sheepdogs, their owners wished not only to trial their dogs, but also to show them, so that, after some time it was inevitable that a Breed Standard had to be written. New Zealand became the first country in the world to adopt a Breed Standard for the Border Collie as we know it today.

In 1927 history was made when a sub-committee of the New Zealand Kennel Club and the Sheep Dog Trial Association submitted a Standard and a scale of points for the Working Collie to both organisations and these were subsequently adopted. When one compares it to the present-day Standards it has varied little over this period of time, except for the teeth, which are now required to have scissor bite, and the height, which was been lowered.

The first Border Collies were registered with the New Zealand Kennel Club on 17th April 1919. Glenn, NZKC registration number 4874b, and Tan, NZKC registration number 4875b, were born on 29th September 1918, bred by McConachy. Glenn was owned by W. Gunn. Their sire was Bruce, and the dam was Fly.

Although New Zealand began exhibiting Border Collies at a more furious rate than Australia, especially in the late 1940s when an Australian judge, officiating in New Zealand, judged about twenty Border Collies, the numbers being shown in New Zealand in the 1950s and 60s began to decline dramatically. However, it was the opposite in Australia, where in the 1950s and 60s dedicated breeders began to establish their type and breed in order to improve the conformation of the dogs. It was at this time – the 1950s, 60s and 70s – that Australia became the leader in maintaining a breed type and in developing the Border Collie as a show dog.

There may have been Border Collies exhibited in the conformation and Obedience rings in Queensland, South Australia, Western Australia and Tasmania during the 1950s and early 1960s, and some of these dogs would have made new records for the breed in their states. However, I will concentrate mainly on the states of New South Wales and Victoria during the early years of the development of the Border Collie breed in the show ring, and will pick up the stories of the other states later, in a more contemporary setting.

NEW SOUTH WALES 1950s & 60s

In New South Wales there are records of Border Collies being exhibited at the Sydney Agricultural Society's Royal Show as early as the 1930s. The 1940s were desolate, especially during the war years; however, in the 1950s the breed's popularity in the show ring began to increase again. At the Royal Shows there were six dogs entered in 1951, four in 1952, 28 in 1953 and 29 entries recorded in 1954. The breed in New South Wales was now firmly established as a show dog, as well as continuing in its other role as a working sheepdog.

Possibly the best-known Border Collie in New South Wales in the early 1960s was Aust. Ch. Ninda Mundai. Winner of the Sydney Royal CCs in 1962 and 1963, Mundai was bred and exhibited by Mr and Mrs Roy O'Donnell. Mundai also ventured to Royal shows in other Australian states, conquering in Queensland, winning the

CCs at the Brisbane Royals in 1961 and 1962, in South Australia at the Adelaide Royals in 1963 and 1964, in Western Australia at the Perth Royal in 1963 and also having the honour of winning Best Opposite Sex In Group at the Perth Royal that year, making her the first Border Collie to win a Royal Show In Group award. Mundai later became the first Border Collie to win a class in-show award all breeds.

Mr Fred Butt's Margian Kennel became an influence in the development of the breed in New South Wales. Aust. Ch. Margian Spats (Best Of Breed 1967, 1968 and 1970 Sydney Royal Shows), Aust. Ch. Margian Jolly Roger and Aust. Ch. Margian Queen can be seen behind some of New South Wales top kennels over the years and are behind many of today's top winning dogs.

Other New South Wales kennels of influence in the 1950s and 60s include Nidgee, Neewah, Yenching, and Kyneton. The Gotrah Kennel of Mrs Peidje Vidler became extremely respected by breeders throughout Australia for many years. From one of the early Gotrah litters came Aust. Ch. Gotrah Duke: born in the late 1950s he was a lovely type dog and this type continues on through the Gotrah dogs up until the present day.

VICTORIA 1950s & 60s

In 1950, there was an announcement in the *KCC Gazette* that a register was being started for Border Collies whereby they may be entered at Championship Shows and Parades. In their first year as a recognized breed there were only two litters registered; however, the increase in popularity was steady from this time on.

In 1954, the previously-known Australian Heeler and Kelpie Club of Victoria incorporated Border Collies as well, and for the next 28 years became known informally as the "3 Breeds Club".

Entries for the Melbourne Royal Show steadily increased from 1951 when there were 11 entries to 17 entries in 1952, 23 entries in 1953, 36 entries in 1960, 43 entries in 1965 to 48 entries in 1969. Ch. Digger was the first Border Collie to win two Melbourne Royal CCs in 1954 and 1955. His record was beaten shortly after by Ch. Bonnie Laddie who won three consecutive Melbourne Royal CCs in 1957, 1958 and 1959

In early 1954, Bonnie Laddie (who later became an Australian Champion) was born and purchased by Pauline and Jim Brien of the Glenine kennel. The first Border Collie to win three consecutive Melbourne Royal CCs, he also won four Specialty Club CCs, one Adelaide Royal CC and five Classic CCs. This top show dog also became a top sire, producing no less than 15 Champions, including Ch. Checkmate Gay Abby (foundation bitch for the Checkmate kennel), Glenine Jeanette (dam of Glenine Ben Cameron, a successful stud dog for the Crestvale kennel in the 1960s), Ch. Kaiapoi Tiki (dam of Glenine Lady Vikki, foundation bitch for the Crestvale kennel) and Epsom Bint (who helped establish the Epsom kennel).

The Epsom kennel of Clive and Molly Blackney was a strong kennel during the 1950s and 60s. Epsom Bint produced many Champions including Ch. Epsom Beauty, Ch. Epsom Mitzy, Ch. Epsom Tinkerbelle and Ch. Epsom Shep. Many progeny from these dogs are behind the great dogs of today. The top stud dogs in Victoria in the early 1970s – Ch. Epsom Thunder (Cheviot kennel), Ch. Epsom Great Glen CDX (Fyneglen kennel) and Ch. Epsom Rex (Glentress kennel) – were descendants of Bint: her name appears five times within a six-generation pedigree of Great Glen and Rex. The Kaiapoi kennel produced the great stud dogs Ch. Kaiapoi Aranui, Ch. Kaiapoi Highland Haze and Ch. Kaiapoi Scotman. Ch. Kaiapoi Aranui

is the sire of Ch. Epsom Thunder, while Ch. Kaiapoi Highland Haze produced the legendary Ch. Checkmate Gay Lady.

The Glenine and Gilhai bloodlines formed the foundation of John and Gloria Whyte's Crestvale kennel. One of their first litters, sired by Glenine Ben Cameron from Glenine Lady Vikki, produced Ch. Crestvale Loch Laddie CD in the late 1960s, who became an influential stud dog in Victoria.

NEW ZEALAND 1960s & 70s

In New Zealand in the 1960s it seemed that there were few Border Collies of show standard. And at this time it appears that there were mostly only two types of people interested in Border Collies: farmers and Obedience competitors. It took until the 1970s before people in New Zealand started really to get interested in Border Collies as show dogs.

Mrs Peg McKenzie (Strathcarron kennel, South Island) was one breeder in the 1960s and 70s who bred some excellent working and Obedience dogs, including many Obedience Champions and titled dogs. Mrs McKenzie utilised many of the English imported bloodlines and working bloodlines which, together, produced her top sire NZ Ch. Ob. Ch. Strathcarron Jazz CDX. She also imported and utilised dogs from Australia, from the Sarasota, Checkmate, and Joseian kennels and, later, from the Gotrah kennel, who blended beautifully with the English imported bloodlines to produce both top Obedience and working dogs and winning show dogs. Working Trials and Obedience Ch. Strathcarron Pedlar CDX UDX WDX TDX, bred by Peg McKenzie and owned by Mrs Judy Harker of Auckland, would be one of the finest examples of the breed as a truly versatile working dog, working in films and commercials and becoming NZ's first Working Trial and Obedience

Champion Border Collie.

During this period many breeders started their kennels through developing the Strathcarron bloodlines, or having their foundation stock or first Border Collies from the Strathcarron kennels. These kennels include Clan-Abby, Marclan, Wayfarer, Dalreoch, Silhouette, and Glendarroch, to name a few.

Mrs Carol Whitfield established the Keenglo kennel in the 1960s and, like Peg McKenzie, believed the Border Collie should be able to work sheep in addition to competing in shows or Obedience trials. She purchased stock from Scottish imported parents and top working bloodlines, as well as later utilising imported dogs from Australia, such as Timmar New Venture (who later became a NZ Champion).

During the mid-1970s, many imports from the Gotrah kennel started arriving in New Zealand, and they were used by the Lanmora, Rimrock, Trywon, Glen-Clova, Marclan and Keenglo kennels. NZ Ch. Ob. Ch. Gotrah Ringleader, owned by Allanah Knapp (Moore) of the Lanmora kennel, competed successfully in both the Obedience and conformation rings in the 1970s, culminating with Best Of Breed at the 1979 NZ National Dog Show. Rocky was successfully utilised at stud with the female Gotrah imports as well as many of the Strathcarron lines. It is interesting that, in the early 1980s, Rocky's grandson, Send-A-Way Midnight, who combined many of the top Strathcarron lines, was later sent back to the Gotrah kennel to introduce fresh bloodlines for future breeding programmes in New South Wales.

With the infusion of many New South Wales Gotrah imports into New Zealand in the 1970s, other breeders in New Zealand wanted to see what the rest of Australia had to offer and ventured to Victoria to view the kennels there. Previous imports

had arrived from Checkmate, Josiean, Willence and Epsom kennel in the late 1960s and early 70s; however, it was the mid-1970s when the Victorian imports began to create a dramatic effect on the Border Collie breed in New Zealand.

The first Border Collie in the Clan-Abby kennel, owned by Judy, Peter and Johanna Vos, was a bitch from the Strathcarron kennel. A male had been previously imported from the Checkmate kennel as a bred-mate for the bitch. Seeing what a wonderful improvement the consolidated Victorian bloodlines had made on her first litter, Judy wanted more improvement and saw Victoria as the state which had the bloodlines she wanted to use to continue the foundation of the Clan-Abby kennel. Her ideal Border Collie was the famous Aust. Ch. Checkmate Gay Lady and so she decided to contact Lady's owners in Victoria, the late Jack and Joan Thompson of Cheviot kennel. After corresponding for some time, the Thompsons offered Lady's daughter from her first litter, namely Cheviot Joanne (who later became a NZ Champion). Lady wanted to be the only bitch on the Thompson's property and she could not tolerate having her daughter taking any of the attention she sought from her owners. Cheviot Joanne was sent to New Zealand in whelp to top Victorian show and stud dog Aust. Ch. Crestvale Sono Thunder, bred and owned by John and Gloria Whyte, whose Crestvale kennel had been a great influence on the development of the Border Collie in Australia during the 1960 and 70s.

From this litter came NZ Ch. Thunderboy Of Clan-Abby, who on February 8th 1979, was the first Border Collie in New Zealand to win an all-breeds in-show award. Border Collies were very seldom considered for a Group placing, let alone in-show placing at all-breeds Championship shows.

Later Judy purchased Cheviot Gay Lord

NZ Ch. Gotrah Lammermuir Kilt.

NZ Ch. Minimbah Red The Rules: Dog CC and Best in Group 1990 Sydney Royal Show.

(Imp. Aust), a male from Aust. Ch. Checkmate Gay Lady's second and only other litter. Gay Lord proved valuable as a stud dog and the Clan-Abby kennel had some new useful bloodlines to continue utilising in their breeding program.

NEW SOUTH WALES TODAY

The Border Collie Club Of New South Wales was inaugurated on 16th January 1980 with 41 members. RNSWCC affiliation was granted in June 1980 and within the first twelve months the club's membership had grown to 110 members. In recent years membership of the club has been maintained at between 250 and 300 members. The club applied for and was granted incorporation in 1981. The club's first show was an Open Show held on October 11th 1980 and was judged by Roy O'Donnell of the Ninda kennel. (Mr O'Donnell was the club's first patron.)

In the early 1970s, one of the most famous dogs bred by Mrs Peidje Vidler's Gotrah kennel was born, Aust. Ch. Gotrah Talybent Roger. A Best In Show winner in 1974, and CC winner at six Royal Shows, he became an outstanding sire, producing many Champions in conformation and Obedience. Talybent Roger, his son and his grandson, have all won Best In Show honours, making a rare occurrence of three generations of Best In Show winners.

Aust. Ch. Gotrah Lammermuir Kilt followed on from Talybent Roger, winning the CC at the Adelaide Royal in 1977 and Best Of Breed at the NZ National Dog Show that same year. He, too, has produced many Champions in conformation and Obedience. One outstanding son is Aust. Ch. and Aust. Obed. Ch. Borcat McAllister UD TD, the second dual-titled Border Collie in Australia.

The Ebony kennel of Ron and Peg Anderson was one producing consistent type and quality. Ebony Lady (foundation bitch) produced Ch. Ebony Ace and Ch. Ebony Clova. Ch. Ebony Ace was the sire of Ch. Ebony Velvet, who later became a top-producing bitch at Tasmania's Sarasota kennel. Ch. Ebony Clova was the dam of Ch. Ebony Mac, the winner of three Sydney Royal CCs, and twice Best In Show at the Border Collie Club of NSW Championship Shows.

Wooleston and Koonanda form the basis of many New South Wales kennels today. The Minimbah Stud used these lines, along with the Margian bloodlines, to produce some of New South Wales most outstanding show dogs during the 1980s. Harvey and Anne Caddy's dedication to the breed began in the 1970s with foundation bitch Ch. Wooleston Wee Lassie CD. She, in turn, produced Ch. Minimbah Black Gypsy, the dam of many Champions including Ch. Minimbah Tradition. Tradition won Best In Show at the BCC of NSW Championship Shows in 1983 and 1984. In turn he, too, produced on, siring one of the most successful show dogs in the history of New South Wales, Ch. Minimbah Hot Pursuit. Toddy was a

Aust. Ch. Lochinbrae of Clan-Abby (imp. NZ): The first Border Collie to win Best in Show at both the NSW and Victoria Border Collie Club Specialty Shows.

wonderful show and stud dog, winning over 20 Best In Show awards, four of these being at the Border Collie Club of NSW Championship Shows, and two Royal CCs and Runner-up Best In Group at the Sydney Royal in 1987. Toddy continued the tradition by producing many Champions, and a Sydney Royal winning son, Ch. Minimbah Red The Rules. Red (as the name suggests) is a red/white Border Collie, who made history in 1990 when he won Best Of Breed and went on to win Best In Group at the Sydney Royal Show.

In the late 1980s and early 1990s the New South Wales show rings were dominated by a NZ import, exhibited by a new Border Collie exhibitor and kennel. Sigrid and Ross Mathew of the Korella kennel were fortunate to purchase Ch. Lochinbrae Of Clan-Abby from Nancy Wilson, whose circumstances caused her to let K2 go to a new home. The Mathews previously were Dachshund breeders, and K2 was Korella's first Border Collie. His temperament and success caused the Mathews' later switch in breeds. While with the Mathews, K2 amassed 11 Best In Show wins and 11 Runner-up Best In Show wins, and he was the first Border

Collie to win Best In Show at both the NSW and Victorian Border Collie Club Specialty shows. K2 produced some lovely progeny including Aust. NZ Jap. Ch. Windygyle Maori Chief, Ch. Windygyle Penny Lane, Ch. Korella Storm Raider and Aust. NZ Ch. Maghera Debonnaire.

The rest of the 1990s in New South Wales has been dominated by another relatively new kennel and exhibitor. Ms Lauren Somers moved down from Queensland to New South Wales, breeding her first litter from her foundation bitch Gotrah Celtic Brie CD TDX to top-winning Queensland dog, Ch. Beechwood Boots 'N All. From this litter Ch. Nahrof First Edition was born, a dog who was to make history in NSW as the winner of over 31 Best In Show awards, the first dog to win three consecutive Best In Show wins at the Border Collie Club of NSW and the only dog to win this event seven times. First Edition, also the winner of four Royal CCs, was awarded Best In Group and Best Opposite Sex In Show at the Brisbane Royal in 1993 and Best In Group at the Brisbane Royal in 1995. First Edition has recently ventured to the USA where he is continuing his outstanding show career and setting new records for the breed.

Other consistent kennels in New South Wales during the 1980s and 1990s have been Sheermyst, Ansavon, Crystalledge, Loadstar, Tuckonie, Auldbrig, Ballyann, Rosebrook, Bobanette, Amberloch, Bordalace and Windygyle.

VICTORIA TODAY
Early in 1980 Mr P. Ruffels and Mrs M. Quinn formed a steering committee with a view to establishing a new club purely for Border Collies. This steering committee subsequently called together all interested parties, and at this meeting, on the 10th July 1980, the Border Collie Club of Victoria was born.

NZ Ch.
Rullion
Gambit: Top
Victorian sire
during the
1980s.

NZ Ch.
Finestyle
Sundancer:
Dog CC
Adelaide,
Melbourne and
Brisbane
Royals.

Maureen and Frank Wilson's Checkmate kennel, notable in the 1960s, continued into the 1970s breeding many Champions, and it produced foundation stock for forthcoming top kennels. Ch. Checkmate Maree became the foundation bitch for the Ebony kennel of Rob and Peg Anderson in New South Wales. Ch. Checkmate Fair Lady was the foundation bitch for Karen Monk and Elaine Monk (now Saxon) at Victoria's Maghera kennel. Checkmate Miss Crystal became one of the foundations of Wayne and Colleen McGrath's Ansavon kennel in New South Wales, Checkmate Lady Lassita produced many champions for the Joseian kennel in Victoria, while the Adams' Glentress kennel in Victoria has used the Checkmate bloodlines extensively in their breeding programs.

In December 1969, the legendary Ch. Checkmate Gay Lady, whom I have mentioned before, was born, and the Victorian Border Collie fraternity was to witness one of the outstanding show bitches of all time. During a brilliant show career in the hands of her owner, the late Mr Jack Thompson, she became the first Border Collie in Victoria to win a Best In Show (all breeds); this was in November 1972. Lady was the most outstanding Victorian show Border Collie during the 1970s and won the CC at the Melbourne Royal Show in 1972, 73, 74, 75, and 1977. Also, at the Adelaide Royal, she won the CC in 1972 and 1973.

It was in fact at Melbourne Royal in 1972 that the renowned English judge, the late Harry Glover, was so impressed with Ch. Checkmate Gay Lady that he decided that she was the ideal upon which to base the first English Standard. He returned home determined to press forward with the move to get a fixed International Sheepdog Society (ISDS) registered variety of working sheepdog, long known as the Border Collie, as an officially recognised breed in the British show world. The rest is history. His efforts paid off and the breed became officially KC-recognised in 1976.

John and Gloria Whyte's Crestvale kennel remained strong throughout the 1970s and still are, up until the present day. Crestvale Gay Gypsy produced some excellent progeny, especially in the litter sired by Ch. Epsom Thunder which produced Ch. Crestvale Sono Thunder (retained by Crestvale) and Ch. Crestvale Gay Serena CD (foundation bitch of the Tullaview kennel). These two litter-mates have had a dramatic effect on the breed throughout Australia and New Zealand, with nearly every current top winning dog or kennel being able to trace their stock to Sono Thunder or Serena.

Patrice and Gary Knight's Tullaview kennel was fortunate to purchase Ch. Crestvale Gay Serena CD – an excellent type bitch who reproduced this type in each litter. Ch. Tullaview Tornado CD was the first of her progeny to be noted: he was the sire of numerous Champions, including Ch. Cheryla Mac Spade (the first dog owned by Kennoway kennel, South Australia), Aust. NZ Ch. Rullion Joy (brood bitch for the Clan-Abby kennel, New Zealand), and Ch. Minimbah Dash 'N Beauty (brood bitch for the Minimbah kennel, NSW) to name a few. Crestvale Gay Serena's other progeny included Ch.

Tullaview Tarena (Kennoway kennel, SA), Aust. NZ Ch. Tullaview Tierre (Marclan kennel, NZ) and Ch. Tullaview Tallahasse (dam of Aust. NZ Ch. Tullaview Trailblazer and Ch. Tullaview Uppity Miss), although the most notable was the famous bitch Ch. Tullaview Temptress (Tullacrest kennel, SA).

Ch. Checkmate Gay Lady's tradition at Melbourne Royal shows was carried on in the late 1970s by an equally exceptional bitch, who would go on to create an unsurpassed record at Royal Shows. Ch. Tullaview Temptress won the Bitch CC at Melbourne Royal in 1978, 79, 80, 81, 82, 83 and 1985. Her first CC in 1978 was at ten months of age and she went on to take Best Puppy In Group and Best Puppy In Show – previously unheard-of results for a Border Collie at this, Australia's most prestigious show. In 1982, as well as winning the CC and Best Of Breed, she went on to take Best In Group. Along with these successes at Melbourne, she also conquered Adelaide Royal, taking Bitch CC in 1979, 82, 83, 84 and 1985. Temptress set new records for the breed, winning many Best In Show all breeds – although her forte was at the Royals.

The Tullaview kennel later bred another successful bitch, Ch. Tullaview Uppity Miss, who, along with Bitch CCs at Adelaide Royal Shows, was awarded Bitch CC at the 1990 Melbourne Royal Show, plus Best Of Breed, Runner-Up Best In Group and Runner-Up Best In Show. This was the first time a Border Collie had won Runner-Up Best In Show at the Royal Melbourne Show.

The Werlak kennel in Victoria continued with the Epsom, Glenine and Crestvale lines to produce, in the mid-1970s, Ch. Werlak Beau Jade. Beau went to the Tullacrest kennel in South Australia at five years of age. Previously he had not been shown. However, he did not need a warm-up to his show-career. He went straight in

and never looked back! He won the Dog CC at Melbourne Royal in 1980 and 1981 as well as winning Dog CC at Adelaide Royal in 1982 and having four Best In Show awards to his credit.

The Rullion kennel of the late Phil and Judy Ruffles were noted for their quality stock, many of which became the foundation stock for other kennels. Ch. Rullion Gambit became an extremely successful stud dog in the late 1970s and early 1980s. Gambit won the Dog CC at the first two alternate Championship shows held by the Border Collie Club of Victoria. He was the sire of Ch. Maghera Croupier (winner of three consecutive Melbourne Royal CCs 1982, 83 and 1984; Best In Show at the Border Collie Club of Victoria's first Championship Show in 1984), of Ch. Ansavon Scotsman and of Aust. NZ Ch. Kennoway Deal'rs Choice, to name a few of his progeny. Also bred by the Rullion kennel were Ch. Rullion Flare (foundation bitch for the Glentress kennel, Victoria), Ch. Rullion Nova (foundation bitch for the Crystalledge kennel, New South Wales), Ch. Rullion Lustre (foundation bitch for the Dakiem kennel, NSW), and Ch. Rullion Triflow Bliss (foundation bitch for the Llanwynn kennel, WA).

Karen Monk and Elaine Saxon's Maghera kennels have been consistent producers of winners throughout the 1980s and up until the present day. The successful Ch. Maghera Croupier (previously mentioned) in turn produced Ch. Finestyle Sundancer (bred by Deidre Dart and co-owned in South Australia with Lynn and Bill Harrison). Ch. Finestyle Sundancer set a new record in Adelaide, with five consecutive Adelaide Royal CCs, 1986 to 1990, and also winning the CC at Melbourne Royal in 1988 and Brisbane that same year, where he made history by taking Best In Group and Runner-Up Best In Show! For the Maghera kennel

Sundancer produced the superb blue and white male, Aust. NZ Ch. Maghera Crystal Rythem. Also a Melbourne Royal CC winner in 1991, Crystal Rythem has twice won Best In Show at the Border Collie Club of Victoria's Championship shows.

SOUTH AUSTRALIA TODAY

Undoubtedly the big change in the breed in South Australia came in the late 1970s with the entry on to the scene of the very successful Victorian-bred bitch Ch. Tullaview Temptress, owned by Lynn and Bill Harrison of the Tullacrest kennel. Around the same time, John and Joyce Sullivan of the Kennoway kennel had success with locally-bred Ch. Cheryla Mac Spade, who helped considerably to strengthen the quality of dogs in the state. Mac Spade was the first dog owned by the Sullivans and he proved to be successful in the show ring, winning Dog CC at Adelaide Royal in 1979, 80, 83, 84, 85, as well as the Dog CC at the Sydney Royal in 1984 and Dog CC in Melbourne at the Royal in 1985. Mac Spade was a Specialty Best In Show winner.

The purchase of Ch. Tullaview Tarena firmly established the Kennoway kennel's breeding programme in the 1980s. Using Victorian and New South Wales stud dogs enhanced the state's success. The 1980s continued with Tullacrest kennel campaigning another successful bitch – this time Temptress's daughter, Ch. Tullacrest Be Tempted, who was also a Bitch CC winner at the Adelaide Royal and twice Bitch CC winner at the Royal Melbourne Show. The Kennoway kennel bred a grandson of Mac Spade, Aust. NZ Ch. Kennoway Colorado. Colorado, too, had a successful show career, including Best In Show at the Border Collie Club of Victoria's Championship Show in 1986 and Dog CC and Best Of Breed the same year at the Royal Melbourne Show.

Victorian-bred Ch. Finestyle Sundancer

Aust. NZ Ch. Loch-N-Legacy To Clan-Abby: Best in Show 1994 Adelaide Royal, runner-up Best in Show Adelaide Royal 1995, twice Best in Show at the Border Collie Club of Victoria's Ch. Shows.

dominated the Dog CCs at the Adelaide Royal from 1986 to 1990 while, as a youngster, Kennoway kennel's Ch. Kennoway Kiwi Connection was awarded Puppy In Show at the 1990 Melbourne Royal Show. Aust. NZ Ch. Kennoway Bailey's Bandit won the Dog CC at the Adelaide Royal in 1991, Dog CC Melbourne Royal 1989 and 1993, and Best In Show at the Perth Royal in 1991.

The 1992 Adelaide Royal saw Tullacrest kennel handling the Vos/Tullacrest's NZ import, Aust. NZ Gr. Ch. Clan-Abby Phantom-Of-Love, to take the Dog CC and later go through to Runner-up Best In Show. Two years later another Clan-Abby import, also handled by the Tullacrest kennel and in partnership with the Vos family, took the ultimate award of Best In Show. Aust. NZ Ch. Loch-N-Legacy To Clan-Abby was given the nod by Mr H. Lehtinen of Finland, and the following year, in 1995, he continued his success at Adelaide Royal with Best In Group and Runner-up Best In Show.

TASMANIA TODAY

The Sarasota kennel of Mrs Tull Lutrell was established in 1967. Many dogs from

NZ Ch. Beechwood Boots 'N All: Best in Show winner (all breeds and Specialty), Best in Show Border Collie Club of Victoria 1987.

Aust. NZ Ch. Trumagik Tartan Trekker.

the Sarasota kennel have become the foundations of leading kennels throughout Australia and New Zealand. These dogs include Ch. Sarasota Saretta (foundation bitch of the Rullion kennel, Victoria), Ch. Sarasota Talisman (Kenkoff kennel, Queensland, and proven as a valuable sire in that state), Sarasota Sarissa CDX (brood bitch for the Strathcarron kennel, NZ), Sarasota Sarah (foundation bitch for the Chatsworth and Aldyson kennels in Tasmania). Syd, Shirley and Allison Munton's Aldyson kennel became Tasmania's most consistent kennel since the early 1980s. Their foundation stock was based on the Sarasota and Crestvale lines, while the infusion of new Victorian lines produced their most successful male, Aust. NZ Ch. Aldyson Mac Duff. Duffy is an all-breeds Best In Show winner in Australia and New Zealand.

WESTERN AUSTRALIA TODAY

The breed in Western Australia has been greatly influenced by Victorian and New South Wales bloodlines. Dedicated breeders such as Max and Pat Johnson (Llanwnen kennel), Irene and Chris Lawton (Quickstar kennel) and Helena Fitzgerald (Borderfame kennel) have produced successful winners over the years. Ch. Quickstar Rough N Tough, Dog CC Perth Royal show and Best In Show winner, was one of Perth's top winning males in the mid to late 1980s. Aust. NZ. Ch. Borderfame Miss Muffin CDX, Best In Show at the Border Collie Club of WA and Bitch CC winner at the Perth Royal Show, is considered to be one of the greatest bitches in the history of the breed in Western Australia. Ch. Borderfame Bravo CDX AD is a multi-Best In Show winner all-breeds and has been a consistent winner throughout the 1990s.

QUEENSLAND TODAY

Queensland has had a recognised Breed Standard and has been awarding Challenge Certificates from as far back as 1950. Early breeders and kennels developed the breed with the infusion of bloodlines from New South Wales, Victoria, South Australia and New Zealand. Mrs Myrtle Layton's Gadgerrie kennel is Queensland's oldest-established kennel, started in 1967. 1986 saw the Queensland-bred bitch Bawntawn Simply Stunin (later to become an Australian Champion) win Puppy In Group and Opposite Sex To Champion Puppy In Show at the Brisbane Royal Show. Bred by Cheryl and Peter Brauers and owned by Noel and Maureen Kay,

NZ Ch. Aberdeenboy of Clan-Abby.

NZ Ch. Clan-Abby Lorna's Love.

Simply Stunin became the foundation bitch for the Trumagik kennel.

One of the most consistent winners in the early 1980s was Ron and Janice McKiernan's Ch. Induru Benjamin Boots. Twice Best In Show at the Cattle, Kelpie and Border Collie Club of Queensland Championship Shows, Ben was the McKiernans' first dog and proved to be a valuable stud dog, producing excellent type for their Cannyben kennel.

During the late 1980s and early 1990s, Queensland saw a locally-bred dog reach new highs in the show ring. A son of Ch. Induru Benjamin Boots, Mac, also known as Ch. Beechwood Boot's N All (bred by R. and J. Edwards and owned by R. and J. McKiernan), was a multi-Best In Show (All breeds and Specialty) winner. He also won Best In Show at the Border Collie Club of Victoria's Championship Show in 1987 as a junior. Other all-breeds Best In Show winners include locally-bred Ch. Gremaric Top Gun (bred and owned by Greg Richens), Ch. Aldyson King Billy

(bred in Tasmania and owned by Lyn Prowse, Townsville) and Ch. NZ Ch. Tamaari Go To The Devil (bred in South Australia and owned by Dell Keats).

In the mid-1990s the Bawntawn kennel imported Aust. NZ Ch. Joy's-Echo Of Clan-Abby, who has been a useful stud and a competitive show dog. Ch. Trumagik Star Trekker, a Royal Challenge winner and Top Border Collie in Queensland 1990, sired Queensland's top winning red and white bitch Ch. Trumagik Touch O Tartan. Touch O Tartan was later mated to her grandsire, which produced another top-winning Queensland-bred dog. Aust. NZ Ch. Trumagik Tartan Trekker began his show career with Puppy In Show at the Brisbane Royal Show 1994, Dog CC, Best Of Breed and Runner-Up Best In Group at the Brisbane Royal Show 1996. At the 1996 Sydney Royal Show his success continued, with Best In Group and Runner-Up Best In Show – the first Border Collie to achieve such heights at the Sydney Royal. Currently the top-winning Border Collie in Australia, Tartan Trekker has amassed 31 Best In Show wins at just three years of age.

NEW ZEALAND TODAY

In the early 1980s Mrs Maria Jackson of the Marclan kennel imported two wonderful bitches from the Tullaview kennel in Victoria belonging to the late Gary and Patrice Knight (now Patrice Smith). These two bitches were Aust. Ch. Tullaview Tierre (who later became a NZ Champion also) and Tullaview Miranda (who later became a NZ Aust. Champion). Other imports in the early 1980s from Victoria included males from the Crestvale kennel and, from similar bloodlines, a female from the Chiaroscuro kennel. The transmigration of dogs between Australia and New Zealand has been of great help in improving the quality of dogs in both countries. Many breeders and owners have taken advantage of the opportunity to send dogs between the countries to be campaigned, and to be utilised by breeders while visiting the other country. The 1980s and 1990s have seen a surge of imports from Australia which have visited New Zealand and offered some wonderful new bloodlines and attributes.

In the mid-1980s the Dornbrae kennel imported Merrybrook Sophie, a bitch from the UK who was brought out in whelp to Scottish-bred Eng. Show Ch. Melodor Flint At Dykebar. Also imported from Scotland was Muirend Border Scotsman, who proved valuable for his new bloodlines. The early 1980s saw the importation from Victoria of Rullion Joy (who later became a NZ and Aust. Ch), a top brood bitch for the Clan-Abby kennel. Joy has produced over ten Champions, including Ch. Thunderline Of Clan-Abby (Specialty Best In Show winner in the South Island) and Ch. Aberdeenboy Of Clan-Abby (Specialty Best In Show winner). Aberdeenboy was later mated to Ch. Clan-Abby Lorna Doone (daughter of the two Victorian imports, Cheviot Gay Lord and Cheviot Joanne) to produce NZ Eng. Show Ch. Clan-Abby Blue Aberdoone – the first Border Collie to be exported back to the UK. Thunderline was the sire of Ch. Clan-Abby Lorna's Love (NZ's first bitch to win a Runner-Up Best In Show all-breeds) and of NZ Fin. Show Ch. Clan-Abby Lorna's Kilt (the first Border Collie import in Finland).

Aust. Ch. Maghera Casanova (who later also became a NZ Champion) came to New Zealand to offer some new bloodlines and to obtain his NZ title. Casanova swept New Zealand by storm, amassing Best In Show (All breeds) and Specialty wins,

BELOW LEFT: Aust. NZ Grand Ch. Joy's Casanova O Clan-Abby.

BELOW RIGHT: Aust., NZ, S. Afr., Zim. Ch. Clan-Abby Casanova Too: Best of Breed National Dog Show 1988, 1989, 1990 and 1991, runner-up Best in Group 1989 and 1990, Best in Group in

*Aust NZ Grand Ch. Clan-Abby
Phantom of Love.*

concluding with Best Of Breed at the 1987 National Dog Show. The sire of over ten New Zealand Champions, his progeny include Aust. NZ Ch. Dajarra Lazer Lad (Best In Show at the Border Collie Club of NSW Championship Show, and Specialty Best In Show winner in NZ), Aust. NZ Ch. Joy's-Echo Of Clan-Abby, Aust. NZ Ch. Casanova Joy Of Clan-Abby, Aust. NZ Ch. Lazer Joy Of Clan-Abby and Aust. NZ. South African Zimbabwe Ch. Clan-Abby Casanova Too. Casanova Too followed in his sire's footsteps, winning Best Of Breed at the 1988 National Dog Show as well as Runner-Up Best In Group, the first time a Border Collie had won a Group award at the National Dog Show. Casanova Too won Best Of Breed at the National Dog Show in 1989, 1990 and 1991, also winning Runner-Up Best In

Group in 1990 and Best In Group in 1991. He later became an all breeds Best In Show winner in New Zealand and Zimbabwe, while making his mark in the South African show ring as well.

Aust. NZ Ch. Lazer Joy Of Clan-Abby was the first Border Collie to win an in-show award at the National Dog Show when, in 1989, she was awarded Intermediate In Group and Best Intermediate In Show. The first South Island-bred Border Collie to win a Best In Show award was Glen-Nevis Snow-Storm, bred by Katherine Stewart and Margaret Pantling. Since that time, Ch. Lochburn Simply X-Quisit has also won an all-breeds Best In Show. The breed had gained recognition in the show ring in New Zealand, and was now consistently winning at Group and in-show level.

When the award of Grand Champion was brought in by the NZ Kennel Club, the first collie of any breed to achieve this title was a Border Collie, Aust. NZ Grand Ch. Joy's-Casanova O Clan-Abby, granted in November 1993. This title was granted to a dog who had won three all-breed Best In Show awards at Championship Show level, as well as obtaining 50 Challenge Certificates. Since that time only one other Border Collie has been granted the Grand Champion title, namely Aust. NZ Grand Ch. Clan-Abby Phantom-Of-Love, who amassed over 21 all-breed Best In Show awards during his show career in Australia and New Zealand.

17 *HEALTH CARE*

For the dog's comfort, and in order to have a responsive working dog, it is essential to maintain a dog in as good health as possible. A dog that is undernourished or anaemic will tire easily and be unwilling to perform too many tasks. Similarly, the dog with aching hips, or a dull but constant pain from bad teeth, will become bad-tempered and quick to turn if it thinks that, by being touched, the pain will intensify. The veterinary surgeon will want to co-operate with you, as the owner of the Collie, in keeping the animal well for as long a natural life as possible, but the dog must be handled well when brought into the surgery to allow a full examination to be made. With large breeds the collection of blood samples for disease screening may be impossible unless the dog is first muzzled or well sedated, as the person withdrawing blood from the dog's forearm is placed in a very hazardous situation. Some veterinary surgeons prefer to collect samples from the jugular vein at the lower side of the neck and this is especially useful when larger volumes of blood are needed for analysis. Co-operate with your veterinary surgeon by attending for the annual booster vaccines and remember it is beneficial, on these visits, to allow the dog to be inspected for early signs of disease. Visits early on in life,

when there are no painful procedures and when rewards can be offered by the veterinary staff for good behaviour, will make future visits all the easier.

Between visits, you should inspect your dog for any changes in coat condition, for breath odour or for any unusual lumps or swellings. Daily brushing and grooming helps you to get to know the dog and pick up any early signs of disease. Improved diet and preventive vaccinations are contributing to a much longer life for all domestic animals. The dog's weight should be watched, and weighing at three-monthly intervals, if suitable scales can be found, helps to detect any gradual change in condition.

SELECTING VETERINARY CARE

The choice of a veterinary surgeon may be based on accessibility, especially if you like to walk your dog to the surgery. Dogs excited by car travel may be frustrated if, after a journey, they are deposited in a waiting-room full of other dogs' odours and no opportunities to work off their pent-up energy. If there is no practice nearby to which the dog can be walked, some people make enquiries from other Border Collie owners they meet before deciding which veterinary practice will have the greatest sympathy to their dog and their requirements for veterinary care. Treatment prices will vary and it is fairly easy to phone around and enquire the cost of a booster vaccine, or the cost of neutering, to judge the level of charges, especially if you are new to an area. Facilities in practices are not all the same, so a practice or veterinary hospital with 24-hour nursing staff residing on the premises and equipment for emergency surgery, will have to charge more than the smaller practice, which adequately provides for vaccination and other injections but requires you to go elsewhere for more complicated procedures.

GENERAL GROOMING AND HYGIENE

Border Collies have relatively easy coats to maintain but they do require daily grooming, especially at times when they are moulting. Knots in the coat are easier to remove when they have only been present for a short time rather than having been left for weeks or more. Grooming your dog is an ideal time to inspect the body closely, to look for any unexpected abnormalities and assess the general condition. The sooner a health problem is noticed, the quicker the vet can be asked for an opinion, and the better the chance of a full recovery in a progressive disease or a tumour.

The Border Collie puppy should be groomed from the earliest age so that the puppy will learn to associate such handling with being a pleasurable experience. Procedures will be easier to carry out if this is started early in life. If a dog is used to being handled in this way, it will be far easier for a veterinary surgeon to make an examination, and a visit to the surgery becomes less stressful for the owner as well as the dog. Before you start to groom the dog, carry out a thorough physical examination to check for any

abnormalities. Always start at the head end, as the hands are cleaner when looking at the orifices on the head, before handling the dog's feet and the anal region.

EYES: Inspect the eyes first for matter or discharges in the corner. There should be no excessive watering and the white of the eye should be briefly looked at to see that it is not red or discoloured. The surface of the eye should be clear and bright and the expression one of alertness. There are specific diseases that affect the eyes, so any abnormal signs should be noted and reported to the veterinary surgeon if necessary.

EARS: A painful ear can be a very irritating complaint for your dog, so the prevention of ear problems is important. If there is a noticeable build-up of wax in the ear canal, this can be easily removed by first softening the wax with an ear-cleaning fluid and then wiping gently with cotton wool. The use of cotton wool buds in the ear is discouraged and all cleaning should be the most gentle possible. There is a range of ear cleaners suitable for the Border Collie and the vet will advise on the one most appropriate for routine use.

If there is an excessive amount of wax in the canal, or if the ear is hot, reddened or swollen, this is an indication of infection or inflammation and veterinary attention should be sought quickly. Should an infection be left untreated, the dog will scratch the affected ear repeatedly, often introducing other infections carried on its soiled hind toenails. Oozing, and the multiplication of harmful bacteria in the moist discharges, will make the ear much worse and treatment becomes more difficult. In some dogs ulcers will be seen in the base of the wide open ear and any cold wind, or inadvertent touching of the ear, may make the dog cry out, having experienced a sharp pain.

MOUTH: Check your dog's gums each day for redness or inflammation. This can develop as the tartar builds up on the teeth and food particles get caught at the gum margin. The decaying food will produce breath odour if not removed and mouth bacteria can produce even worse halitosis. The teeth and gum margins have pain receptors, so any tartar build-up can lead to a disease which puts the dog off its food and even causes bad temper. With some Border Collies it may be difficult to examine the condition of the back molar teeth until the dog is given a general anaesthetic or a deep sedative.

Canine toothpastes are now available, which can be used to help prevent a build-up of tartar. If the dog's teeth are cleaned regularly, you will avoid a state of dental neglect so advanced that your Border Collie needs a general anaesthetic to have the teeth scaled and polished at the veterinary practice. Start brushing a dog's teeth at about four months of age but avoid the areas where the permanent teeth are about to erupt. At first, the puppy will want to play but, little by little, will become used to having all its teeth cleaned while young and small, rather than waiting until you have a fully-grown dog that objects to the procedure.

Puppies lose their milk teeth between four and six months and sore gums will be apparent at that age. Massaging the skin just below the eye will help when the molar teeth are about to erupt. While grooming the older dog, look for signs of abnormalities such as mouth warts, excess saliva or white froth at the back of the mouth.

NOSE: Again, remove any discharges and look for cracking or fissuring. There is little point in worrying about a 'cold wet nose' as a health indicator.

SKIN AND COAT: Examine the whole of your dog's body when grooming. Tell-tale black dirt or white scurf may indicate a parasite infection. Patches of hair loss, redness of skin and abnormal lumps may first be found during grooming. Your Border Collie's coat will normally have a slight shine, and oil from the sebaceous glands will give it water-proofing grease that gives the smooth feel as the hand is run over the hair.

NAILS AND FEET: Nails should be worn short, as over-long nails may splinter painfully, especially in cold weather when the nail is brittle. If the dog is regularly walked on hard surfaces such as concrete, paving stones or rocks, the nails will wear down naturally. Tarmac and grass does little to wear nails down at exercise times. If the nails are left to become too long, they are difficult for the dog to wear down; the heel takes more of the weight of the leg and the nails may split, with painful consequences.

Clipping nails is a delicate task. If you cut too short, into the quick, blood will flow and the dog will find it painful. The dog may then become very wary of anyone who tries to get near its feet with nail clippers held in the hand. Exercising the dog on concrete may be safer for the beginner than attempting to cut across the nail with new, sharp clippers.

Make a habit of feeling the area between the toes, where tufts of hair attract sticky substances. Clay soils can form little hard balls between the toes, and tar or chewing gum can be picked up on a walk with equally damaging effect. You will notice any cuts and pad injuries when handling the feet for grooming.

PERINEUM AND GENITAL AREA: Check for swollen anal sacs or unexpected discharges. Segments of tapeworms might be seen near the rectum. The bitch's vulva should not discharge except when signs of her being on heat are present. The prepuce of the male dog should have no discharge and the penis should not protrude, except if the dog is unwisely excited during the grooming or handling.

GROOMING: Once the first physical examination has been carried out, a grooming routine for the Border Collie should be followed. Here is one I recommend, based on a large kennel which trains working dogs:
1. Using your finger-tips massage the coat against the normal backward lie of the hairs. This will loosen up the dead hairs and encourage the skin to secrete the sebum oil that gives the healthy shine.
2. Use a bristle brush, to pick up the hair you have loosened, again working against the lie of the coat.
3. Using a metal-toothed comb, you can now work your way in a methodical order over the dog's body, combing with the lie of the coat, paying particular attention to the feathering down the hind legs, tail and around the neck and ears.
4. Finally, to finish, bring a shine to the coat; use a bristle brush down the back and limbs. Brush the neck and head, praising the dog or offering a small food reward.

PREVENTATIVE CARE

VACCINATIONS
The use of vaccines to prevent disease is well-established for human as well as for animal health. The longer life expectancy of the animal, and the comparative rarity of puppy disease and early death, is something that has become taken for granted in the last 40 years. Yet many older dog breeders remember the very ill puppies that died of distemper fits or were left twitching with chorea for the rest of their lives. The appearance of parvovirus in 1979 was an unpleasant shock to those who thought that veterinary treatment could deal with all puppy diarrhoeas. There were many deaths in puppies under 12 months old until the use of vaccines gave protection. Some died of sudden heart failure caused by the parvo virus damaging the heart muscle. Immunity would protect the puppy, either through their mother's milk, or by the early use of vaccines to stimulate the puppy's own body defences as they became old enough to respond to an injected vaccine.

The vet is the best person to advise on the type of vaccine to use and at what age to give it, since vets have a unique knowledge of the type of infection prevalent in a locality and when infection is likely to strike.

An example of this is in the Guide Dogs for the Blind Association's breeding programme where, for over 25 years, early vaccination was given to the six-week-old puppy. No isolation after this early vaccination was needed. The procedure was contrary to general advice given in the 60s and 70s when puppy disease was at an acceptably low figure. Later, when parvovirus infection was widespread in the early 80s, the mortality rate of GDBA puppies was much lower than among the puppies of breeders who had kept their puppies in kennels until 12 weeks or longer before selling them. The temperament of some breeds was also suspect, due to a longer enforced isolation after vaccination. Proper socialisation did not take place, as the new owners of such puppies were advised not to take them out until four months of age when a final parvo booster had to be given. This meant that there were no opportunities to mix with people and other dogs, until an age when the older puppy had already developed a fear of being handled by strangers or was suspicious of other dogs met outside the home.

DISTEMPER: Always considered the classical virus disease, it has become very rare where vaccine is used on a regular basis. From time to time distemper is seen in larger cities, where there is a stray or roaming dog population unprotected by vaccination. This may subsequently lead to infection of show, or other kennel dogs, that do not have a high level of immunity.

The virus has an incubation of seven to 21 days and infection is followed by a rise in temperature, loss of appetite, a cough and often diarrhoea. Discharges from the eyes and nose may be watery at first but often become thick mucoid with a green or creamy colour due to secondary infections. The teeth are affected when the puppy of under six months of age is infected by the virus; enamel defects shown as brown marks last for life and are known as 'distemper teeth'.

The 'hard pad' strain seen in the 60s is now considered to be nothing more than the hyperkeratosis of the nose and footpads that occurs after all distemper infections; the name is still in use when dog illness is written or talked about. In over half of all dogs affected with distemper, damage to the nervous system will show as fits, chorea (twitching of muscles) or posterior paralysis. Old dogs may develop encephalitis (ODE) due to latent distemper virus in the nervous tissue.

The vaccines in use today are all modified live vaccines and are highly effective in preventing disease. The age for a first injection will partly depend on the maker's instruction sheet and partly on a knowledge of the amount of protection passed by the mother to the young puppies. Maternally derived immunity (MDI) might block the vaccine in the young puppy, but blood sampling bitches during their pregnancy was used as a method of estimating how soon the puppy would respond to vaccine. The use of a first vaccine at six weeks is now becoming more widespread; this allows for the all-important early socialisation period of the puppy's development.

PARVOVIRUS: This is probably the second most important virus disease and, like distemper, is largely preventable by the correct use of vaccination. The speed with which an infection could spread from kennel to kennel surprised many, but the disease is caused by a very tough virus that can be carried on footwear that has walked though virus-infected faeces. The virus may then persist for up to a year; it is untouched by many commonly-used kennel disinfectants. The sudden death of puppies caused by damage to the heart muscle, often just after sale, is no longer seen but the gastro-enteritis form still occurs.

The sudden illness takes the form of repeated vomiting in the first 24 hours followed by profuse, watery diarrhoea, often with a characteristic sour smell and a red-brown colour. The cause of death was often from the severe dehydration that accompanied this loss of fluid. However, once it was understood that puppies should be treated with intravenous fluids similar to the treatment of human cholera victims, the death rate fell. Fluids by mouth are sufficient in less severe cases, provided they replace the essential electrolytes. The traditional mixture of a level teaspoonful of salt and a dessert-spoonful of glucose in two pints of water has saved many lives.

Vaccination of the young puppy is recommended, although the MDI may partially block the effectiveness of the vaccine, as is seen with distemper. A live vaccine at six weeks, followed by a further dose at 12 weeks, will protect most puppies. The four-month booster is no longer in common use, but it is now more usual to see parvovirus in the recently weaned puppy or the five-month-old puppy, where immunity no longer protects that individual against infection.

HEPATITIS: This disease, produced by an adenovirus, is now quite rare but one form (CVA-2) is often associated with 'kennel cough' infection in dogs. After infection, the virus multiplies in the lymphatic system and then sets out to damage the lining of the blood vessels. It was for this reason that the cause of death was liver failure, so the name hepatitis was given as, on post mortem, the liver was seen to be very swollen and engorged with blood. Other organs are also damaged and about 70 per cent of recovered dogs are found to have kidney damage. The eye damage known as 'blue eye' seen on recovery is not recognised in the Border Collie but was quite common in certain other breeds. Vaccination at six and 12 weeks, using a reliable vaccine that contains the CAV-2 virus, is very effective as a prevention against this disease.

LEPTOSPIROSIS: Caused by bacteria, it differs from the previous group of viral infections as protection has to be provided by at least two doses of a killed vaccine, and a 12-monthly repeat dose of this vaccine is essential if the protection is to be maintained. The type of leptospirosis spread by rats is the most devastating to the dog and frequently results in jaundice, then death from kidney and liver failure unless early treatment with antibiotics is available.

The other serotype of leptospira that damages the dog's kidney is less often seen since vaccination and annual boosters have been regularly used. Gun dogs and dogs such as Border Collies, that walk and work in the country where rats may have contaminated water courses, are especially at risk, although sometimes dogs kept entirely in kennels may be affected if rats cross the exercise yards and leave infected

urine for the dog to sniff at or lick up.

KENNEL COUGH: As a troublesome infection that causes harsh coughing in dogs, originating from the trachea and bronchial tubes, kennel cough has become one of the best known diseases. Traditionally dogs became infected in boarding kennels but it has recently been suggested it should be called 'infectious bronchitis', as any dog coming within droplet infection distance of another dog coughing at a show, or in public exercise areas, may catch the illness. There are five known viral and bacterial agents that may all, or perhaps only two of them at a time, cause the disease known as kennel cough. Vaccination by nose drops of a Bordetella vaccine can give protection, and these drops are often given just a week before a dog goes into kennels. The normal booster vaccine given contains protection for three of the other known causes.

The disease develops within four to seven days of infection, so it may not be seen until after a dog has just left the kennels. The deep harsh cough is often described as 'if a bone or something was stuck in the throat'. The dog coughs repeatedly. Even with treatment, coughs last for 14 days but in some dogs the cough lasts as long as six weeks. Infection may then persist in the trachea, and if the dog is a 'carrier', it may get subsequent bouts of coughing if stressed. This explains why some non-coughing dogs put into board may cause an outbreak of kennel cough. Once only a summer-time disease, kennel cough outbreaks now occur at any time of the year, often after a holiday period when more dogs than usual are boarded

RABIES: The virus disease is almost unknown to most UK veterinarians due to a successful quarantine policy that has kept the island free of rabies in dogs and in wild life such as foxes. Inactivated rabies vaccine is available in the UK; it has been used for many years in dogs intended for export. Elsewhere in the world, both live attenuated vaccines and inactivated vaccines are used on an annual basis.

BOOSTERS: Thanks to the development of effective canine vaccines by the pharmaceutical industry, most of the diseases described above are now uncommon in Europe and North America. The need for an annual booster is essential to keep up a high level of immunity where killed vaccines are used, and with live virus vaccines it probably does no harm to inject repeat doses every year. It is easy to become complacent about the absence of infectious disease in Border Collies and it is false economy to overlook the need for revaccination.

PARASITES

INTERNAL PARASITES
ROUNDWORMS: The most common worm in puppies and dogs up to one year of age are *Toxocara* and *Toxascaris*. Puppies with roundworms will start to pass worm eggs into the environment as early as three weeks and most eggs are released when puppies are about seven weeks of age. This is the most dangerous time for the exercise areas to be contaminated with eggs, and for any young children who play with the puppies to get the slightly sticky worm eggs on their hands. Then they may lick their fingers and consequently catch *Zoonotic Toxocariasis*.

   Adult dogs also pass roundworms, which might be seen emerging from the rectum of the nursing bitch that develops diarrhoea. Worms may also appear in the vomit, if the worm moves forward from the intestine into the stomach by accident.

   Control of worms depends on frequent dosing of young puppies – from as early as

two weeks of age and repeated every two to three weeks until they are three months old. To prevent puppies carrying worms, the pregnant bitch can be wormed from the 42nd day of pregnancy with a safe, licensed wormer such as fenbendazole. The wormer can be given daily to the bitch until the second day after all the puppies have been born. Routine worming of adults twice a year, with a combined tablet for round and tapeworms, is a good preventative measure. If there are young children in a household, even more frequent worm dosing may be advisable to reduce the risk of roundworm larvae migrating to the child and possible subsequent eye damage.

TAPEWORMS: They are not known to kill dogs but the appearance of a wriggling segment coming through the rectum, or moving on the tail hair, is enough to deter all but the most unsqueamish dog lover. Responsible, regular worming of dogs is needed, to avoid the harm that dog worms can do to other creatures. The biggest threat is from the *Echinococcus* worm that a dog obtains if feeding from raw sheep offals. The worm is only six millimetres long but several thousand could live in one dog. If a human should swallow a segment of this worm it may move to the person's liver or lungs, in the same way as it would in the sheep. A major illness would be the unpleasant result, another example of a zoonotic infection.

   The most frequently found tapeworm is *Dipylidium caninum*. It is not a long tapeworm compared with the old-fashioned *Taenia* worms, but when segments break off they may be recognised, as they resemble grains of rice attached to the hairs of the dog's tail. The tapeworm has become more common in dogs and cats since the number of fleas has increased; the intermediate host of this worm is the flea or the louse. When dogs groom themselves they attempt to swallow any crawling insect on the skin's surface and, in this way, may become infested with tapeworms even though worming twice a year is carried out. Flea control is just as important as worming in preventing tapeworm infection. Three-monthly dosing with tablets is a good idea – less frequently if the dog is known to be away from sources of reinfection. The other tapeworms of the *Taenia* species come from dogs eating raw rabbits (*T. serialis* or *pisiformis*) or from sheep, cattle or pig offals (*T. ovis, hydatigena* or *multiceps*).

HOOKWORMS: These are less frequently found as a cause of trouble in the UK but are prevalent in other parts of the world. The hookworm does damage to the intestine by using its teeth on its lining. *Uncinaria* may be the cause of poor condition and thinness. Diarrhoea is seen as permanently soft, discoloured faeces that can respond dramatically to worming. The other hookworm, *Ancylostoma*, may be found to be the reason for anaemia and weakness. Exercising dogs over grass used by wild foxes for excretion and scent marking allows the dog to reinfect itself with hookworm eggs.

OTHER INTERNAL PARASITES: *Giardia* is a parasite that occurs in dogs in kennels. It should be investigated in dogs with diarrhoea that have come through quarantine or those that have been kennelled. It is a protozoal organism that likes to live in stagnant surface water; it is of especial interest because a similar strain is a cause of dysentery in humans, especially where water-borne infection is blamed for the illness. It may be necessary routinely to treat all dogs in kennels with a drug such as fenbendazole to prevent a continuing problem. Whipworms are found in the large intestine and are identified when faeces samples are

examined after mucoid dysentery affects a dog. Treatment is effective using a reliable anthelminthic. Heartworms are unknown in most parts of the UK but are a great problem in other countries. Bladder worms are only detected when urine samples are examined; they are similar to the Whipworms and fortunately are rare. Any obscure illness in a dog should require the examination of fresh faeces samples.

ECTOPARASITES

External parasites may cause intense irritation and skin diseases from scratching and rubbing. In recent years the cat flea has become by far the most common ectoparasite of Border Collies, but more traditional sarcoptic mange, lice and ringworm skin infections do appear from time to time. Demodectic mange may have a hereditary basis as it is seen more frequently in certain strains and litters.

FLEAS: The flea that hops may never be found in the Border Collie's coat but its presence may be detected by the flea dirt or excreta containing dried blood. Grooming your dog over white paper or a light table top may reveal black bits that turn dark red like blood spots when moistened. Once the flea dirt is found, a closer inspection of the dog may show fleas running though the coat at skin level. At one time the fleas preferred to live in the hair down the spine towards the tail root but now they are found in the shorter hairs of the abdomen or the neck. This may relate to the fact that cat fleas are the most commonly found variety in dogs. Such fleas prefer a softer hair structure for their 'living space'. All fleas are temporary visitors who like to feed from the dog by biting to suck blood, but in their development and egg-laying stages they may live freely off the dog thereby escaping some of the parasitic dressing put on their host's coat. Re-infestation then becomes possible and many flea treatments appear to be ineffective unless the flea in the environment is eliminated at the same time.

There is a wide range of antiparasitic sprays, washes and baths available and the Border Collie owner may well be confused as to how and when to apply these. There is the further problem that some dogs seem able to carry a few fleas on them with very little discomfort, while others show intense irritation and will bite pieces out of themselves in an attempt to catch the single flea. A cat in the household or crossing the garden may drop flea eggs, and in a warm place they can hatch out and develop into more fleas waiting to jump onto the dog.

Flea eggs and immature larvae may lie dormant for months waiting to complete their development and become ready to bite. Adult fleas too can wait for months off an animal until able to find a host to feed from, so treating the dog is only tackling part of the problem; the kennels or the house has to be treated as well. Vacuum cleaning and easy-to-clean sleeping quarters for the dog help enormously in dealing with a flea infestation once an environmental spray has been applied. The choice of aerosol spray, medicated bath, tablet by mouth or agent that stops larval development is a wide one, and experience will show which method is most suitable for each dog affected.

LICE: These may be found in the dog's coat occasionally – especially in a dog leading an outdoor life, more than the average pet dog. Lice spend their whole life on the dog and fairly close contact between dogs is necessary to spread the parasites. Large numbers of lice cause intense irritation with hair loss. Biting lice can produce anaemia when they are present in large enough numbers to remove blood continuously, at a rate similar to a bleeding ulcer. Liquid treatments applied as a total bath soak are best. Lice eggs can be transmitted from dog to dog on grooming brushes. The lice and their eggs are visible to the naked eye, and should be spotted during the normal grooming routine.

MANGE MITES: These mites cannot be seen during grooming. If they are suspected, scrapings from the skin surface are sent for examination under the microscope. The two forms of mange, *Sarcoptes* and *Demodex,* can be distinguished in this way, but bare skin patches of low-grade mange infection may at first seem similar when a dog is examined. There are a number of differences in the two forms of mange, and blood tests are now available to aid diagnosis, but one simple distinction is that sarcoptic mange is very itchy and spreads from dog to dog, while demodectic mange in the older dog usually remains as a scaly, hairless patch and, although an obvious blemish, does not cause a lot of itching. Antiparasitic baths with pyrethroids or amitraz, and topical applications of organophosphorous washes will have to be repeated, but are usually effective.

TICKS: Ticks are large enough not to be missed and can be expected in those dogs working where sheep, hedgehogs etc. leave tick eggs about. Applications of pyrethroid or other 'spot' liquids on the neck and rump will keep ticks off a dog for a month. Baths are also effective. Ticks may be removed by first soaking them in vegetable oil, then gently coaxing and lifting the tick's head away from the dog's skin. Ticks can carry very serious infections, and should therefore be dealt with promptly and disposed of carefully.

CHEYLETIELLA: These cause surface irritation of dogs and intense itching in humans living with the dogs who happen to get bitten. The so-called 'moving dandruff' show up as white flecks on a black dog's skin, but may be more difficult to see on a light-coloured dog. Antiparasitic shampoos will kill the surface feeders but carrier dogs in kennels may show very few symptoms at all.

MALASEZZIA: This is a yeast-like surface organism that appears in dogs with low resistance to infection. A patchy coat and dull hair should make the Border Collie owner suspect the presence of yeasts in unusually large numbers. Once identified, baths and general hygiene, with improved nutrition, help the dog to overcome this problem. The yeast will also be found in the ear canal and if shown to be present on a stained smear in large numbers, then the ear should be treated with a suitable preparation of Miconazole, Nystatin and Malaseb shampoo.

RINGWORM: Ringworm is found in dogs as a fungal infection of the hair. The signs of a 'ring' are not always present, and some dogs show quite a violent itchy skin response once infected. Cattle ringworm can be transmitted to country dogs. Ringworm spores can remain in the environment and in old woodwork for a long time. Diagnosis by skin tests is slow but reliable, as the 'Woods' lamp, which uses ultraviolet light, does not identify all types of ringworm. Treatment with anti-fungal washes, or the antibiotic griseofulvin, may be used to eliminate the mycotic infection.

ACCIDENTS AND FIRST AID
A few simple procedures described here do not suggest that there are no other things that can be done as 'first aid', but in most cases the sooner the patient gets to the veterinary surgery, the better the chance of a full recovery. For this reason, splinting broken bones is now out of favour, and more pain may be caused in trying to tie on a splint than if the dog is quickly transported to a place where any shock and pain can be treated professionally. X-rays will better show the nature of a fracture and what is the best method of treatment.

TRAFFIC ACCIDENTS: Border Colllies, being solid dogs, seldom go underneath vehicles but they tend to get severe chest injuries if hit in front, or pelvic and limb injuries if struck on the side. Fractures of the long bones of the leg are another common result of injury with a fast-moving car. Any dog hit by a car will be distressed and because of fright and pain will tend to bite, even when its familiar owners are present to attempt to help. First, assess the injuries by noting any gaping holes and where blood is being lost. Do this before touching the dog's head. Some frightened dogs may try to run away at that point, so a lead or scarf round the neck will help to steady the dog, and a tape muzzle may have to be used before a dog is lifted into a vehicle for transport to the surgery.

A pressure bandage applied to a bleeding area is the best way of staunching blood flow, but improvisation with whatever cloth is to hand is acceptable in a life-saving situation. The dog may be breathing rapidly or gasping with 'air hunger' signs. In this case, the mouth and nostrils should be wiped free of dried blood or saliva to help unblock the airway. If you suspect a spinal injury, slide a board under the dog before picking it up. Otherwise, a blanket is the best way of allowing two or more persons to pick up an injured dog without aggravating the injuries.

CHOKING AND VOMITING: Try to find out the cause of any sudden attack. Grass awns may enter the throat and airways in the summer months, and at any time of year a dog that has been playing ball or stick retrieval games may get an obstruction at the back of the throat. Even a fine bamboo cane may become wedged across the upper molar teeth. In the case of one gundog that had been out shooting all day, a length of cane was retrieved from the upper part of the oesophagus the same evening. Poisonous substances may cause retching and vomiting; and thirsty dogs have been known to drink from toilet bowls and unsuspectingly drink bleach and other cleaning substances.

Having initially looked for a foreign body, your first aid measures should be aimed at providing as good an air supply as possible. If there is any blistering or soreness of the lips or tongue, use honey or salad oil to coat the inflamed surfaces. A vomiting dog should be prevented from drinking water and regurgitating it as fast as it is swallowed. Ice cubes in a dish left to melt may be a way of helping the dog, as it will drink the iced water more slowly.

COLLAPSE AND UNCONSCIOUSNESS: As in the road accident, assess the dog before touching to determine the cause of the incident, so that appropriate first aid can be given. The dog running in a field on a warm day may have had a circulatory collapse; the dog convulsing may be throwing an epileptic fit. The elderly dog found semi-conscious in the morning after voiding urine and faeces may have had a 'stroke' or vestibular disease. Each condition in turn will need different treatment, but, as a general rule, pull the tongue forward to ensure there is an airway to the lungs, keep the animal cool and avoid unnecessary noise and commotion. Look for any drugs or poisons that a dog may have swallowed, gently feel the left side for gas distending the abdomen, and check the pupils of the eyes and their response to a bright light. The veterinary surgeon will be better able to deal with the situation if a timetable of events, and any contributing factors, can be given to him in a concise manner.

INSECT STINGS: Stings occur more often in the late summer. Usually the foot swells rapidly or, if the dog has caught a wasp in its mouth, the side of the face swells up and the eye may become partly shut. Vinegar is a traditional remedy to apply to the sting area. If an antihistamine tablet is available, this can be given to the dog immediately to stop further swelling. Biting flies cause swellings on the body and may be the cause of the 'hot spots' or acute moist eczemas that Border Collies can suffer from. Calamine lotions cool the skin but the dog should be discouraged from attacking its own skin, because, if licked, calamine causes vomiting.

SHOCK: This occurs to a greater or lesser extent with nearly all accidents. Keep the patient warm, wrapping a blanket, coat or wool garment around the body of the dog. Unless you have reasons to think an anaesthetic will be given, or other contra-indications exist such as throat damage, offer fluids by mouth in small quantities. Oral rehydration solutions can be obtained from the veterinary surgeon and a packet should be kept in every emergency first aid kit. As an alternative, a solution of half a teaspoon of salt and half a teaspoon of bicarbonate of soda dissolved in a litre of water may be given, a few dessert-spoonfuls at a time.

SKIN DISEASES

Fleas are probably still the most common problem. Flea bites may not be obvious, especially in a dense-coated breed. Once a dog becomes sensitised to the proteins injected by the flea when it first bites, any subsequent contact with flea saliva may bring on an itchy rash, even though no live fleas are found on the dog. The various other causes of parasitic skin disease have already been outlined in the section on external parasites.

OTHER PRURITIC SKIN CONDITIONS:

Anal sac irritation will cause a dog to nibble at the hair around the tail base, or it may cause licking and nibbling anywhere around the hindquarters. The glands may be so impacted that they cannot be emptied out during the dog's normal straining to pass faeces. An infected lining of one or both sacs may also be the cause of irritation, and this can often be detected by a fruity odour to the sac's contents or, at its worst, a smell like rotten meat.

Bacterial dermatoses result from multiplication of skin bacteria such as *Staph. intermedius*. Red blotches and ring-like marks around a central pustule are most clearly seen when the hairless areas of the abdomen are inspected. Skin swabs may be used to identify the bacteria present, and this information can then be used to choose the most appropriate antibiotic for the infection causing the irritation.

HAIR LOSS AND ALOPECIA:

A Collie's coat is normally shed twice a year, but sometimes the growth of new hair is delayed and the coat appears thin, lifeless and, if it is groomed excessively, bare patches develop. Investigations into the possibility of thyroid disease may be needed when there is a failure of hair to grow. Other hormonal skin disease may cause symmetrical hair loss in the flanks of a bitch, or bare tail-head areas (stud tail) in some dogs. Feminisation of the older male dog will have hair loss as one of the signs of a Sertoli cell tumour. Veterinary advice should be sought.

DIGESTIVE DISORDERS
SICKNESS AND DIARRHOEA:

Occasional sickness is not a cause for concern in the younger dog. The dog is adapted to eating a wide range of different foods, and part of its protection against food poisoning is the ability to reject unsuitable foods by returning them from the stomach by reflex vomiting. If there is a yellow coloration to the vomit, it means that the bile from the liver, which normally passes into the small intestine after leaving the bile duct, has, for some reason, been passed forward to enter the stomach. The bitter bile acids will cause reflex vomiting as soon as they reach the stomach wall, and will be sicked up, together with any food left in the stomach.

Bacterial infections, such as those of *Salmonella* and *Campylobacter* can only be detected by the culture of faeces. The importance of strains of *E. coli* in the cause of dog diarrhoea is an interesting development; renewed interest in this organism that was, at one time, thought to be harmless, is accompanied by human deaths from the 057 strain found in cooked and raw meat.

Repeated sickness, starting off with recognisable food followed by slime, or food followed by mucus alone, is a more serious sign. It may be associated with obstructions due to a foreign body, or to infection such as pyometra or hepatitis. Some outbreaks of diarrhoea will start with food being vomited, as this will stimulate the intestine. As soon as food enters the small intestine, the stomach empties itself reflexly, by vomiting any food remaining within the stomach. Sometimes a reversal of the normal flow of food will cause the appearance of a faecal vomit.

Diarrhoea is the passage of frequent loose or unformed faeces: it is associated with infections and irritation of the intestine. The rapid transit of food taken in by mouth means that water cannot be absorbed by the large intestine, and soft or runny stools result from the incomplete digestion and water reabsorption. When blood is present it may appear as streaks from the large intestine. If blackish and foul-smelling, it means that the blood has come from the small intestine and has been subjected to some of the digestive fluids. The blood condition is then known as dysentery.

Chronic diarrhoea is a problem where the looseness of faeces lasts more than 48 hours. It may be associated with malabsorption, where the lining of the intestine is incapable of absorbing digested food. There are other diseases such as food intolerances, bacterial overgrowth, lymphoid and other tumours that may cause maldigestion, where there is some failure of the digestive juices to breakdown the food. Other causes are exocrine pancreatic insufficiency (EPI), inflammatory bowel diseases, or any disturbance in gastric or liver function. Investigations by the veterinary surgeon will include blood tests and faecal laboratory examinations. These may be followed by X-rays or endoscope examinations.

The treatment of sickness and diarrhoea involves, firstly, withholding solid food for 24 hours, giving small quantities of replacement fluids as soon as the dog stops vomiting (proprietary electrolyte fluids are probably best), then introducing a highly digestible food (with low fat is best) in small quantities – about one third of the normal amount fed on the second day of the illness. The amount should be increased slowly until, by the fourth day, a full ration of food is given again. In the recovery period fats should be avoided, as well as milk and dairy products, because of the dog's inability to digest lactose.

GASTRIC DILATION: This disease is better known as bloat, and 'torsion' can be a problem in any of the larger breeds. It is especially associated with feeding regimes where a highly digestible food can be swallowed rapidly and, if this is followed by the drinking of large quantities of water, the situation contributes to the development of the bloat. Feeding immediately after strenuous exercise has been blamed too. When a dog is fed with a meal in the late afternoon or evening, there is the greater risk of the dog lying down, so that abdominal movement associated with walking or jumping up does not allow for eructation, or the dispersal of gas from the stomach. Greedy feeders that swallow air as they gulp down their food are considered at greatest risk, but it does seem associated with the flat slab-chest dogs that have large deep chests and thus loosely suspended stomachs.

The bloated stomach may rotate as a 'torsion' or volvulus, and become the gastric dilation and volvulus condition known as GDV, which means an acute emergency. The dog needs to be rushed to the veterinary surgery for treatment of shock and for the deflation of the stomach. Affected dogs seem uncomfortable, become depressed and look at their flanks with expressions of disbelief. At first, the left side just behind the ribs is the only side to bulge; percussion with the finger tips will produce a drum-like resonance over the left ribcage edge and over the distended abdomen behind. Within a few hours both sides of the abdomen appear distended behind the ribcage, the dog becomes more uncomfortable and lies down a lot as the pain increases. The gas-filled stomach presses on the diaphragm restricting the breathing, the colour of the tongue becomes more purplish and breaths are more frequent and quite shallow. Some time at this stage, the weight of the enlarging spleen attached to the greater curvature of the gas-filled stomach makes the stomach twist in a clockwise direction.

The signs of discomfort become more noticeable as the stomach's exit to the oesophagus is pinched off by a 180-degree rotation. If a stomach tube is passed through the mouth down the oesophagus at this stage the tube can be pressed down no further than just beyond the entrance level of the oesophagus into the abdomen. No gas will pass back up the tube, even though the stomach is still tight-filled with gas.

Emergency treatment at the veterinary surgery will usually mean setting up an intravenous drip to deal with the shock. Decompression of the stomach will be attempted, possibly first by passing the stomach tube as described above or, probably more successfully, by inserting a wide bore (18 G needle) canula at the point behind the left rib arch that shows the most distension by the gas. The finger should then be kept on the needle hub protruding through the skin, partially to hold it in place as the size of the stomach reduces, and partially to vent the gas out slowly or in pulses. This ensures that the blood in the veins can start to flow towards the heart again, once the abdomen size returns to normal.

Frequently a laparotomy will be necessary to empty the stomach or to provide a means of fixing the stomach to the abdominal wall so that an adhesion will make it less likely that the gas distension will again appear. A number of operation techniques are used; some involve suturing the stomach wall to a rib, while others rely on a tube to vent gas from the stomach, and the aim is to have a permanent adhesion to prevent rotation of the stomach at a later date. Some veterinary surgeons believe that feeding a complete canned food diet to the dog is the best preventive available.

CONSTIPATION: This disorder usually occurs either through the dog eating too many bones whose chalky residue clogs up the rectum, or, in older male dogs, it may be associated with enlargement of the prostate gland. Occasionally a tumour inside the rectum will cause straining and apparent constipation. Treatment with oily lubricants and enemas should be followed by high-fibre diets. Soluble fibre, as found in oatmeal, is thought to add to the moist faecal bulk and thus retain water from the large intestine lumen, so that the faeces are not bone-hard and painful to pass. Allow exercise, or place the dog in the garden 30 minutes after feeding, as this will stimulate the reflexes for normal defecation.

BREEDING AND REPRODUCTION

There are no specific problems in the Border Collie and both mating and whelping should proceed with the minimum of trouble (see Chapter 13 Breeding Border Collies).

THE OLDER BORDER COLLIE

GERIATRIC CARE: Border Collies are a relatively long-lived breed: 12 to 15 years of age was considered a good age for a working dog but a number may be able live to 17 years or more, provided they avoid arthritis and injuries. The tendency for older Border Collies to eat less is more common than in other breeds where, if the food is available, overeating leads to adiposity and will significantly shorten the dog's life. Some of the oldest dogs are the leanest dogs, so dietary control helps if you wish your dog to live longer. After about 12 years of age it may be of advantage to divide the daily ration into two small feeds to help absorption and digestion; any tendency to overweight must be checked and regular weighing helps to control the dietary intake. The older dog will use up less energy in exercise and, if housed for most of the day, fewer calories will be burned up to keep the dog warm. Some reduction in calorie intake is desirable and there are special diets prepared for the older dog that are higher in fibre and lower in energy than the diet for the younger dog,

Keep a careful watch on the condition of the mouth as breath odour is one of the first signs of dental disease or of decay of food trapped between the gums and 'ledges' of tartar that may have built up on the teeth. Border Collies may have cracked teeth from chewing bones, or iron bars, earlier in their life, and only in old age does the tooth root become infected and an abscess develop. The back upper molar teeth are often affected and an abscess will show as a swelling immediately below the eye if the carnassial tooth has infected roots. Chewing as a form of jaw exercise is a method of keeping the teeth healthy, but when there is a build-up of plaque on the tooth surface, cleaning the teeth using an ultrasonic scaler, followed by a machine polisher, is the better way of keeping a healthy mouth.

Monitor the length of your dog's nails, since less exercise and possible arthritis sometimes lead the older dog to put less weight on the affected leg and nail overgrowth occurs. Careful trimming to avoid cutting into the 'quick', or live part of the nail, will help many older Collies. The elbows, too, should be inspected for calluses on their outer side, as dogs that are stiff do not move as often as they might to relieve their body weight on the surface they sleep on. The skin over the outside of the elbow has little padding from fat or muscle and bone lies just underneath, so leathery skin or a callus can easily occur. In extreme cases the callus develops cracks and fissures and a bacterial infection is set up so that the surface becomes pink and oozing.

URINARY INCONTINENCE: This is one of the problems found in many older dogs. Leakage from the bladder, resulting in damp patches in the bedding overnight, may be remedied by taking up the water bowl after 7pm to prevent evening drinking. Also effective is the use of one of the sympathomimetic group of drugs to promote bladder storage. A urine sample should be examined: sometimes a mild cystitis bacterium will be found in the urine. Treatment with an appropriate antibiotic will reduce bladder sensitivity and storage will be better. If large quantities of urine are being voided day and night, then investigation of urine-concentrating powers and blood biochemistry tests are necessary, to look for major disease. Diabetes insipidus or mellitus, Cushing's disease, liver disease and nephrosis may all be first detected as the dog being 'incontinent' when left shut indoors for more than a few hours. Blood tests are necessary to distinguish many of these conditions of the older Border Collie.

18 BREED ASSOCIATED DISEASES

This is a breed originating from working stock, so selection over many generations of those Collies best able to gather sheep on the hillside and the lowlands, has led to a very sound breed with few hereditary disorders. However, there is always the risk that the use of popular bloodlines may lead to an unexpected concentration of genetic factors, as was shown with certain eye problems that were, until recently, a problem in some groups within the breed. Any young Border Collie affected with blindness, or even with an inability to distinguish moving objects, would not survive long enough to be used for breeding but, as with many hereditary diseases, the carrier state allows genetic factors to miss several generations before the problem is seen again. There is also the problem, with late-onset hereditary disorders, that litters may have been born before one, or both, of the parents is discovered to be affected with a specific disorder.

INHERITED EYE CONDITIONS

COLLIE EYE ANOMALY (CEA): This is known in some countries of the world as *Scleral Ectasia,* and other terms are also in use. It affects, principally, the Rough and the Smooth Collie and the Shetland Sheep dog breeds and, to a much lesser extent, the Border Collie. It is caused by a defect during the very earliest development of the eye in the unborn puppy. It is therefore described as 'congenital and hereditary'.

In its most severe form it can cause total blindness and retinal detachments. In one study of Rough Collies in Norway, 40 per cent had Collie Eye Anomaly and this was also found in some other European countries that had imported the breed. Collie Eye Anomaly has been recorded as affecting 90 per cent of that breed in some states in the USA. The overuse of sires in localised areas must contribute to this apparent concentration of a disease in certain countries.

It is important to identify all affected dogs and remove them from a breeding programme. Examination and certification of puppies should be done at an early age by veterinary surgeons who have specialised in ophthalmology. Eye tests of puppies can be made at six to eight weeks. Because the disease is hereditary and due to a recessive gene, every attempt should be made to eliminate it from future breeding stock, and pet owners should be educated about the dangers of allowing their dogs to breed without having them examined for eye disease.

The disease can only be seen with the ophthalmoscope used by the veterinary surgeon to examine the retina at the back of the eye. Chorio-retinal dysplasia may be seen as an unpigmented zone close, and lateral to, the optic disc, the head of the optic nerve that connects the eye to the brain. This fault can be recognised, on examination, as a pale zone, or a lack of pigmentation, allowing the white inner surface of the sclera to be seen. Ectasia means a bulging, and, in some cases, the tough outer sclera of the eye has a weakness, so the bulge is outwards and the condition is then known as a 'coloboma'. These, and other changes, will be noted as part of the routine eye examination at the time of certification. The International Sheep Dog Society is responsible for administering the certification scheme for this breed. The British Veterinary Association and the Kennel Club operate a certification scheme for eyes in the UK, and the Canine Eye Registration (CERF), in the US, is a registry that records dogs that physically appear to be free of inherited eye diseases.

RETINAL ATROPHY: Retinal atrophy is now well known as a cause of poor vision and blindness. The International Sheep Dog Society has a very good control scheme involving the inspection and certification of all dogs' eyes, and this has been very successful in reducing the frequency of retinal disease. Progressive retinal degeneration (PRD), known in the UK as Progressive Retinal Atrophy (PRA), is a disease of the retina at the back of the eyeball and, in the early stages, can only be recognised by the use of an ophthalmoscope. The Border Collie breed may be affected by PRD type 1 and PRD type 2. These diseases are more popularly known in many countries as PRA or retinal atrophy but, fortunately, they are not as common in the Border Collie as in some other breeds.

CENTRAL PROGRESSIVE RETINAL ATROPHY (CPRA): CPRA is the abbreviation for Central Progressive Retinal Atrophy, or Type 2 Progressive Retinal Degeneration. The disease is a pigment epithelial dystrophy, according to some authorities, characterised by a loss of vision at the centre of the retina, so that dogs can see moving objects quite well, but stationary objects may not be picked out by the dog against their background. The vision is better in dim light, as at dusk, and worst in very bright light, as at the middle of the day. Total loss of sight and a noticeable blindness is unusual with this disease.

GENERALISED PROGRESSIVE RETINAL ATROPHY: Known also as PRD Type 1, this disease is caused by a recessive gene and, for this reason, may appear unexpectedly in a litter of pups where there has been no history of blindness in parents or grandparents. It is known as 'night blindness' in Red Setters and, once present, always leads to total loss of vision, with blindness developing in a few months or years. Cataracts may also develop later in the disease but, fortunately, these are rare in the Border Collie and all Collie breeds. In affected non-Collie breeds, cataracts make the blindness very obvious.

PRIMARY LENS LUXATION: Subluxation and luxation of the lens is a condition where the ligament, or zonule, that holds the lens at the centre of the eye weakens, the lens then lacks support and a partial displacement may occur. Both eyes may be affected, but usually one eye shows disease in advance of the other. The displaced lens may eventually become a cataract and opaque or, if the lens falls forward to touch the inner side of the cornea, it may become an oedema seen as a white patch that suddenly develops on the cornea, at the front of the eye. There is, potentially, a risk of fluid building up within the eye (glaucoma) after the lens luxates.

CATARACT: The Border Collie is rarely affected with cataracts unless there has been some injury to the eye that causes the lens to become opaque. The hereditary cataract seen in many breeds of dog has not been recognised in any Collie breed.

OTHER EYE CONDITIONS
Unusual eye colour:
1) The partially pigmented iris is due to a Merle factor and it causes a very striking appearance to the dog's face. One or both eyes may be affected. Various terms have been used: a 'Wall eye' is a blue or white iris or part of the iris. 'China Eye' is a blue iris or part of an iris. 'Watch eye' is a blue or yellow-brown iris or part of the iris. The lack of pigment does not affect the dog's vision and the Merle eye is not considered a health problem. The Merle coat colour gene is dominant and has been associated with deafness.
2) Corneal opacity due to a fat type of deposit. The condition known as lipid keratopathy or corneal lipidosis was thought to have a hereditary basis. The veterinary surgeon should be consulted about any scars or white marks seen on the eye surface.

EYELID DISORDERS
THE PROMINENT THIRD EYELID OR MEMBRANA NICTITANS: The third eyelid is an important structure in the protection of the eye. It helps produce some of the fluid (tears) that lubricates and protects the eye surface; the eyelid edge can move across the eye, rather like a car windscreen wiper, to remove dust, or other foreign body irritants on the eye surface. Eversion refers to the rolling over of the lid, but it is rarely seen in Border Collies.

ENTROPION AND ECTROPION: The condition of entropion can be an inherited defect of the eyelid structure. It is rarely seen in Border Collies. It is an inturning of the eyelids; there may be excessive tear formation and the overflow of tears is seen on the faces of light-coloured dogs. When entropion does appear in the breed it is often the result of an injury to the eye, through a dog fight, for example, or some other injury to the eyelids. Once diagnosed, the severe cases will need surgery to evert the eyelid edge. Ectropion is the opposite condition to entropion; it is a looseness of the eyelids, with undue exposure of the pink lining of the lid. Ectropion can be a hereditary disease in some breeds with loose skin on the head but, in the Border Collie, ectropion is usually the result of injury.

BONE AND JOINT DISEASES
(With hereditary influences)

HIP DYSPLASIA (HD)
The problem of Hip Dysplasia was a major consideration in the breeding of German Shepherds and some of the Retriever breeds; the problem is still widespread, existing in most dog breeds. Any breed can be considered to have a problem where more than 5 per cent of the breed are showing recognisable signs of hip dysplasia.

The working guide dog (a few of which are Border Collies) is rarely disadvantaged by hip dysplasia as it does not affect the daily life of the dog; the dog walks at a slow pace, does not have to jump up and does not do agility work. Hip dysplasia may be the cause of pain to the dog. A sudden pain or discomfort in the young dog may be associated with a rupture of the round ligament of the hip, that allows for subluxation of the joint with a short period of pain. Fractures of the edges of the acetabulum may also cause some of this pain, when the head of the thigh bone (femur) partially comes out of the hip joint. In the older dog, pain from the disease of osteoarthritis can develop, secondary to an existing hip dysplasia. The disease of Hip Dysplasia is not entirely a hereditary one, and environmental factors such as feeding, exercise and even the position the young dog is made to sit in, all may be responsible for up to 60 per cent of the occurrence of the hip dysplasia changes as seen on X-ray, as the disease has only a moderate inheritability of 30 to 45 per cent.

In the UK the BVA/KC hip scheme commenced in 1978 for German Shepherds, and in 1983 for other breeds, including the Border Collie. Hip X-rays are examined of dogs over 12 months of age and a 'score' is allocated, based on nine features of each hip joint. The breed average for Border Collies is 13, with a range of between 0 and 89 scored in the breed. The higher the score, the worse the condition. Anyone considering breeding should find out the scores for the intended parents; there would usually seem to be little justification for attempting to breed from any stock that has an above-average score. It must be remembered that low scores on hips do not always improve when the puppies are examined: some of the matings of 0/0 hip score dogs in other breeds have produced litters of puppies with a hip score little better than the breed average. This policy of only using low hip score parents may be modified by breeding from higher-scoring bitches that have other characteristics that could be of especial value to the breeder, in a programme to seek a particular type of dog.

In the USA, a similar scheme is operated by the Orthopaedic Foundation for Animals (OFA), and a high standard X-ray plate is needed for evaluation by the organisation's radiologists. Established in 1966 as the world's largest all-breed registry, a seven-point scoring system is used for hips ranging from 'excellent' to 'severe dysplasia'. Dogs must be at least two years old to receive a breeding number from the OFA, although preliminary evaluations will be made by the OFA on dogs younger than 24 months, to help breeders choose their future stock. A slightly different approach is taken by the University of Pennsylvania Hip Improvement Programme (PennHIP). Here, two views of the hind limb are required to measure the amount of displacement or 'joint laxity' in the hips. This method of evaluation overcomes the objection that some dogs appear to have very unstable hip joints, but when X-rayed in the extended position, they appear to have normal hip structure. A third hip evaluation scheme is operated in the USA by the Institute for Genetic Disease Control in Animals (GDC). Similar open registries of blood lines are used in Norway and Sweden to help breeders select stock for mating. The normal dog can be certified at 12 months of age, and the information is then available on a progeny report held in a database.

GUIDELINES FOR HIP IMPROVEMENT
1) Score all stock, using the BVA/KC scheme or similar schemes that are available outside the UK. This necessitates having X-rays of all young breeding stock.
2) As far as practical, breed only from stock with a hip score better than the breed average.
3) Follow recommendations about feeding and exercise to avoid undue injury and stress to the growing hip joint.
4) Regularly review all inherited diseases in the dog group e.g. in a kennels, or enquire about litter mates or parents. Expect to get evasive replies when asking others about their dogs' hip scores, as not all are low ones!

OSTEOCHONDROSIS

Another disease with a hereditary basis, osteochondrosis is seen in many large and giant breeds of dogs; it is also known as OD or OCD. The Border Collie is less likely to suffer from elbow osteochondrosis, or from the condition of an un-united anconeal process, which may be detected in breeds such as the German Shepherd on X-ray at, or just after, six months.

OSTEOARTHRITIS

Usually seen affecting the older dog, this condition, which limits joint movement, starts as an erosive joint disease due to a loss of the cartilage on the joint surface. As the disease progresses, additional bone may be laid down round the edge of the joint, possibly as a result of inflammation and an attempt to support the joint. The disease develops slowly, leading to lameness, pain, the grating feeling known as crepitus and then joint instability. The joint feels thickened from the outside, and there is limited movement when the joint is bent to stretch it or flex it. If a joint is not moving, then the muscles around it weaken or atrophy, so that the leg becomes wasted. X-rays should be taken to assess the degree of new bone building up around the joint. A management plan for the dog can be drawn up, and pain control is the first priority in treatment. Osteoarthritis is thought to be aggravated by the dog being overweight, and dietary control is an important way of helping a dog with joint pain or swelling. Although not considered a hereditary disease, osteoarthritis is often the result of hip dysplasia and osteochondrosis, both of which have a genetic basis.

CRUCIATE LIGAMENT RUPTURE

The stifle, or 'knee' joint, is not robustly constructed but, as long as Border Collies are kept lean and fit, there is not a great risk of this injury. Once a dog becomes overweight, the stifle, that depends on a number of ligaments and cartilages to hold it together and give free movement, may become at risk. The stifle is used in jumping and for forward propulsion. Overweight dogs that are suddenly asked to perform tasks, even ones as simple as jumping out of a Range Rover or an estate car rear door, may land heavily and damage the ligaments.

The cruciate ligaments are those crossing the centre of the stifle joint and there are two other collateral ligaments that support the sides of the joint. The kneecap, or patella, also has ligaments that run at the front of the joint and these, too, can fail to support the stifle joint, throwing a greater strain on the two ligaments at the centre. It is usually the front ligament in the centre of the stifle joint – the anterior cruciate ligament – that takes the greatest strain when the dog jumps or turns awkwardly, and this may tear or, at the worst, completely break in half. The tearing of the ligament happens because a weakness has been developing in the fibres so, after partial tearing and stretching, the ligament ruptures. The result is a very lame dog. Often the stifle joint is so unstable that the two bone ends that form the joint can be slid over each other. This instability is used in the 'draw forward' test.

Cruciate rupture usually happens suddenly during extreme exercise and it does not improve with enforced rest, as with many other injuries. Heavy dogs will usually require a surgical operation to repair the torn ligament. There are a number of techniques employed, but most require a ligament implant inserted through or around the joint. Provided the operation is done before arthritic changes develop in the joint surface, the results are very good, since the joint is stabilised again.

PANOSTEITIS

This may be found as one cause of sudden lameness, most often in a fore leg, but sometimes the lameness will alternate from front to back legs. The lameness is quite severe and it might suggest that a bone has been broken but if an X-ray is taken, it will show no damage to the bone structure at all. It is believed that this is an auto-immune condition, as it does not appear until six months of age and only infrequently does it cause lameness in the middle-aged or elderly dog. Treatment involves resting the dog for a few days, then giving controlled exercise until the dog eventually walks soundly again. Non-steroidal anti-inflammatory tablets can be given, and severely lame dogs may benefit from corticosteroid injections.

SKIN DISORDERS

The Border Collie is fairly resistant to skin disease, and most skin problems in the breed are probably the result of skin parasite infections and there is no known hereditary basis for such infections.

COLLIE NOSE: This condition, with crusting around the edges of the nostrils, and the loss of dark pigment, with a dermatitis that may spread up the nose, sometimes affecting the eyelid and lip margins, may be found in Collies. It occurs most frequently in sunny climates and ultra-violet light exposure was once thought to be a factor. It is more probably an auto-immune skin condition in which the T-cells are involved, and there is probably a breed predisposition in Collies to the disorder.

DIGESTIVE SYSTEM DISORDERS

BLOAT

The sudden accumulation of gas in the stomach will cause distress and, if left untreated, eventual death. Gastric dilation and torsion of the stomach (GDV) can be a problem in any of the larger breeds. It is especially associated with the Giant Breeds and Setters but it may be found in Collies as an acute emergency. The feeding routine should be such as to avoid hungry dogs swallowing food rapidly, then being left unexercised and unobserved. In the UK, the kennels for the Guide Dogs for the Blind Association feed in the morning before the two work periods during the daytime, so that gas cannot accumulate in the stomach. Any dog with a tendency to bloat will be seen at the earliest stage of discomfort. Often a silicone-base tablet can be given at this stage to stop bubbles of gas being held in the stomach. Dogs known to 'bloat' can be made to eat more slowly by supervising them and feeding them on their own, when there is no competition from other dogs stealing their food. Canned dog food seems less likely to cause bloat than some of the complete or semi-moist diets. The treatment of gastric dilation is dealt with in the previous chapter.

DIARRHOEA FROM BACTERIAL OVERGROWTH

The condition now known as SIBO (small intestine bacterial overgrowth) is a disorder that may be the cause of persisting diarrhoea, increased appetite and weight loss. To explain it simply, it is a disorder where too many bacteria are living in the small intestine for the dog's health; these bacteria take some of the best nutrients out of the food eaten that passes from the stomach to the small intestine. Diagnosis has to be confirmed by blood tests, then a month-long course of antibiotics, together with a modified low fat diet, is usually sufficient to clear the disorder entirely. The diet may be supplemented with Vitamin B and trace elements such as are found in a number of pet health tablets.

255

COPROPHAGIA

The eating of faeces is a habit acquired by dogs kept in kennels. Dogs who are adequately supervised when they defecate will have little opportunity to explore the smells or the taste of recently voided faeces. The flavouring agents and palatable residues that are found in faeces after prepared foods have been apparently digested to a dog's satisfaction, must be blamed for the dog's subsequent nose investigation then taste exploration, before ingestion of the faeces. Treatment of such a behaviour pattern, which is associated with boredom, should be undertaken.

Deterrents such as garlic, paprika and even fresh pineapple have been used to curb a dog's desire to eat faeces. Blood tests for SIBO (as above) should be taken. The habit may not be so revolting as first thought, since rabbits use the method of eating faeces taken from their own rectums as a way of further digesting cellulose for food, and many free-range animals will eat faeces from herbivores left on the ground, as a way of obtaining extra Vitamin B.

EXOCRINE PANCREATIC INSUFFICIENCY (EPI)

This is uncommon in Border Collies, and in all breeds there now seems to be a decrease in the illness compared to 20 years ago. This may be due to more accurate diagnostic tests being used, and the fact that, once identified, litters from the same blood lines have not been bred from again. One third of all cases of EPI are found in breeds such as Labradors, Collies and Golden Retrievers, and about two thirds in the German Shepherd, which is the most commonly affected breed. The disease may not show up until middle age, when it appears as a chronic diarrhoea with weight loss due to a failure in the digestive enzymes in the small intestine. The EPI blood test is used to confirm a diagnosis. The response to treatment, using low fat diets, and supplements of digestive enzymes in dried pancreatic extract combined with drugs to lower stomach acidity is good. Unfortunately long-term treatment adds to the expense of medication.